Pro Wrestling's Black World Champions

Pro Wrestling's Black World Champions

(3rd Edition)

David L. Shabazz

South Carolina * Kentucky

Pro Wrestling's Black World Champions

Copyright © 2025 by David L. Shabazz

Third Edition -- First Printing

All Rights Reserved
Published in the United States by Awesome Records

No part of this book may be reproduced or utilized in any form by any means, electronic or mechanical, including photocopying, recording or by any information storage and retrieval system, without permission in writing from the publisher.

Library of Congress Control Number: 2025912401

ISBN-10: 1-893680-17-7
ISBN-13: 978-1-893680-17-3

Manufactured in the United States of America

To my brother and mentor Julian L.D. Shabazz

Table of Champions

Introduction 10
   "Somebody Like You..." 13
THE TRAILBLAZERS 22
   ETHEL JOHNSON 23
   BEARCAT WRIGHT 28
   BOBO BRAZIL 35
   "SAILOR" ART THOMAS 43
   ERNIE LADD 47
BLACK WORLD HEAVYWEIGHT WRESTLING CHAMPIONS 54
   Ron Simmons 55
   Jacqueline 62
   The Rock 67
   Booker T 75
   Jazz 87
   R-Truth 91
   Xavier 98
   Awesome Kong 101
   Vix Crow 105
   Layla 109
   Mark Henry 113
   Mercedes Mone 120
   Naomi 129
   Kofi Kingston 134

    Bobby Lashley 142

    Bianca Belair 150

    Big E 155

    Nyla Rose 162

    Big Ryck 165

    Jay Lethal 168

    Jonathan Gresham 173

    Athena 178

    Rich Swann 182

    Moose Ojinnaka 187

    Tyrus 192

    Swerve Strickland 196

    Trick Williams 200

BLACK TAG TEAM WORLD CHAMPIONS 204

    Soul Patrol 205

    Doom 215

    Sasha Banks & Naomi 223

    Lethal Consequences 227

    Men On A Mission 229

    Swerve In Our Glory 239

    The Acclaimed 243

    Tha Gangstas 246

    Street Profits 252

    The Prime Time Players 257

    The New Day 261

Private Party 267
The Hurt Syndicate 269
Bianca Belair and Jade Cargill 282
Blunt Force Trauma 287
Harlem Heat 291

Conclusion 299
References 300
Acknowledgements 309
Index 310

Introduction

"My champion is black," was the opening statement uttered by Swerve Strickland at the press conference following a career-defining victory. Strickland had just wrestled the title away from champion Samoa Joe at the *Dynasty* pay-per-view on Sunday, April 21, 2024, to become the first African American male world heavyweight champion in All Elite Wrestling (AEW). Two weeks later, Bianca Belair and Jade Cargill won the women's tag team championship at WWE's pay-per-view held in Lyon, France. Their victories are further evidence of the progress African Americans have made in the modern professional wrestling industry. The idea to release a new edition of this book came shortly after publication of the second edition in 2022. Wrestling fans were appreciative and more eager to know about the history and legacy of the black wrestlers than I had imagined.

This third edition of *Pro Wrestling's Black World Champions* has expanded tremendously but is still built on the foundation laid by my brother Julian's original article and subsequent eBook which was first published in 2009. Very little controversy still exists over who should be called the first Black heavyweight world wrestling champion. Ron Simmons has been universally recognized by wrestling promotions and historians as the first black world heavyweight champion. However, that is not to discredit the black wrestlers who came before him. Historically, African Americans were only allowed to compete against other Black wrestlers - especially in the deep South. Thus, many of the wrestling promotions within the territories created their own Colored (and later Negro) champion. Some were even elevated to the status of "world" Colored or Negro champion. The validity and reliability of their championship status remains challenging when records of Black wrestlers during that time period were either non-existent, poorly kept or not kept at all. Therefore, this book only details the careers of Black champions from major independent wrestling promotions and those Black champions in the territories after they were either organized and governed by or were affiliates of the National Wrestling Alliance (1948) or its predecessor the National Wrestling Association (1930).

This book is divided into three parts. The first part opens with an essay on black world champions that focuses on a controversial monologue designed to promote a championship match between Triple H and Booker T. After the essay, the lives of the African American singles world champion forerunners are explored. Each wrestler won a heavyweight title in a promotion that may not have been a true "world" championship but at least sanctioned some matches outside of the continental United States. We believe it is more accurate to refer to them as trailblazers. They should be recognized and celebrated for integrating the sport and allowing the black wrestlers of today to be seen as worthy of holding a bona fide world championship. The five trailblazers profiled are Ethel Johnson, Bearcat Wright, Bobo Brazil, Art Thomas and Ernie Ladd. According to the book *National Wrestling Alliance: The Untold Story of the Monopoly that Strangled Pro Wrestling*,

> "Recognition by the members of the National Wrestling Alliance as world heavyweight champion was acknowledged as the pinnacle of professional wrestling for more than 40 years. While great credibility was brought to the AWA and WWWF titles by champions Verne Gagne and Bruno Sammartino respectively, the NWA world heavyweight title remained the most cherished crown in the industry…The champion needed to be able to fluctuate between being the all-encompassing 'good' guy and a heel, depending on the night's specific opponent…He was responsible for boosting the esteem of the local headliner, and, rather than come off as an invincible superhero, was to make his rival look as if he was capable of winning the prized championship" (Hornbaker 2007, pp. 196-197).

In the second part, we explore the lives of the world champions recognized by the major promotions – World Wrestling Entertainment (WWE/WWF), All Elite Wrestling (AEW), Total Non-Stop Action/ Impact Wrestling (TNA/NWA), World Championship Wrestling (WCW), Extreme Championship Wrestling (ECW) and Ring of Honor

(RoH). Finally, the last section profiles the all-black tag team world champions which is new to this edition. This third edition also lists the major accomplishments and significant title reigns for each wrestler. With the exception of the trailblazers and others who have passed, many wrestlers are still active performers. Many of their accolades will have changed by the time this publication becomes available. Some wrestlers will have longer profiles due to the number of titles they have held, their longevity in the business and outside activities that helped build their popularity and overall entertainment value. This publication is not intended to present full biographies of each wrestler. Instead, the profiles provide a biographical sketch of the black singles wrestlers and all-black tag teams who have held world championship titles in professional wrestling.

"Somebody Like You Doesn't Get To Be A World Champion"

Professional wrestling is a unique form of entertainment. It combines athleticism, and showmanship with the ability to execute a compelling storyline. A defining moment in the modern history of professional wrestling is the battle for supremacy between World Championship Wrestling (WCW) and the former World Wrestling Federation (WWF) known as the Monday Night Wars. It was a television ratings war that ended on March 23, 2001, with the WWF purchasing WCW. When Booker T challenged Triple H for the WWE's world heavyweight championship in 2003, he was berated in a promo by the champion. The promo was a build up to their match at WrestleMania 19 which was held on March 30 at Safeco Field in Seattle, Washington. The speech was known for the racial overtones but also a subtle yet overt show of the wrestling company's perceived superiority. To examine the promo rhetorically, Triple H's monologue has to be examined as well as the occasion for context, the intended audience, the subject and the purpose or objective he hoped to achieve.

The Promo

The nine-minute promotional segment was delivered on the March 3, 2003, episode of Monday Night *Raw*.[1] For the first minute, Booker T was in the middle of the ring and he was smiling brightly. He introduced himself as the five-time WCW world heavyweight champion – although he uttered the phrase six times. He had just emerged victorious at the *Royal Rumble* and was happy to announce that he was going to *WrestleMania* to challenge for the world title. Just as Booker T finished saying one of his signature catchphrases "Can

---

[1] Watch the promo here - https://www.youtube.com/watch?v=50yDO_iXBG0

you dig that, suckas," he was interrupted by Triple H who was accompanied to the ring by his Evolution group member Ric Flair. Triple H told Booker that he was confused about why he was in the WWE. During the promo, he said: "You're not here to be a competitor, you're here to be an entertainer…Come on Book, dance. Entertain me. That's your job." He told Booker that he was in the WWE to make people like him laugh. The audience erupted and started shouting asshole at Triple H. At another point, Triple H's attacks became more personal as he commented on Booker T's "nappy hair" and use of Ebonics by pronouncing the word "suckas" instead of "suckers." As the crowd quieted down, he recognized Booker's reign as a five-time WCW champion but said "that place was a joke." He explained the comment by referencing actor David Arquette and former WWF booker Vince Russo once laying claim to be WCW world champion. Triple H ended by saying the event – WrestleMania – was larger than life and that Booker would face a champion who, as "the game," is also larger than life. Booker T's smile had transformed into an angry stare. The segment ended with Booker T saying he was going to prove his worth at WrestleMania and become world champion again. Triple H sarcastically offered him good luck and left the ring with Flair who smiled but did not speak at any point during the segment.

Monday Night War

The Monday Night War was a battle between television programs owned by the World Wrestling Federation (WWF) and World Championship Wrestling (WCW). The television ratings war began on September 4, 1995, when WCW starting airing its wrestling program *Nitro* on Monday nights at the same time. Previously, *Raw* was the only wrestling program on Monday nights. The move was seen as a direct challenge to the WWF. WCW dominated the Nielsen ratings for most of the mid-1990s. Under the direction of Eric Bischoff with the financial resources of Ted Turner at his disposal, WCW acquired many of the previous household names from WWF including Hulk Hogan, Bret Hart and "Macho Man" Randy Savage.

Scott Hall and Kevin Nash wrestled their final matches for the WWF on May 19, 1996. On May 27, 1996, Hall who was known as Razor Ramon in the WWF, appeared live on WCW television. After hinting that a "big surprise" was coming, he was joined on June 10 by Nash, who was known as Diesel and "Big Daddy Cool" in the WWF. Hall and Nash collectively were known as "The Outsiders" and they declared war on WCW. The gimmick worked well because WWF's *Raw* was aired on taped delay at the time while WCW's *Nitro* was live. Audiences could see Hall and Nash on WWF and WCW within days of each broadcast which gave credibility to the "takeover" storyline. The group officially became the New World Order (nWo) on July 7, 1996, at the *Bash at the Beach* pay-per-view. Bischoff held a six-man "Hostile Takeover" match with WCW wrestlers against The Outsiders in what appeared to be a two-on-three handicapped match until "Hollywood" Hulk Hogan appeared and revealed himself as the third member. The Monday Night War ended due to a loss of credibility when actor David Arquette – who had no professional wrestling experience – was made world champion and the huge financial strain mostly from the millions of dollars that high profile wrestlers were being paid, which the new AOL Time Warner conglomerate no longer wanted to incur. Vince McMahon bought WCW on March 26, 2001, which officially ended the Monday Night War.

The following year, McMahon found himself in a trademark dispute with the World Wildlife Foundation over use of the acronym WWF. To avoid further legal issues, the company changed its name to World Wrestling Entertainment (WWE) in 2002. The war was over but the WWE decided to turn the real-life situation into a storyline. Turning real situations into story lines has been a staple of professional wrestling. To further profit from the war, the WWE would marginalize WCW in the subsequent story lines. Booker T was essentially the face of WCW. The promo was developed after Booker T won the right to challenge Triple H for the world heavyweight championship.

Critical rhetoric examines how artifacts and texts create or maintain practices that control certain groups or individuals. It seeks to reveal how texts reinforce the notion of who should be in power and who should not be empowered. To analyze the rhetorical situation, the analysis will start with the wrestlers Triple H, Booker T and how they related to the audience.

Connecticut Blueblood

Hunter Hearst Helmsley (Triple H) is a professional wrestling character portrayed by Paul Levesque. Levesque was born in Nashua, New Hampshire where he was known for his athleticism. In high school, he was an avid bodybuilder and played baseball and basketball. At age 19, he placed first at the 1988 Mr. Teenage New Hampshire contest. He started training under wrestler Killer Kowalski in 1990 and made his in-ring debut in 1992 with Kowalski's International Wrestling Federation. After wrestling on the independent circuit, he signed a one-year deal with World Championship Wrestling (WCW) in 1994. After contract negotiations failed, he left the company and signed with the World Wrestling Federation in 1995 as the "Connecticut blue blood" Hunter Hearst Helmsley (Marvez, 2001). As a blue blood character, he was a natural heel. He came to the ring with his hair in a pony tail wearing a knee-length tailcoat with a bottle of perfume in hand. In promotional vignettes, he presented himself as a proper gentleman in speech and etiquette. He initially had a brief winning streak. However, after losing a match to "The Hitman" Bret Hart, Sable became his valet. He was later managed by "Mr. Perfect" Curt Hening and won the intercontinental championship from Sable's real-life husband at the time, Marc Mero. He was also briefly managed by Mr. Hughes, an African American wrestler. After losing the title to The Rock, he feuded with Goldust (Dustin Rhodes). During this feud, Chyna became his manager. Helmsley later dropped the snobbish blue blood gimmick and was a founding member of DeGeneration X (DX) along with Chyna, Sean Michaels and "Ravishing" Rick Rude during what became known as the Attitude Era. DX was known for the phrase "suck it" while using a crotch chop gesture. Triple H nicknamed himself "the game" as a symbolic metaphor to show that he is bigger than the sport.

As a wrestler, he is a bona fide champion having won many titles in WWF/E. He is a 14-time world champion, five-time intercontinental champion, two-time world tag team champion and WWE tag team champion. During a feud with The Corporation's Mr. McMahon, he lost the WWF Championship on September 16, 1999, but regained it September 26. During the feud, he (storyline) "married" Mr. McMahon's daughter Stephanie as another way to anger the company chairman. This began the McMahon-Helmsley Era. The storyline eventually turned real as Triple H is now married to Stephanie McMahon and currently serves as the company's chief content officer.

The Hero

Booker T, whose real name is Booker T. Huffman, was born in Plain Dealing, Louisiana. In high school, he was once a drum major; the top student leader in a marching band. He made his wrestling debut in the early 1990s under as the character G.I. Bro. His character was portraying an American soldier. G.I. Bro was a hero figure or what the industry would call a babyface. At the time, America was in a conflict with Iraq as the rhetoric turned into Operation Desert Shield and later Operation Desert Storm. The WWF's resident American hero Sgt. Slaughter was waning in popularity. Thus, the G.I. Bro character was apropos. He would go on to become a dominant tag team champion in the Global Wrestling Federation and World Championship Wrestling. While in WCW, he briefly reverted back to the G.I. Bro character, but the gimmick was not well received. Booker T is the most decorated wrestler in WCW history. When he signed with the WWE, he represented the best of WCW. Booker T was the last world heavyweight champion when the company was sold.

Although their paths were very different, Triple H and Booker T debuted in professional wrestling during the same period. For Triple H, he was managing a Gold's gym which naturally gave him access to athletes including wrestlers. Booker T was living with his siblings and trying to survive. In his youth, he once served time for armed robbery. Afterwards, he followed older brother Lash (Stevie Ray) into a wrestling career.

WrestleMania 19

WrestleMania 19 was a pay-per-view event held in Seattle, Washington on March 30, 2003. This WrestleMania signaled many firsts. It was the first WrestleMania held in the state of Washington, the first under the new company name World Wrestling

Entertainment (WWE), and the first since the company divided its roster and television programs under different brands – *Raw* and *SmackDown*. NXT, which is also nationally televised, is the WWE's developmental promotion. According to the WWE, the event set a record attendance at Safeco Field drawing 54,097 fans (Bernstein, 2003). While the match at *WrestleMania* was billed as a main event, the marque match-up for the *Raw* roster saw The Rock win over Stone Cold Steve Austin. There was also a street fight between Hulk Hogan and company owner "Mr." McMahon, and then the main event featured Brock Lesnar defeating Kurt Angle for the WWE Championship.

There were 10 matches on the card which lasted a total of 3 hours and 55 minutes (Powell, 2003). The fight between Triple H and Booker T was the seventh match. It was the fourth longest match of the night lasting 18 minutes and 45 seconds. Triple H won by pinfall after Ric Flair injured Booker T's leg by throwing him into the steel ring steps. Journalist John Powell gave the WrestleMania card a 10/10 ranking overall. He gave the match between Triple H and Booker T a 7.5/10 noting that fans were largely disappointed in the outcome (Powell, 2003).

Who deserves to be a champion?

If the outcome is predetermined, how is the champion chosen? Because pro wrestling is not a true athletic competition, the champion is subjectively chosen either by one person called a booker or sometimes by a committee. "The winners and losers are determined prior to the opening bell by the person in charge of the show, known as the booker. The booker makes the matches and chooses who goes over in the end. The job of the wrestlers once the action begins is not to injure one another or inflict as much pain as possible. It's actually quite the opposite" (Ucchino, 2024). Traditional wrestling storylines tend to focus on the good versus evil trope personified by the villain (heel) and hero (babyface). Because Triple H portrayed the heel, fans were disappointed when challenger Booker T, the hero, did not win. In the promo leading up to the match, Triple H said "The fact is Booker, someone like you doesn't get to be a world champion. You see, people like you don't deserve it. That's reserved for people like me." He drew instant heat from the crowd with those comments. That was the desired response he and the writers/bookers were expecting. On face value, those comments alone are enough to be considered racist. Triple H is white and Booker T is black. Without further explaining the comment, the audience was left to interpret it as racially charged. However, he continued to berate Booker and solidified the comment as racial when he attacked Booker's personal character. Triple H commented on Booker's "nappy hair" and broken English when he calls his opponents "suckas." Many in the audience booed as the comments made them feel uneasy.

Booker's namesake is the educator, author and prominent African American leader and Civil Rights pioneer Booker T. Washington. Washington was born into slavery but elevated himself to become a part of the black elite. He was known for emphasizing education and self-help with the goal of building community pride and economic strength within the African American race. The wrestler Booker T had to face similar hardships which he was able to overcome throughout his early years at Global Wrestling (GWF) and later World Championship Wrestling. People like to root for the underdog. Triple H was the pompous, aristocratic champion and Booker T was the average, hardworking guy fighting to prove his worth. Triple H downplayed Booker T's accomplishments as a way of devaluing WCW, their primary competition. "I laughed my ass off thinking about you challenging me for the world heavyweight championship. You see Book, I understand you've been the five-time WCW champion. I get all that. But let's face it. That place was a joke," Triple H said. He made the remark in reference to poor decision making when the company put the championship belt on actor David Arquette and even former WWF booker turned WCW booker Vince Russo. "Let's face it Book, you championshipped that place right into the ground." Ironically, the WWF also had an executive hold their world championship title – the chairman himself Vince McMahon. He won the belt on an episode of *SmackDown* that aired September 14, 1999. The person he won the belt from was none other than Triple H. So, if the WCW belt lost value due to non-wrestlers holding the belt, then the same should apply to the WWF championship title.

Since the WWF/E left the National Wrestling Alliance and Vincent K. McMahon took over in the early 1980s from his father, they have been on a quest to claim wrestling supremacy. All of the champions from the NWA and WCW never reached the pinnacle in the WWE except for Ric Flair. Flair briefly held the WWE Championship after winning the *Royal Rumble* in 1992. But even then, it was good promotion for the WWF because Flair left the WCW in 1991 and was stripped of the title "world champion" by both the WCW and NWA. He signed with the WWF and proclaimed himself the real world's champion. He was no longer recognized as champion but the NWA did not return his $25,000 deposit, so Flair maintained possession of the "Big Gold" title belt. Flair became the WWF Champion which solidified his claim to be the real-world champion. It was also a subtle shot behind the scenes at the NWA and WCW for not coming to terms with Flair and losing their most profitable asset. Booker T never held the WWE championship. Neither did Ron Simmons, who was renamed Farooq. Even NWA legend Harley Race would only win the King of the Ring tournament in the WWF. At *WrestleMania III*, the defining moment was Hulk Hogan body slamming the 500-pound Andre the Giant. It was portrayed as an almost impossible feat of strength. However, Harley Race body slammed Andre years before. Even Hogan and a few other wrestlers had body slammed the giant before *WrestleMania III*. The only wrestlers to hold the WWF/E world title from other companies had to be first reborn into a WWE superstar. WCW's Mean Marc, Vinnie Vegas and Stunning Steve became mega-stars in the WWF as The Undertaker, Diesel and "Stone Cold" Steve Austin.

The Monday Night War was reminiscent of the Yellow Journalism period when Joseph Pulitzer's *New York World* face intense competition from William Randolph Hearst's *New York Journal*. The two newspapers both ran the same yellow kid comic strip at one time and would lure employees away from the competition by offering more money. When faced with still competition from WCW, WWF turned sensational and created the Attitude Era. This period featured sensationalism with Austin drinking beer in the ring, Sable emphasizing her sex appeal, a character named Val Venis and The Godfather who was accompanied to the ring by several (storyline) whores. After the war ended, WWE toned it down but did not necessarily return to the family-friendly programs.

The wrestling champions at every level are determined by the bookers and the politics of the promotion. Technical wrestling skill alone is not enough to become a pro wrestling champion. The fans have to like you (or hate you) by way of ticket sales and/or viewer ratings. And the promoters have to give you a push and want you to become champion. Tony Khan's AEW has had success giving black wrestlers an opportunity from the company's inception. Despite having to fight for a title that he had already won five times in WCW, Booker T did eventually win the world heavyweight championship in WWE. Unfortunately, Booker T never won the promotion's other world title, the WWE Championship, which is the oldest and most prestigious of the two. He lost the match but won the hearts of the fans. Triple H maintained his heel status. His monologue was effective in garnering interest in the match. Unfortunately, he appeared to get caught up in the moment and go off-script – unless the bookers wrote the "nappy hair" and "suckas" comments for him. If that was the case, Triple H could have objected and delivered an attack without getting personal. Black Entertainment Television (BET) ranked Booker T as the best black wrestler of all time (Tynes, 2025). His reputation and legendary status remain despite the outcome of that match. The fight was really about WWF/E showing they had conquered WCW. Since the match was at *WrestleMania*, the WWF/E controlled the narrative. Regardless of how fans felt, that was a fight Booker T was never supposed to win.

THE TRAILBLAZERS

ETHEL JOHNSON

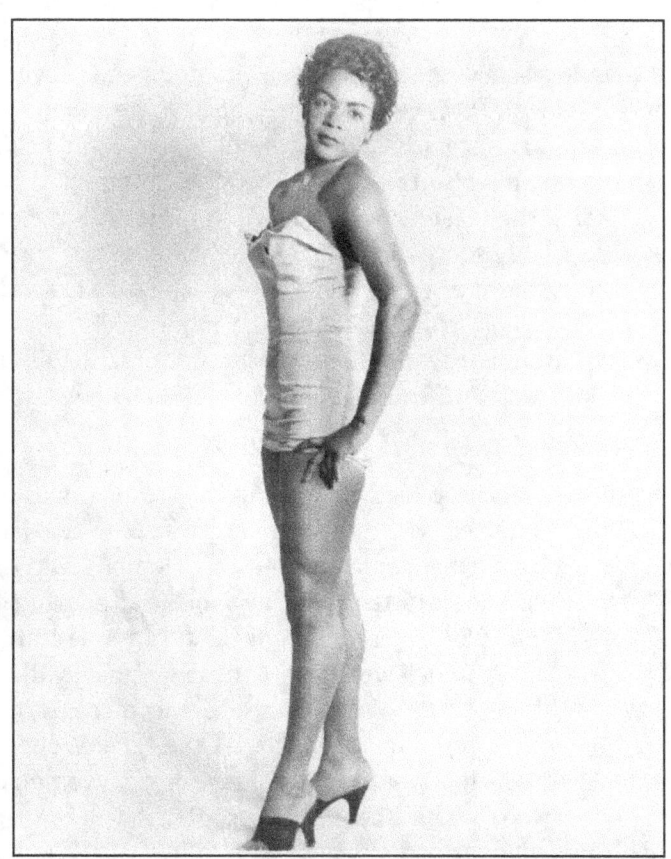

"Negro men have been competing in pro wrestling almost since the origin of catch-as-catch-can matches in the United States... They have met with success in such faraway places as Thailand (Siam), Burma, and Indonesia. Then why wouldn't the Negro girl athletes stand an equal chance of making the grade? That's the way I figured it. And from the tremendous fan support given Negro girls' matches I have not been wrong in my figuring." – Billy Wolfe

It takes a tremendous amount of confidence, self-determination and a strong will to compete in a sport where females have been marginalized. In the 1950's, America was segregated particularly in the deep South where Jim Crow laws enforced racial discrimination. To be female and African American in 1950's America compounds the obstacles one must overcome to be a professional wrestler. At that time, to be black and female was seen as a double negative to many in American society. However, a divinely positive attitude is what Ethel Johnson and her sisters Babs Wingo and Marva Scott held onto not only in the ring but also the arenas, the locker rooms and on the road where finding shelter for African American artists and athletes wasn't always easy. "Johnson endured harassment from fans, threats to her safety, and systemic discrimination, even as she excelled and captured titles. Many of her struggles reflect the larger societal issues of her era, yet Johnson, Babs, and Marva fought on, breaking down barriers and opening doors for future generations of women wrestlers" (WOL 2025).

Ethel Blanche Wingo Hairston, who wrestled under the name Ethel Johnson, started wrestling when she was only 16. Hairston was born in Georgia but her family moved to Columbus, Ohio when she was very young. She started training shortly after her sister Babs Wingo broke the color barrier as the first African American female to desegregate professional wrestling. Johnson signed with promoter Billy Wolfe in the 1950s. Wolfe was also the manager/husband of Mildred Burke; the top female wrestler at the time. Wolfe joined the NWA in 1949 which widen opportunities for the women under his management throughout the territories. He and Burke trained the women to wrestle instead of using them as eye-candy and sideshows (Hornbaker, 2007). Wolfe had at least six African American wrestlers including Mary Horton, Louise Greene, Ramona Isbell and Kathleen Wimbley, who traveled with his company across the U.S. and Canada. Johnson used the name Rita Valdez on wrestling tours throughout Latin America (Annino, 2024). According to an article in *Jet* magazine, Wolfe said his Black female wrestlers earned as much as $300 per week. "My Negro girls are the hottest thing in the sport," Wolfe was quoted. Johnson was the middle sister between the elder Betty (Babs) and younger sister Marva Scott. Throughout their wrestling careers, all three sisters held a version of the Colored Women's world title on the independent circuit at least once. Johnson was a petite 5'5" tall and weighed 110 pounds. However, she used her athleticism and wit to outperform many larger opponents. She was known for the standing drop kick.

Johnson was trained by Mildred Burke who was the inaugural National Wrestling Alliance (NWA) women's world champion. Burke openly bragged about her salary which was extremely rare for a female.[2] "Burke was a megastar, an undefeated champion who wore diamonds and furs and talked openly about her $50,000 annual income – a real figure, which became a part of her character as well" (Erdman, 2018). The Wingo sisters were popular enough to earn a shot at Burke's world title. Burke defeated Babs Wingo in a best-two-out-of-three falls match on Oct 2, 1953. She also defeated Johnson in a title match. Johnson competed against the top female wrestlers in the sport at the time including NWA women's champions Burke and June Byers. Johnson and Burke once held the NWA women's world tag team titles. They won the titles on July 9, 1956 by defeating Penny Banner and Betty Jo Hawkins in Calgary, a major city in the Canadian province of Alberta. Johnson also lost a competitive match for the AWA women's world championship to inaugural title holder Penny Banner. She was also Texas Colored Women's champion twice, Ohio Women's Tag Team champion with sister Marva and a three-time Colored Women's world champion (Malcolm, 2022).

Because of her stunning physical appearance, Johnson's publicity photos featured her in pin-up style poses. She was considered the first African American sex symbol in professional wrestling (Laprade & Murphy, 2017). In one of her final matches, she participated in an intergender match teaming with Dominic DeNucci to defeat Marva Scott and Jerry Jaffee. In 184 recorded matches, she finished her career with an impressive 153-25-6 record. According to her obituary, she expressed her feelings about women's professional wrestling, "We loved it, we ate it, we slept it, we talked about it, it was

---

[2] A salary of $50,000 in 1950 is equivalent to approximately $670,000 in 2025.

our life." Details of the Wingo sisters and other African America female wrestling pioneers has been chronicled in the documentary Lady Wrestler: The Johnson died on September 14, 2018 at age 83. She was inducted into the WWE Hall of Fame in 2021 and is a two-time inductee into the Women's Wrestling Hall of Fame – initially as a singles competitor in 2023 and again in 2025 in the tag team category with her sisters Babs Wingo and Marva Scott.

Major Championships and Accomplishments

Title	Promotion	Dates
Texas Negro Women's Champion	Houston Wrestling	Feb 8, 1957
NWA World Women's Tag Team Champion	Big Time Wrestling	w/June Byers (July 9, 1957)
Texas Negro Women's Champion	Southwest Sports	May 26, 1959 June 1, 1959 Sept 27, 1960 Oct 4, 1960
Ohio Women's Tag Team Champion		w/Marva Scott (Oct 8, 1959)

Honors	Sponsor	Year
WWE Hall of Fame	World Wrestling Entertainment	2021
Women's Wrestling Hall of Fame	Women's Wrestling Hall of Fame	2023 & 2025

BEARCAT WRIGHT

"Due to the scripted nature of professional wrestling, championships are held by wrestlers selected by the promotions. Therefore, it would be wrong to state that African Americans have not succeeded due to lack of ability. Their inability to rise to the top of the profession stems rather from lack of opportunity." (Hogg, p. 40)

Every field of endeavor has a trailblazer and sports is no exception. For African American men, there was Jack Johnson who became the first black heavyweight boxing champion in 1908. In 1945, Jackie Robinson became the first black player in Major League Baseball (MLB) by joining the Brooklyn Dodgers. The following year, Kenny Washington integrated professional football by signing with the Los Angeles Rams. In professional wrestling, Edward "Bearcat" Wright, is arguably the most important trailblazer for Black wrestling champions.

He not only made it possible for Black wrestlers to be the franchise player at major wrestling promotions, but also played a significant role in desegregating the sport.

By all accounts, Jamaican-born Bearcat Wright was a good wrestler and an extremely proud man. Wright was a controversial figure who worked all over the world throughout his career. At first, he followed in the footsteps of his father the original "bearcat" Wright as a boxer. Wright had a promising boxing career with several amateur fights and a reportedly brief but undefeated 8-0 professional record. However, the excitement and opportunity to earn a significantly higher income, lured Wright away from boxing. According to the book *The Pro Wrestling Hall of Fame: Heroes and Icons*, Wright was quoted as saying: "In my first two bouts, on successive nights, I earned $225. That was more than I cleared in twenty-two bouts as a pro fighter" (Johnson et al., 2014, p. 251). Wright was probably including exhibitions and/or amateur fights in that number. While the exact number of professional boxing matches may be questionable, it is clear that he was making more money as a professional wrestler. In 1959, he made his pro wrestling debut. The tall, huge man was very popular with fans and always drew money as a box-office attraction. At 6'7" tall, he was a good ring worker and agile for his size.

During the time, segregated matches were the norm especially in the deep South. Even though Wright was a popular and successful performer, he nonetheless shared the frustrations of many African American athletes of his day. In most areas of the United States, promoters had a ban on integrated matches and it was unheard of for a Black wrestler to be on top as the promotion's primary champion. Wright repeatedly wrestled against the same Black wrestlers in town after town. While the money was good, he had reached a ceiling and wanted more opportunities to expand his fan base as well as increase his earning potential. He saw the response of the fans to his popularity and finally he'd had enough of what he felt was second-class treatment of Black wrestlers.

It was after yet another segregated match in Gary, Indiana in 1960 when Wright grabbed the house microphone and announced that he'd never wrestle in a segregated arena again. He was promptly suspended by the Indiana State Athletic Commission but his plea was heard by many. When the National Association for the Advancement of Colored People (NAACP) came out in support of Wright, the Commission decided not to pursue the issue and rescinded their ban against Wright. Thus, professional wrestling was desegregated in the state of Indiana. This action set a precedent for other states to follow.

Wright continued to wrestle throughout the territories and things began to change when he went to Boston. According to wrestling historian Don Luce, former Olympic freestyle wrestler and two-time AWA world heavyweight champion Ed Don George was the first promoter to recognize Wright's potential to become a major box office draw. Luce was quoted as saying "Ed Don George was the first promoter to build Bearcat Wright up as a major attraction. His career took off after this" (Cosper, 2019, p. 158). In 1961, Wright started working for Tony Santos who ran Big Time Wrestling in Boston, Massachusetts. At the time, Big Time Wrestling was an independent territorial promotion that had broken ties with the NWA.

Boston was where Wright first won a major singles wrestling title. He defeated Killer Kowalski in April 1961 at the Boston Garden for the Big Time Wrestling world championship. The promotion called the championship a world title, but Big Time was primarily a regional promotion in the New England territory. Big Time recognized Edouard Carpentier as champion after he defeated the recognized champion Lou Thesz, who was the NWA world heavyweight champion. The decision was disputed and the belt returned to Thesz. Thus, Big Time's (and other territory wrestling promotion's) "world" championship was based on Carpentier's claim to the NWA's world title after a controversial decision stemming from his match with Thesz.

Two years after winning the BTW championship, he captured the World Wrestling Association (WWA) version of the title when he defeated "Classy" Freddie Blassie. Wright created more controversy with that organization by refusing to lose the title. Bearcat Wright's stand became a real threat to the WWA. Not only was he physically imposing, he was feared because of his enormous strength. Wright would routinely demonstrate feats of strength such as ripping phone books in half and crushing apples with his bare hands in front of the audience. In a rematch with Blassie, Wright was scheduled to drop the title but had already shown his unwillingness to lose. "Wright double-crossed Blassie, holding down his weakened opponent for a pin after a headbutt, and triggering a commotion in the front office" (Johnson & Oliver, p. 253). The WWA brought in Judo expert Gene LaBell to ensure the belt changed hands. Once Wright saw LaBell, he knew the promotion was taking measures to ensure the title would return to Blassie. Instead of facing a shoot match against LaBell and Blassie, Wright refused to enter the ring and left the arena. Not only was he stripped of the title, the WWA urged other promotions to boycott Bearcat Wright. After this, his career started to decline. He did have a series of matches for the NWA world heavyweight title against Gene Kiniski but was unsuccessful. Wright also won the IWA world heavyweight title twice during his time in Australia's World Championship Wrestling promotion. He also won the NWA Vancouver tag team title with Enrique Torres and the IWA world tag team title in Sydney, Australia with Mark Lewin, NWA Hawaii tag team title with Sam Steamboat, and NWA Florida tag team title with Bobby Shane. His in-ring career ended in 1975 with a tour of Japan facing New Japan Pro Wrestling stars. His last known match was a victory over Haruka Eigen in Tokyo.

Bearcat Wright's proud stand and often controversial nature may have given promoters headaches, but in many ways his stance opened previously closed doors for Black professional wrestlers. Wright himself remained popular with fans and was a trendsetter for those African American wrestlers who followed his footsteps. He popularized many of the movements that later became stereotypical for Black wrestlers such as the claw and the flying dropkick. In the 1970s, Wright wrestled in Japan facing several top competitors in the New Japan Pro Wrestling promotion, including the NJPW founder and legend Antonio Inoki. He passed away on August 28, 1982 at the age of 50, but his groundbreaking legacy of triumph and success lives on. Wright was inducted into the legacy wing of the WWE's Hall of Fame in 2017.

Major Championships and Accomplishments		
Title	Promotion	Dates
NWA Hawaii Tag Team Champion	50th State Big Time Wrestling (Polynesian Pro Wrestling)	w/ Luther Lindsay (July 28, 1965) – 160 days w/ Sam Steamboat (July 21, 1971) – 80 days
AAC World Heavyweight Champion	Big Time Wrestling / Atlantic Athletic Commission (Boston)	April 4, 1961 – 56 days
NWA United States Heavyweight Champion	NWA San Francisco (Big Time Wrestling)	Dec 2, 1967 – 77 days April 13, 1968 – 82 days
NWA Florida Tag Team Championship	Championship Wrestling from Florida	March 9, 1972 – 61 days
NWA Brass Knuckles Champion	Championship Wrestling from Florida	March 28, 1972 – 48 days
NWA Canadian Tag Team Champion (Vancouver)	NWA All-Star Wrestling	w/ Enrique Torres (April 13, 1964) – 42 days
NWA Pacific Coast Tag Team Champion	NWA All-Star Wrestling	w/ Whipper Billy Watson (July 9, 1962) – 29 days
NWA Pacific Northwest Tag Team Champion	Pacific Northwest Wrestling	w/ Shag Thomas (Oct. 28, 1965) – 70 days w/ Shag Thomas (Jan 13, 1966) – 18

		days w/ Billy White Wolf (March 20, 1966) – 59 days
IWA World Heavyweight Champion (Australia)	World Championship Wrestling (Australia)	Aug 19, 1966 - 15 days Aug 19, 1967 – 13 days
IWA World Tag Team Champion	World Championship Wrestling (Australia)	w/ Mark Lewin (July 29, 1966)
WWA World Heavyweight Champion	Worldwide Wrestling Associates (NWA Los Angeles)	Aug 23, 1963 – 115 days
WWA International Television Tag Team Champion	Worldwide Wrestling Associates (NWA Los Angeles)	w/ Mr. Moto (July 19, 1963) – 71 days

Honors	Sponsor	Year
WWE Hall of Fame	World Wrestling Entertainment	2017
Wrestling Observer Hall of Fame	Wrestling Observer Newsletter	2019

BOBO BRAZIL

Bobo Brazil was another pioneer in the sport of professional wrestling for Black Americans. He was one of the most dominant performers and was able to transcend racial barriers due to his popularity among fans. Brazil is the first African American wrestler to have a legitimate claim to the National Wrestling Alliance's (NWA) world heavyweight championship title while the NWA was still a major conglomerate and considered the most respected wrestling organization in the world.

He was born Houston Harris on July 19, 1924 in Little Rock, Arkansas. Baseball was his favorite sport growing up. Harris worked odd jobs and eventually started playing baseball for the House of David Negro League team. While playing baseball, he was introduced to pro wrestling. Harris started training under former wrestler Joe Savoldi who originally gave him the name BuBu Brasil, "the South American Giant." A promoter's flyer misspelled his name and he would be known as Bobo Brazil for the rest of his career (Greer, 2021).

Wrestling under the name Bobo Brazil, he was "over" with fans of all races throughout his entire career. Standing 6'8" tall and weighing nearly 270 pounds, Brazil is often referred to as "the Jackie Robinson of professional wrestling" because of his immense success in crossing over and breaking down racial and ethnic barriers in the ring (Arnold, 2021). Pro wrestlers routinely came from football, boxing and other mainstream sports; so, it should come as no surprise to learn that Brazil was an inspiration to other athletes outside of wrestling, especially African American athletes. Former boxing heavyweight champion Joe Frazier was quoted in a February 6, 1970, *New York Times* article: "I was about 17 when I got interested in boxing and the guys I remember hearing about were Joe Louis, Sugar Ray Robinson, Hurricane Jackson and Bobo Brazil." (Sledge, 2020). Later in his own career Bobo mentored former boxer-turner-wrestler Rocky Johnson.

Bobo Brazil battles the Sheik. Boxer Joe Louis was the guest referee.

Bobo Brazil's first recorded match was in March 1948 in Benton Harbor. The match against Armand Myers ended after a 30-minute time limit draw. (Johnson & Oliver, 2012). Brazil went on to have classic feuds with The Sheik that ran for decades. Their feud increased the popularity of both athletes and was a huge financial draw for both wrestlers and the promotion. Brazil was the first World Wide Wrestling Federation (WWWF) United States heavyweight champion when the title was created in 1963. Brazil was a seven-time United States champion serving as both the first and last person to hold the belt. His final reign – which was his longest, lasted from February 1971 until the title was retired in March 1976.

Brazil was very popular with wrestling fans from different racial backgrounds especially during his prime. He became so popular that he was instrumental in crossing racial barriers and being allowed to wrestle against many of the top white stars of his day. The National Wrestling Alliance (NWA) sanctioned a title match where Brazil defeated "Nature Boy" Buddy Rogers for the NWA world heavyweight title in 1962. However, it was a gimmick match and the title change was not officially recognized by the NWA. "Brazil returned the title the next day after the match, after Rogers claimed he had been injured before the bout. The (local) promotion debunked Rogers's injury claim and billed Brazil as the world champ. However, the NWA did not recognize the title switch; it was likely just a promotional gimmick to avoid having Brazil lose. The local promotion could bill him as the uncrowned champ, and Rogers could continue to be the touring champion" (Klein 2012, p. 54).

Brazil won a recognized version of the championship title on September 2, 1966, when he defeated Buddy Austin in Los Angeles for the World Wrestling Association (WWA) world title. He actually held that belt twice, winning it again on January 12, 1968. When the WWA rejoined the NWA, there was a unification bout between Brazil and NWA champion Gene Kiniski. The match ended in a draw with Kiniski retaining the NWA title and thus becoming the only recognized world champion. Later in his career, Brazil wrestled and put over a young Ric Flair after many matches throughout the South. Brazil dropped the United States heavyweight championship to Flair in 1977, launching what would become the first of many major championships for the 16-time world heavyweight champion. In an interview with Ric Flair, he said: "I worked with many (Black wrestlers) over the years. Bobo Brazil was one of the best."

Bobo Brazil's long career was filled with championships and success all over the world. While he was not the first African American wrestler to win a major championship in the territories, he not only further integrated the sport but also built his own legacy as one of the most popular babyface wrestlers of all time. Whereas Bearcat Wright has been largely ignored for his contributions due to being labeled difficult to work with, Bobo Brazil's modest demeanor allowed him to transcend racial barriers more easily. He faced discrimination just like the other black wrestlers, but was popular due to his low-key demeanor making him more amenable to promoters. "Promoters who were willing to book African American wrestlers were enamored with only one: Bobo Brazil. With his athleticism and charisma, Brazil was a TV star and a natural draw at the box office. And sadly, most promoters did not feel the 'need' to have more than one African American in their territory at a time" (Cosper 2019, p. 191). Brazil was fortunate to wrestle integrated matches early on in his career. In 1994, he was inducted into the World Wrestling Federation (WWF) Hall of Fame. Bobo Brazil died on January 20, 1998, at the age of 74, silencing a career that spanned over four decades.

Major Championships and Accomplishments		
Title	Promotion	Dates
NWA United States Heavyweight Champion (9 times)	Big Time Wrestling (Detroit)	January 28, 1961
		August 1967
		July 29, 1971
		August 19, 1972
		December 23, 1972
		January 13, 1973
		January 25, 1975
		April 19, 1975
		April 21, 1976
NWA World Tag Team Champion (7 times)	Big Time Wrestling (Detroit)	w/ Sailor Art Thomas (1960s?)
		w/ Lord Athol Layton (August 8, 1970) – 133 days
		w/ Guy Mitchell (July 21, 1973)
		w/ Tony Marino (May 11, 1974)
		w/ Tony Marino (June 15, 1974)
		w/ Tony Marino (1974?)
		w/ Fred Curry (November 1974)

NWA United States Heavyweight Champion	Big Time Wrestling (San Francisco)	October 16, 1965 – 28 days
NWA Florida Tag Team Champion (2 times)	Championship Wrestling from Florida	w/ Sweet Brown Sugar (Sept 29, 1979) – 10 days w/Dusty Rhodes (Sept 9, 1980) – 39 days
NWA United States Heavyweight Champion	Mid-Atlantic Championship Wrestling	July 7, 1977 – 22 days
NWA Canadian Tag Team Champion	Maple Leaf Wrestling	w/ Whipper Billy Watson (May 22, 1958) – 21 days
NWA Toronto United States Heavyweight Champion	Maple Leaf Wrestling	February 6, 1977 – 21 days
NWA International Heavyweight Champion (2 times)	Japan Pro Wrestling	June 25, 1968 – 2 days December 1, 1972 – 3 days
NWA Americas Heavyweight Champion (3 times)	NWA Hollywood Wrestling (Worldwide Wrestling Associates)	October 4, 1968 – 98 days February 7, 1969 – 14 days April 10, 1981 – 7 days
WWA International	Worldwide Wrestling	w/ Wilbur Snyder

Tag Team Champion (4 times)	Associates	(June 3, 1954) w/ Wilber Snyder (Sept 6, 1954) – 37 days w/ Sandor Szabo (Nov 29, 1954) – 51 days w/ Primo Carnera (Nov 28, 1956) – 93 days?
WWA World Heavyweight Champion (2 times)	Worldwide Wrestling Associates	Sept 2, 1966 – 14 days January 12, 1968 – 341 days
WWA World Heavyweight Champion (2 times)	World Wrestling Association (Indianapolis)	July 24, 1981 – 79 days November 1981 (?)
WWWF United States Heavyweight Champion (7 times)	Worldwide Wrestling Federation (WWF/WWE)	April 6, 1963 -63 days July 9, 1963 – 64 days Oct 22, 1963 – 240- days Aug 24, 1967-29 days Nov 24, 1968 – 57 days Feb 10, 1969 – 687 days Feb 19, 1971 –

		1,837 days (Final champion before belt was deactivated on March 1, 1976)

Honors	Sponsor	Year
International Pro Wrestling Hall of Fame	Pro Wrestling Hall of Fame and Museum	2023
NWA Hall of Fame	National Wrestling Alliance (NWA)	2013
Pro Wrestling Hall of Fame	Pro Wrestling Hall of Fame and Museum	2008
World Wrestling Federation Hall of Fame	World Wrestling Federation/ World Wrestling Entertainment	1994
PWI Editor's Award	Pro Wrestling Illustrated	1998
Wrestling Observer Hall of Fame	Wrestling Observer Newsletter	1996

"SAILOR" ART THOMAS

Arthur Thomas was a trailblazer when he entered professional wrestling with his seaman pedigree and chiseled physique. Thomas was born January 30, 1924, in Gurdon, Arkansas. It was a small town with a population at that time of slightly more than 1800. In 1935, Thomas moved to Madison, Wisconsin with his mother. After his mother died, young Art Thomas lived in different orphanages. He eventually dropped out of school and joined the United States Merchant Marine academy. In wartime, the merchant marines serve as an auxiliary unit for the United States Navy. During World War II, Thomas delivered ammunition and supplies to the Navy seamen and served on a construction battalion that built an aerodrome in Guam.

After two years of military service, the young war veteran joined a traveling bodybuilding troupe. In the late 1940's, while working for Greyhound and training at the YMCA, Thomas met local Madison wrestler and promoter Jimmy Demetral. At first, Thomas was not interested in professional wrestling. As he continued to travel, he soon met another wrestling promoter in California who also thought Thomas was a good candidate for the sport. He then began to seriously consider pro wrestling and went back to train with Demetral who booked him in local carnival shows. In 1954, Thomas officially joined the world of professional wrestling. Thomas was originally used as a "plant" among the crowd. When the babyface (good guy) was being overpowered, he would emerge from the crowd and save the "face" from the heels or bad guys. Eventually, he became a regular in-ring performer and was one of the top box-office draws in the business at the time. After seven years of training and working with Demetral, Thomas had a wrestling match at Madison Square Garden in 1961 where he impressed promoters and his career took off.

Because Thomas did not have an amateur wrestling background, his moves were somewhat limited. Legendary wrestler and promoter Bill Watts once described Thomas as a difficult in-ring performer. Watts said Thomas would forget the moves they had planned and he would have to revert to a shoot match where he used take-downs in order to gain control of the match due to Thomas' strength and physicality. He was known for doing up to 300 free hand (bodyweight) squats per day to develop his legs and core. After continuing to work on wrestling maneuvers to match his physique, he eventually moved up the ranks because audiences wanted to see him in person.

Sailor Art Thomas challenged "Nature Boy" Buddy Rogers for the NWA United States heavyweight title in 1961. He lost the match but the card drew a crowd of over 31,000 fans. Due to drawing huge crowds, they continued to feud throughout the territories. From 1961-63, Thomas fought Rogers first for the United States heavyweight title six times with former boxer Jersey Joe Walcott serving as special referee for three of those matches. Their feud continued after Rogers won the NWA world heavyweight title. Thomas fought Rogers multiple times but never captured the title. He also had two NWA world title matches against Lou Thesz in 1963-64 after battling "Classy" Freddie Blassie in 1962 for the WWA world title in four unsuccessful attempts. After proving himself as a bona fide main event performer who could draw money, Thomas was given a few title reigns. He briefly held the WWA international television tag team championship with Thesz and the NWA Detroit world tag team championship with frequent tag team partner Bobo Brazil. In March 1968, Thomas teamed with Thesz and former boxing legend Joe Louis in a six-man tag match to defeat Louie Tillet, Tarzan Tyler and The Great Malenko in Florida.

In 1972, Thomas defeated Baron von Raschke in Detroit for the World Wrestling Association's (WWA) world heavyweight championship. Thomas was recognized as the champion in Detroit. Both Billy Red Cloud and Raschke were recognized as champion in Indianapolis. There was no undisputed champion at the time in the WWA until, of course, the unification bouts took place. Raschke defeated Red Cloud for the sole claim in Indianapolis and won the match over Thomas for the title in Detroit. Thomas worked another job while wrestling and could not be available to defend the title on a regular basis. His career as a bodybuilder and pro wrestler lasted over thirty years, as he was popular all across the globe. He had seven children and died a month after a cancer diagnosis. Arthur Thomas died on March 20, 2002. He was 79. In 2016, he was inducted into the legacy wing of the WWE's Hall of Fame.

Major Championships and Accomplishments		
Title	Promotion	Dates
NWA Tag Team Champion	Big Time (NWA Detroit)	w/Bobo Brazil (1965?)
NWA International Tag Team Champion	Maple Leaf Wrestling (Toronto)	w/John Paul Henning (July 25, 1963) – 84 days
WWA World Heavyweight Champion	World Wrestling Association (Indianapolis)	April 25, 1972 – 25 days
WWA International Television Tag Team Champion	World Wrestling Associates (Los Angeles)	w/Lou Thesz (Nov 22, 1961)

Honors	Sponsor	Year
WWE Hall of Fame	World Wrestling Entertainment	2016

ERNIE LADD

Ernest "Ernie" Ladd was a one-of-a-kind athlete who took his natural gifts to the highest level through a combination of charisma and hard work. Nicknamed "The Big Cat," Ladd was a legendary competitor in both football and pro wrestling. Not only was he a legend inside the ring, he was also a manager and the first African American to book wrestling matches for a major wrestling promotion. He was born on November 28, 1938, in Rayville, Louisiana. His birthplace was a small, predominantly African American town located in Northeast Louisiana. According to Ladd, three weeks after he was born, he moved to Marshall, Texas and then on to Orange, Texas, where he was raised. He attended Emma H. Wallace High School where he was a gifted two-sport athlete excelling in basketball and football. Ladd's high school football coach Willie Ray Smith was the father of NFL legend Charles "Bubba" Smith. His talents landed him a basketball scholarship to attend Grambling State University. At Grambling, he was also a two-sport athlete playing basketball for a year but excelling in football under coach Eddie Robinson.

In 1961, Ladd was simultaneously drafted by the National Football League's (NFL) Chicago Bears in the fourth round and the American Football League's (AFL) San Diego Chargers. He decided to sign with the Chargers. Ladd was one of the biggest and largest men in professional football at the time but was known for his quickness and agility. At his peak, Ladd stood 6'9" tall and weighed 330 pounds of solid muscle. He could run the 40-yard dash in 4.9 seconds. At San Diego, he was a member of the original Fearsome Foursome. The Fearsome Foursome were the Chargers starting defensive front line consisting of defensive end Ron Nery, defensive tackle Bill Hudson, defensive end Earl Faison and Ladd at defensive tackle. The Foursome helped the Chargers reach the American Football League Championship game five times. They won the AFL championship in 1963 dominating the Boston Patriots 51-10. Ladd was an AFL All-Star from 1962-65.

During his playing years, Ladd developed a contentious relationship with the Chargers management especially his coach who he blamed for breaking up the Fearsome Foursome defensive line. During the 1964 All-Star game, Ladd was refused cab service and later organized a protest against racial discrimination. He started the 1965 season on suspension. Ladd eventually agreed to a 10% salary cut which also made him a free agent. After leaving the Chargers in 1965, he played one season for the Houston Oilers (1966-67) and for the Kansas City Chiefs (1967-68). Knee injuries dating back to Grambling began to take a toll. He played in 112 consecutive football games over his eight-year career. Ladd was a member of the Chiefs when they won the AFL Championship.

Ladd started wrestling in 1961 – the same year he was drafted to play professional football. His first foray in professional wrestling was a publicity stunt. But as his popularity grew, Ladd continued to wrestle part time during football's off-season. One day, Ladd was challenged by "The Destroyer" Dick Beyer to come over to what Beyer called "a man's sport." Like many at the time, Ladd considered wrestlers to be phony until he stepped into the ring. He grew to love wrestling and he was making much more money. According to *Forbes*, the average NFL player's salary in 1970 was $23,000. Ladd was making as much from wrestling just during the football offseason. So, at 28 years of age with several more productive football years, Ladd decided to take a year off from football and discovered he could make significantly more money in pro wrestling. In an interview with *The New York Times* Ladd once said: "After a few years, I was making so much money wrestling in the off-season that I figured I could make a lot more by giving up football and wrestling full time…That first year wrestling, I made $98,000 and after that never made less than a hundred grand a year. That was big money back in the 60's" (Litsky, 2007).

Ladd developed his in-ring technique with training from Tiger Conway, Beyer and others. He was also drawn to the flamboyance of other wrestlers including "Classy" Freddie Blassie. At his 1994 WWF Hall of Fame induction speech, Blassie said: "And while 'The Cat' Ernie Ladd played football with the San Diego Chargers. I had a hand in teaching him to wrestle." [3] In the early 1960s, talk show host Regis Philbin was just starting out with *The Regis Philbin Show*, a late-night, weekend talk show in San Diego. With a small budget, Philbin turned to the local wrestlers to attract more viewers. His "go-to" wrestler was Blassie, who made frequent appearances on his show. Ladd also made guest appearances on Philbin's show with Blassie. "In San Diego, people would sometimes come down for the weekend, and I'd be

---

[3] https://www.youtube.com/watch?v=fLilWn-yNiU

lucky enough to get them on the show," Philbin was quoted. "But I always liked wrestling." (Blassie & Greenberg 2004, p. 90-91.) With in-ring training during the offseason and character development from television appearances, Ladd was ready when he began wrestling full-time in 1969. At 6'9" and weighing 300 pounds, Ladd was an imposing figure. He was the first Black character to successfully portray a "heel" or bad guy. During the 1970s, he was known in some territories as "The King" and "The Big Cat" in others. Ladd won the WWA heavyweight championship after defeating Dick the Bruiser in 1980. His title run was short but memorable. He lost the belt back after a month in a rematch.

Ladd's charisma allowed him to verbally joust at the same level as his physical skill. He would routinely insult his competitors calling them names like "pork chop belly" and referring to the program hosts – including a young Vince McMahon – not by name but as "Mr. TV announcer" only. During the later years, he served as a manager for Afa and Sika, The Wild Samoans. Ladd stopped performing in-ring and became a manager because he was also a booker in the Mid-South Wrestling promotion. He was the first African American to be a booker in the territories. Ladd retired from wrestling in 1986. His athletic prowess and accomplishments have been duly noted. He was inducted into the San Diego Chargers Hall of Fame in 1981. In pro wrestling, he is among a handful of wrestlers to be inducted into both the WCW Hall of Fame (1994) and the WWE Hall of Fame (1995). Ernie Ladd died in 2007 at age 68.

Major Championships and Accomplishments		
Title	Promotion	Dates
WWA World Heavyweight Champion	World Wrestling Association (Indianapolis)	Nov 1, 1980 – 28 days
NWA Central States Tag Team Champion	Central States Wrestling/Heart of American Sports Attractions	w/Bruiser Brody (Feb 3, 1980) – 46 days
NWA Florida Heavyweight Champion	Championship Wrestling from Florida	July 16, 1977 - 15 days
NWA Southern Heavyweight Champion	Championship Wrestling from Florida	Oct 1979?
NWA Georgia Tag Team Champion	Georgia Championship Wrestling	w/Ole Anderson (Oct 5, 1979) – 10 days
NWA Americas Heavyweight Champion	NWA Hollywood Wrestling/Worldwide Wrestling Associates	July 28, 1972 – 126 days July 12, 1974 – 35 days
WWA International TV Tag Team Champion	NWA Hollywood Wrestling/Worldwide Wrestling Associates	w/Edouard Carpentier (Feb 1, 1964) – 26 days
NWA American Heavyweight Champion	World Class Championship Wrestling/NWA Big Time Wrestling	May 11, 1981 – 24 days
NWA Texas Heavyweight Champion	World Class Championship Wrestling/NWA Big Time Wrestling	Jan 8, 1965 – 112 days
Mid-South Louisiana	Universal Wrestling Federation /	Jan 18, 1980 – 421

Champion	NWA Tri-State Wrestling	days
		Jan 16, 1981 – 47 days
Mid-South North American Heavyweight Champion	Universal Wrestling Federation / NWA Tri-State Wrestling	Feb 14, 1978 – 105 days
		Aug 15, 1978 – 460 days
		Dec 25, 1978 – 53 days
		Oct 16, 1984 – 416 days
NWA United States Tag Team Champion	Universal Wrestling Federation / NWA Tri-State Wrestling	w/The Assassin (April 5, 1978) – 18 days
WWA World Tag Team Champion	World Wrestling Association (Indianapolis)	w/Baron von Raschke (Feb 24, 1973) – 147 days
WWC North American Heavyweight Champion	World Wrestling Council (Puerto Rico)	Oct 21, 1974 – 33 days

Honors	Sponsor	Year
Honoree	Cauliflower Alley Club	2005
NWA Hall of Fame	National Wrestling Alliance	2013
Pro Wrestling Hall of Fame	Professional Wrestling Hall of Fame and Museum	2018
Southern California Pro Wrestling Hall of Fame	Southern California Pro Wrestling Hall of Fame	2020
WCW Hall of Fame	World Championship Wrestling	1994
WWF Hall of Fame	World Wrestling Federation	1995
Wrestling Observer Newsletter Hall of Fame	Wrestling Observer Newsletter	1996
AFL Champion	American Football League	1963
San Diego Chargers Hall of Fame	San Diego Chargers	1981
GSU Hall of Fame	Grambling State University	1989

BLACK WORLD HEAVYWEIGHT WRESTLING CHAMPIONS

Ron Simmons

"We changed the face of wrestling and we gave a lot of good black men a lot of opportunities that just didn't exist before Ron." – Big Van Vader

If there's anyone worthy of being referred to as "The Blueprint" among modern black professional wrestlers, it is Ron Simmons. As a dual sport standout in both football and wrestling, he is one of the most influential athletes in the history of professional wrestling. Simmons is universally recognized as the first black world heavyweight champion from a major wrestling promotion. He held the world tag team title in both the NWA and WCW and three times in the WWF/WWE. He also played a direct role in elevating the status of other African American wrestlers allowing them to also pursue and win championships.

Before lacing up his wrestling boots, Simmons was an outstanding college football player. He was a consensus All-American nose guard at Florida State University. He played for head football coach Bobby Bowden. Simmons had an outstanding senior year at Florida State where he finished eighth in the voting for the Heisman Trophy. After his heralded college career ended, he was drafted by the Cleveland Browns of the National Football League (NFL). He also played pro football for the Ottawa Rough Riders of the Canadian Football League (CFL) and the Tampa Bay Bandits of the United States Football League (USFL).

After retiring from professional football, Simmons began training with famed wrestling trainer Hiro Matsuda and began his career as a pro wrestler. With his physique and football credentials, Simmons made a striking appearance and rapidly rose to the top in the NWA and eventually World Championship Wrestling (WCW). In 1986, he joined Jim Crockett Promotions which was the dominant wrestling company within the NWA. He first appeared on the card at the *Great American Bash*. As a rookie, Simmons scored signature wins over Ivan Koloff, The Barbarian and Rodney Anoa'i, the future champion known by the ring name Yokozuna. He remained undefeated for over a year until eventually losing to Ivan Koloff.

In 1989, he teamed with Butch Reed to form the tag team Doom. Both members originally dressed in black hooded robes and wore black face masks. Doom made a massive impact and appeared unstoppable until losing to the Steiner Brothers in February 1990. Doom eventually defeated the Steiner Brothers on May 19, 1990, to win the NWA world tag team titles. In January 1991, Doom became recognized as the first WCW world tag team champions when Jim Crockett Promotions – the largest federation within the NWA – broke ties with the organization and became a major independent promotion. A month later, Doom lost the titles to the Fabulous Freebirds. Simmons returned to singles wrestling and began a quest for the singles world title. He achieved that goal the following year. Whereas black wrestlers before Simmons held versions of the world title, Simmons won the internationally recognized WCW world heavyweight championship on August 2, 1992, by defeating Big Van Vader (Leon White). Defeating Vader was a big deal. Vader was a former triple crown heavyweight wrestling champion, the first man to hold the heavyweight championship in both All Japan Pro and New Japan Pro Wrestling, and a former offensive lineman (center) for the University of Colorado and later the NFL's Los Angeles Rams.

The historic title reign was not originally planned. Vader was in a feud with Sting. The title match was supposed to be Vader against Sting but Sting was injured and had to withdraw from competition. Promoter Bill Watts decided to put the belt on Ron Simmons. "The arena was in Baltimore. I come waltzing in just as I normally do," Simmons said. "I get told by (WCW matchmaker) Bill Watts that I'm gonna be up for the world championship tonight." A shocked and surprised Simmons replied: "What? Tonight? Me? How? Why? How did this come about?' His exact words to me were at that point was 'Hey, why not you? Tonight, we're gonna make history here, okay?" (Mathews, 2023).

Vader had everyone on edge as suspense heightened throughout the entire match. In the end, Simmons caught and pinned Vader with a powerbomb. Simmons held the title for several months before losing it back to Vader. In a 2014 interview reflecting on the match, Vader said:

> "Ron and I went in there and we had what I consider to be my best match ever, which is really saying a lot because I've had a lot of big, historic matches and that was a good one. That 'pop' when Ron finally pinned me and took the belt was unbelievable…We changed history. We talked about it. We

changed the face of wrestling and we gave a lot of good black men a lot of opportunities that just didn't exist before Ron" (Giri, 2014).

After the historic tag team and singles championship run, Simmons moved on to compete briefly for the original Extreme Championship Wrestling (ECW) promotion and then on to the WWF. On the WWF's roster, Simmons remained popular in various roles as Farooq, leader of the Nation of Domination and later forming the Acolytes which morphed into the Acolyte Protection Agency (APA) with tag team partner John "Bradshaw" Layfield (JBL). A less significant but immensely popular with fans and lingering part of his legacy is the four-letter word "damn." After something goes wrong, Simmons would utter the word "damn" to himself but loud enough for others to hear. His partner Bradshaw noticed fans in different cities would say "damn" back to him during matches. After seeing the crowd reaction, he embraced it and officially debuted the one-word catchphrase in 2007 during a segment with King Booker and John Cena.

Throughout his career, Simmons was a triple crown champion in WCW. He won the world heavyweight title, world tag team title and United States tag team title. In the WWE, he held the tag team championship three times with Bradshaw. Simmons was inducted into the WWE Hall of Fame in 2012. "I'm absolutely satisfied with what I have accomplished in my career. I'm proud of not only things I've done (in the ring)," he said in an interview. "When it comes to winning the championship, I'm proud of the way it impacted people lives. It opened the door for other Blacks to come into the business. And people of all races still write me to this day saying how much it changed their lives." Despite being a triple crown champion in WCW, Simmons faded from world title contention as a singles wrestler in the WWF/E. He was used mostly as a mentor and tag team wrestler. Because of his strength and build, he emphasized power moves over technical wrestling and the fans loved him for that. He never held a singles title in the WWE, but his legacy was sealed through leadership in the Nation of Domination and the Acolytes (APA). Since the sport was integrated, Ron Simmons became the prototype for the future black male wrestling world champions.

Major Championships and Accomplishments		
Title	Promotion	Dates
NWA Florida Heavyweight Champion	Championship Wrestling from Florida	Dec 2, 1986 – 49 days
OVW Southern Tag Team Champion	Ohio Valley Wrestling	w/ Bradshaw (April 10, 2003) – 50 days
WCW World Heavyweight Champion	World Championship Wrestling	August 2, 1992 – 150 days
WCW/NWA Tag Team Champion	World Championship Wrestling/National Wrestling Alliance	May 19, 1990 – 281 days
WCW United States Tag Team Champion	World Championship Wrestling	w/Big Josh (Jan. 14, 1992) – 34 days
WWF Tag Team Champion (3 times)	World Wrestling Federation (WWF/WWE)	w/Bradshaw (May 25, 1999) – 35 days w/Bradshaw (July 25, 1999) – 15 days w/Bradshaw (July 9, 2001) – 29 days

Honors	Sponsor	Year
Inspirational Wrestler of the Year	Pro Wrestling Illustrated	1992
Stanley Weston Award	Pro Wrestling Illustrated	2021
WWE Hall of Fame	World Wrestling Entertainment	2012

Jacqueline

Jackie Moore, who wrestled under her real name Jacqueline, is a pioneer and the prototype for black female professional wrestlers. She had the skill, the look, the personality and wrestling acumen which allowed her to rise to the top of the profession. For many years, females in the sport of wrestling were primarily used as "arm pieces" and "eye candy," especially in today's brand of sports-entertainment. Moore, a skilled wrestler, kickboxer and martial artist, never relied on her looks or physique to capture the attention of wrestling fans. She started her career under the tutelage of General Skandor Akbar. Being the only female in the wrestling school, Jacqueline had to train with the men. However, training with male wrestlers paid huge dividends later in her career.

Jacqueline DeLois Moore was born in Dallas, Texas. As a young girl, Moore grew up a fan of the von Erich wrestling family. She made her in-ring debut with the local World Class Championship Wrestling (WCCW) promotion. The Dallas-Fort Worth based promotion was once owned by family patriarch Fritz von Erich (Jack Adkisson). Performing under the name Sweet Georgia Brown, Moore competed in the United States and Japan. In 1991, she joined the United States Wrestling Association (USWA) as Miss Texas. Originally, as a heel valet for Team Texas, she routinely attacked their opponents and interfered in matches to give Team Texas the edge. As Miss Texas, she was the inaugural United States Wrestling Association's (USWA) women's champion. Jaqueline traded the title with Lauren Davenport and another wrestler who also used the name Sweet Georgia Brown, a name Moore once used in the WCCW. On her eighth title run, she defeated Candi Devine to win both the USWA belt and the Universal Wrestling Federation (UWF) women's championship on December 4, 1994. Moore was the last UWF women's champion. She held the title until the promotion folded in 1996. She would win the USWA title a record 14 times before leaving for the WWF. The USWA and WWF had a partnership and would occasionally share wrestlers. Jacqueline was scheduled to appear in the WWF in 1994 but was sidelined due to injury.

Instead of immediately going to the WWF, Jaqueline joined Jim Cornette's Knoxville, Tennessee-based Smoky Mountain Wrestling. She joined the promotion in October 1995 as a member of Cornette's Militia under the name Sgt. Rock; however, the company folded in December before she had the chance to compete in the ring. She was later hired by World Championship Wrestling (WCW) in 1997. In

WCW, she made a name for herself as a strong, athletic manager for male wrestlers including "Taskmaster" Kevin Sullivan and briefly for Harlem Heat. She is mostly known for feuding with Sullivan's ex-wife Woman (Nancy Benoit) and eventually helping Chris Benoit defeat Sullivan in a *"loser must retire"* match by hitting him with a wooden chair. In another notable moment during her stint at WCW, Jacqueline won an intergender match against male wrestler Disco Inferno on October 26, 1997, at the annual *Halloween Havoc* pay-per-view.

Jacqueline re-joined the World Wrestling Federation in 1998 as the on-camera "girlfriend" of "Marvelous" Marc Mero. This instantly set up a feud with Mero's real life estranged wife and women's champion Sable. After months of feuding, Jaqueline eventually defeated Sable to become the first African American WWF women's world champion. After a two-month reign, she lost the title to Sable. However, Jacqueline won the WWF women's title for a second time in 2000 after defeating male wrestler Harvey Wippleman (Bruno Lauer). Wipperman won the belt from Miss Kitty (Stacy Carter) while dressed in drag under the name Hervina.

During her tenure in WWF, Moore also participated in mixed-gender matches where she wrestled both men and women – something she trained for since the start of her career. In 2004, she defeated Chavo Guerrero, Jr. to become the WWF cruiserweight champion. She lost the title in a rematch to Guerrero and was released from the company soon after. In November 2004, she joined Total Nonstop Action (TNA). Jacqueline continued to wrestle women and referee men's matches before transitioning to working behind the scenes. Her last match with TNA was in 2013. Jaqueline is one of the most decorated female wrestlers in history. She was inducted in the WWE Hall of Fame in 2016 and the women's wrestling hall of fame in 2024. She is now retired but continues to make appearances at wrestling events and trade shows.

Major Championships and Accomplishments		
Title	Promotion	Dates
USWA Women's Champion (14 times)	United States Wrestling Association	March 2, 1992 – 42 days
		Aug. 24, 1992 – 28 days
		Oct. 17, 1992 – 16 days
		Nov. 23, 1992 – 14 days
		Jan. 30, 1993 – 58 days
		April 3, 1993 – 121 days
		Aug 23, 1993 – 63 days
		Dec 5, 1994 – 35 days
		Jan 16, 1995 – 63 days
		March 27, 1995 – 21 days
		April 24, 1995 – 218 days
		Dec. 20, 1995 – 21 days
		Jan 15, 1996 – 91 days
		Aug 23, 1996 – 73

65

		days
UWF Women's World Champion	Universal Wrestling Federation	Dec. 5, 1994
WWF Women's Champion	World Wrestling Federation (WWF/WWE)	Sept. 21, 1998 – 54 days Feb. 1, 2000 – 53 days
WWE Cruiserweight Champion	World Wrestling Entertainment (WWE)	May 6, 2004 – 9 days
WWC Women's Champion	World Wrestling Council	Sept. 8, 1990 – 32 days

Honors	Sponsor	Year
WWE Hall of Fame	World Wrestling Entertainment	2016
Women's Wrestling Award	Cauliflower Alley Club	2022
Women's Wrestling Hall of Fame	Women's Wrestling Hall of Fame (WWHOF)	2024

The Rock

Dwayne Douglas Johnson is not only one of the most famous pro wrestlers of all time, but also one of Hollywood's most successful actors. Johnson's movies have grossed over $10 billion worldwide making him one of the highest grossing Hollywood actors. Before he was a top box office draw and businessman, he wrestled full time for eight years in the WWF/WWE. Debuting on the circuit as "Flex Kavana," he later became known as "Rocky Maivia" – as homage to his famous wrestling father "Soul Man" Rocky Johnson and grandfather, the High Chief Peter Maivia. Unfortunately, being pushed as a third-generation wrestler didn't advance his professional wrestling career.

He unexpectedly reached superstar status as a heel when he started referring to himself in third person as "The Rock."

As a wrestler, The Rock is a triple crown champion in the WWE. He is a 10-time world heavyweight champion in the World Wrestling Federation (WWF/WWE). The Rock is also a two-time intercontinental champion and has held the world tag team belt five times. Johnson was born in Hayward, California. He is the son of former wrestler Rocky Johnson, a Black Canadian and Samoan mother Ata Maivia[4]. His father and tag team partner Tony Atlas were the first black world tag team champions in the WWF. His maternal grandmother was the first female professional wrestling promoter when she took over Polynesia Pacific Pro Wrestling after the death of her husband Peter Maivia.

Wrestling is in Johnson's blood; however, it was not the first sport where he found success. As a high school football player, he was named "player of the year" and received a full scholarship to play football at the University of Miami. At Miami, he was a member of the 1991 national championship team and as a senior was named pre-season All-American. After college, he played pro football briefly for the Calgary Stampeders of the Canadian Football League (CFL).

When his football career ended, Johnson began his career as a pro wrestler in 1996 with the Tennessee-based United States Wrestling Association. He was a two-time USWA world tag team champion before signing with the WWF later that same year. In the WWF, he took the ring name Rocky Maivia and was heavily promoted as the WWF's first third generation wrestler. Despite his relative ring inexperience, he rapidly rose through the ranks. On February 13, 1997, he defeated Triple H for the intercontinental championship.

---

[4] The Rock has acknowledged his respect for both his Samoan and Black family heritage on both his television show Young Rock and on social media - https://www.nzherald.co.nz/talanoa/dwayne-the-rock-johnson-announces-special-trip-to-samoa-20-years-after-chief-bestowal/3X3UZMA5JFBTRMSZ3S33XT3SHQ/

Maivia was a clean-cut babyface touted as the blue chipper. Fans began to resent his fast ascent. After losing the title, Rocky remerged as a heel and a member of the Nation of Domination led by Farooq (Ron Simmons). Rocky began to insult the audience and other performers for booing his matches. To punctuate his heel turn, he started referring to himself in third person as The Rock. He began a feud with Farooq and eventually overthrew him to become leader of The Nation. As The Rock's popularity grew, infighting within the Nation reached a climax. In October 1998, he was defeated by Mark Henry with help from D'Lo Brown again turning babyface in the process.

The Rock was the second black male to wear a recognized world heavyweight title in one of the major organizations and the first black world champion in the WWF/E. He accomplished this feat on November 15, 1998, when he defeated Mankind (Mick Foley) for the WWF world heavyweight championship. He subsequently held that title on eight occasions. The Rock is also recognized as a two-time WCW world heavyweight champion. He won the title during The Invasion storyline against Booker T and avenged his title loss to Chris Jericho. After the Invasion storyline ended, the title was renamed the World Heavyweight Championship.

During The Rock's most recent return to the WWE, he became a member of The Bloodline, a villainous group originally led by Roman Reigns. While the Bloodline has found new leadership in Solo Sikoa, Reigns is the OTC (original tribal chief) and The Rock is now known as "the final boss." The Bloodline has a deep Samoan history made up of three families: Anoa'i, Fatu and Maivia. The roots of the family tree go back to Amituana'i Anoa'i and Peter Maivia who were blood brothers. For his wrestling gimmick, The Rock used his real-life status as a Samoan "high chief." Some of the family members are Afa and Sika (The Wild Samoans), Jimmy "Superfly" Snuka, Yokozuna, Rikishi, twins Jimmy and Jey Uso, Umaga, Solo Sikoa, and females Nia Jax, Tamina and Naomi by marriage to Jimmy Uso. The Rock's daughter, Ava Raine (Simone Garcia Johnson), is currently signed to the WWE's NXT brand where she serves as general manager. She is the first fourth generation wrestler in the WWE.

As his acting career grew, The Rock also had more signature matches. The first was defeating Hulk Hogan in an "Icon versus Icon" match in 2002. The following year, also at *WrestleMania*, he pinned Stone Cold Steve Austin in what was Austin's last match. As a charismatic performer, The Rock's signature moves are the Rock Bottom and the People's Elbow. He is also known for raising his eyebrow and referring to himself as "The People's Champion." The Rock received an honorary people's championship belt at the 2024 WWE Hall of Fame ceremony from Lonnie Ali, the wife of boxing legend Muhammad Ali.

The Rock's in-ring wrestling talent is complemented by his tremendous charisma and ability to connect with fans. His interviews and catchphrases added words to the American pop cultural lexicon and he has parlayed that crossover appeal into a successful career in film, television and music. In 2012, Johnson created Seven Buck Productions with his first wife, producer and IFBB professional bodybuilder Dany Garcia. In 2019, he was named one of *Time* magazine's 100 most influential people in the world. The Rock's career is perhaps summed up best by one of his catchphrases: he is the most electrifying man in sports entertainment.

As popular as so many black wrestlers have been over the years, none has yet come close to the level of fame The Rock has achieved. Even though he's spending more time making movies these days than wrestling, he still makes sporadic appearances in the ring, much to the delight of his "millions and millions" of fans. He is also a board member of TKO Group Holdings, the parent company of UFC and WWE. Now, Johnson not only owns a piece of the company that give him his big break, but he also owns the trademark to his moniker "The Rock."

Major Championships and Accomplishments		
Title	Promotion	Dates
USWA World Tag Team Champion	United States Wrestling Association	w/ Bart Sawyer (June 17, 1996) – 14 days
		w/ Bart Sawyer (July 8, 1996) – 7 days
WWF/WWE Champion	World Wrestling Federation	Nov. 15, 1998 – 50 days
		Jan. 24, 1999 – 7 days
		Feb. 15, 1999 – 41 days
		April 30, 2000 – 21 days
		June 25, 2000 – 119 days
		Feb. 25, 2001 – 35 days
		July 21, 2002 – 35 days
		Jan 27, 2013 – 70 days
WCW Champion	World Wrestling Federation	Aug. 19, 2001 – 63 days
		Nov. 5, 2001 – 34 days
WWF Intercontinental	World Wrestling Federation	Feb. 13, 1997 – 73

Champion		days
		Dec. 8, 1997 – 264 days
WWF Tag Team Champion	World Wrestling Federation	w/ Mankind (Aug 30, 1999) – 8 days
		w/ Mankind (Sept. 20, 1999) – 2 days
		w/ Mankind (Oct. 12, 1999) – 6 days
		w/ The Undertaker (Dec 18, 2000) – 1 day
		w/ Chris Jericho (Oct. 22, 2001) – 8 days

Honors	Sponsor	Year
Miami Hurricanes - NCAA National Championship	National Collegiate Athletic Association	1991
Match of the Year – (against Mankind)	Pro Wrestling Illustrated	1999
Match of the Year (against Hollywood Hulk Hogan)	Pro Wrestling Illustrated	2002
Wrestler of the Year	Pro Wrestling Illustrated	2000
Wrestling Observer Hall of Fame	Wrestling Observer Newsletter	2007
Triple Crown Champion - Intercontinental title - WWE Heavyweight title - World Tag Team title	World Wrestling Entertainment	Feb 13, 1997 Nov 15, 1998 Aug 30, 1999
Man of the Century	Muscle & Fitness	2015
Mr. Olympia Icon Award	International Fitness and Bodybuilding Federation (IFBB)	2015
NAACP Image Award	National Association for the Advancement of Colored People	2017

| 100 Most Influential People in the World | *Time* magazine | 2019 |

Booker T

"You didn't have a recognized world champion, African American world champion until 1992. And I'll go on record as saying that if Booker T doesn't become world champion soon in his career, it will be a travesty." -Julian L.D. Shabazz[5]

---

[5] From an appearance on BET Tonight with host Tavis Smiley, June 28, 2000 - https://www.youtube.com/watch?v=z07bhr446h8

Booker T. Huffman is arguably the most decorated wrestler of his era. He has held the top title in three major wrestling promotions and is among a handful of wrestlers recognized as both a triple crown champion and a grand slam champion (four major titles) in the two largest North American wrestling promotions – World Championship Wrestling and World Wrestling Entertainment.

Booker T is a six-time world heavyweight champion. He won the WCW world heavyweight championship five times and the WWE world title once. He is the second black world champion in WCW (after Ron Simmons) and the second black world champion in WWE (after The Rock). He was the final world champion and United States heavyweight champion in WCW simultaneously. He was the first African American to win the world television championship in WCW – a title he held for a record six times. Booker also held the world tag team title 10 times in WCW with his older brother Stevie Ray as Harlem Heat. He was also a world tag team champion three times in the WWE partnering with Test, Rob van Dam and Goldust. After winning the WWE's King of the Ring tournament in 2006, he embraced the trappings of royalty and began the King Booker persona along with his wife Queen Sharmell. After leaving the WWE, Booker joined Total Nonstop Action. In TNA, he held the world tag team title with Scott Steiner and was the inaugural TNA legends champion (now the television champion).

During his active years, Booker T was the consummate in-ring performer due to his athletic background. In high school, he once was a drum major in the marching band. His signature scissors kick and spinaroonie moves were incorporated into wrestling from band and hip-hop break dancing. He may not have reached the crossover appeal at the level of The Rock, but he has remained at the top of the business since first winning the WCW world heavyweight championship on July 9, 2000. He captured the vacated belt by pinning Jeff Jarrett. However, his dominance in the mid-1990's, came as one-half of the Harlem Heat (with his brother Stevie Ray), who held the WCW world tag team titles for a record 10 times.

Booker T was born in Plain Dealing, Louisiana in 1965. He is the youngest of eight children. By age 13, both his parents had died.

He lived with an older sister for three years then at age 17, he moved in with his older brother Lash (Stevie Ray). At the time, Booker was a single parent of a son. While working at a Wendy's restaurant, he was arrested for armed robbery and served 19 months in prison. After serving time, he was making ends meet by working for a storage company. One day his brother Lash discovered wrestler/promoter Ivan Putski was opening a wrestling school to complement his Western Wrestling Alliance independent promotion. He suggested they give wrestling a try and Booker agreed. Booker had always been an athletic person. He didn't play organized sports in school. Instead, he was a high school drum major in the marching band performing and entertaining huge crowds. He was really interested in learning to become a wrestler; however, he was a single father barely earning enough to survive. Fortunately, his supervisor at the storage company gave him the money upfront to attend Putski's wrestling school. Booker told *Slam Wrestling*: "It was $3,000 to go to the school. At the time, I was just working a regular job and raising my son as a single-parent. I was just trying to make everything work. It just so happened that the guy who I worked for at the American Mini Storage wanted to see me succeed. So, he put the money up for me. He was a damn good boss," (Powell, 2021).

Former WWF wrestler Scott Casey, one of the school's trainers at the time, took an interest in Booker. After eight weeks of learning mostly ring psychology, he debuted on the television show *Western Wrestling Alliance Live!* as G.I. Bro. This was a black patriotic character in reference to the Gulf War. He did not want to dance nor do the typical shuck and jive talk similar to the roles most black wrestlers were given. The character was personally important to Booker because he only wanted to portray a positive image of African Americans. "That's been my prime motivation and my prime objective since day one of getting into the wrestling business...I have worked to break that stereotype. That's why when you see me come to a wrestling venue or an event, I am always going to be dressed better than anyone else because I don't just represent myself, I represent a whole race of people who are watching these shows," he said (Powell, 2021).

His vision; however, ended before it could really take off as WWA closed its doors. After the company folded, the brothers wrestled on the Texas independent circuit. One day they had a match against one another which impressed Akbar enough to sign them on the spot. They joined the Dallas-based Global Wrestling Federation as the Ebony Experience. They would win the GWF tag team championship in 1992. They held the tag team titles for a record three times. In August 1993, they joined World Championship Wrestling as Harlem Heat. Billed from Harlem, NY, Booker was renamed Kole and Stevie Ray was renamed Kane. In 1994, they were managed by "Sister" Sherri Martel and resumed using their ring names Booker T and Stevie Ray. In December, they won their first world tag team championship by defeating Stars and Stripes. Harlem Heat went on to have feuds with the best tag team talent in WCW including Sting & Lex Luger, Rick & Scott Steiner, the Road Warriors, Faces of Fear (Meng & Barbarian), American Males, Public Enemy and the Outsiders - Scott Hall and Kevin Nash. When Stevie Ray was forced to take a few months off to allow an ankle injury to properly heal, Booker made the transition into singles wrestling.

On December 29, 1997, Booker T defeated Disco Inferno to become the WCW world television champion. Chris Benoit's interference caused him to lose the title to Fit Finley. He won a highly competitive best of seven series of matches against Benoit to earn the right to face Finley. Booker regained the title on June 14, 1998. He later traded the title with both Scott and Rick Steiner. In 1999, Booker convinced Stevie Ray to leave the New World Order and Harlem Heat reunited. They won the world tag team titles at *Road Wild*, *Fall Brawl* and *Halloween Havoc* pay-per-view events. After a dispute over recruiting a new female manager named Midnight, the duo parted ways again. On April 17, 2000, Eric Bischoff criticized several wrestlers including Booker T. The wrestlers banned together and formed the Misfits in Action (MIA) and Booker reverted back to his original character G.I. Bro and briefly served as leader of the group. After a brief stint with MIA, Booker promoted Hugh Morrus to General Rection and left MIA on June 19, 2000. He left the stable because his years of hard work were finally being noticed and taken seriously. He was promoted by Vince Russo to main event status. In one of the most controversial moves that shifted the paradigm in modern professional wrestling, Russo was fed up with the autonomy and control Hulk Hogan had over the company and fired Hogan publicly during a live broadcast on July 9, 2000, at the *Bash at the Beach* pay-per-view. The original world title match was scheduled to be Hogan vs the reigning champion Jeff Jarrett. When the bell rung, Jarrett immediately laid down in the middle of the ring. This move resembled the infamous "Fingerpoke of Doom" where Hogan won the title by poking Kevin Nash with one finger and Nash laid down allowing Hogan to get the pinfall victory. This was largely seen as the beginning of the end of World Championship Wrestling (Finnegan & Finnegan, 2024). Russo was at ringside during the match and threw the belt into the ring at Hogan. Hogan put one foot on Jarrett for the pin then immediately left the ring.

Russo then entered the ring and said: "I came back for every one of the guys in that locker room that week in, week out bust their ass for WCW. I came back for the Booker T's. I came back for every single guy in MIA. I came back for the Animals. I came back for (Jeff) Jarrett. I came back for the guys behind that curtain that give a shit about this company…Jeff Jarrett is still the official WCW champion but he will defend that title in this ring tonight. And he will defend that title against (the guy) back there who for 14 years has been busting his ass in WCW and can't get a break because of Hulk Hogan. And I'm talking about Booker T."[6]

An impromptu match between Jarrett and Booker T was instantly added to the card and Booker won the first of his five world heavyweight titles with WCW. When the company folded Booker T was the most decorated wrestler in WCW history winning 21 titles overall and he was both the reigning United States and world heavyweight champion. When WCW was bought by the WWF, Booker T ironically made his debut at the *King of the Ring* pay-per-view. He relinquished the US title to Chris Kanyon and lost the world title to Kurt Angle initially but won it back in a rematch. He won the WCW tag

---

[6] https://www.youtube.com/watch?v=lmt66vr7xKc

team title with Test and later with Goldust. He flirted with the WWF Hardcore championship winning and losing the title twice at *Insurrextion*. On July 7, 2023, he won the Intercontinental championship by defeating Christian. Booker and Rob van Dam defeated Ric Flair and Batista to win his third tag team title in WWF/WWE. After Kurt Angle was stripped of the United States title in 2004, Booker won the title in an 8-man elimination tournament. Booker T won the United States title again but it was his victory over Bobby Lashley to win the 2006 King of the Ring tournament when he created the memorable King Booker character.

King Booker with Queen Sharmell

As King Booker, he started using the mannerisms of an English monarch and spoke with a fake British accent. He even added Sir William Regal and Sir Fit Finley to his royal court. Booker was unsuccessful in his attempt to defeat Lashley for the United States title but won the world heavyweight championship from Rey Mysterio at *The Great American Bash* pay-per-view on July 23, 2006. The win made him a triple crown champion. King Booker proclaimed himself the only "king" and feuded with Jerry "the king" Lawler and Triple H over using the title. His last match for WWE was a lost to John Cena. He and Sharmell were granted their release in October 2007. On November 7, 2007, at *Genesis*, Booker T debuted in TNA Wrestling as Sting's mystery partner. Booker and Sharmell also participated in mixed gender tag team matches. On October 23, 2008, Booker introduced the TNA Legends Championship. He later formed the Main Event Mafia and teamed with Scott Steiner to win the TNA world tag team title. They lost the titles to the British Invasion at *Bound for Glory* which was his last match under contract. On May 21, 2010, he returned for one night to challenge Ron Van Dam for the TNA world heavyweight championship in a losing effort. He wrestled briefly in Puerto Rico's International Wrestling Association and Carlos Colon's World Wrestling Council before returning to the WWE as a part time wrestler and commentator.

Booker T became one of the few wrestling stars to win championships in different major wrestling federations. He held titles in WCW, WWF/WWF and TNA. He is a grand slam champion in both WWE and WCW. Booker is now a commentator full time for the WWE as well as owning and operating Reality of Wrestling. He has pinned two autobiographies: *Booker T: From Prison to Promise* (2012) and *Booker T: Wrestling Royalty* (2015). Booker T is a two-time WWE Hall of Famer. He was inducted into the WWE Hall of Fame as a singles competitor in 2013 by his brother Stevie Ray. In 2019, Harlem Heat was inducted into the WWE Hall of Fame. Additionally, Booker T inducted his wife Queen Sharmell into the WWE Hall of Fame in 2022.

Major Championships and Accomplishments		
Title	**Promotion**	**Dates**
GWF Tag Team Champion	Global Wrestling Federation	w/ Stevie Ray (July 31, 1992) – 7 days
		w/ Stevie Ray (Sept. 1992)
		w/ Stevie Ray (Feb 26, 1993) – 70 days
Tag Team Champion	Reality of Wrestling	w/ Stevie Ray (Feb 21, 2015) – 21 days
TNA Legends/Television Champion	Total Nonstop Action	Oct. 23, 2008 – 143 days
TNA World Tag Team Champion	Total Nonstop Action Wrestling	w/ Scott Steiner (July 19, 2009) – 91 days
WCW World Heavyweight Champion	World Championship Wrestling	July 9, 2000 – 50 days
		Sept. 17, 2000 – 8 days
		Oct. 2, 2000 – 55 days
	World Wrestling Federation	March 26, 2001 – 120 days
		July 30, 2001 – 20 days
WCW World Television	World Championship	Dec. 29, 1997 – 49

Champion	Wrestling	days
		Feb 22, 1998 – 67 days
		May 1, 1998 – 1 day
		May 3, 1998 – 1 day
		June 14, 1998 – 29 days
		March 14, 1999 – 56 days
WCW United States Heavyweight Champion	World Championship Wrestling	March 18, 2001 – 128 days
WCW World Tag Team Champion	World Championship Wrestling	w/ Stevie Ray (Dec 8, 1994) – 164 days
		w/ Stevie Ray (May 3, 1995) - 28 days
		w/Stevie Ray (Sept 17, 1995) 1 day
		w/Stevie Ray (Sept 27, 1995) 117 days
		w/Stevie Ray (June 24, 1996) – 5 days
		w/Stevie Ray (July 27, 1996) – 58 days
		w/Stevie Ray (Oct 1, 1996) – 26 days

		w/Stevie Ray (Aug 14, 1999) – 9 days
		w/Stevie Ray (Sept 12, 1999) 36 days
		w/Stevie Ray (Oct 24, 1999) – 1 day
World Tag Team Champion	World Wrestling Federation	w/Test (Sept 25, 2001) – 13 days
		w/Goldust (Dec 15, 2002) – 22 days
		w/Rob Van Dam (Feb 16, 2004) – 35 days
WWF Intercontinental Champion	World Wrestling Federation	July 7, 2003 – 33 days
WWF United States Heavyweight Champion	World Wrestling Federation	March 18, 2001 – 128 days
		July 27, 2004 – 66 days
		Oct 18, 2005 – 35 days
WWF Hardcore Champion	World Wrestling Federation	May 4, 2002 (twice) – less than one day

Honors	Sponsor	Year
Inspirational Wrestler of the Year	Pro Wrestling Illustrated	2000
Tag Team of the Year	Pro Wrestling Illustrated	1995 & 1996
Triple Crown Champion - World Tag Team title - World Heavyweight title - US Heavyweight title	World Championship Wrestling	May 3, 1995 July 9, 2000 March 18, 2001
Triple Crown Champion - World Tag Team title - Intercontinental title - World Heavyweight title	World Wrestling Federation (WWF/WWE)	Nov 1, 2001 July 7, 2003 July 23, 2006
Grand Slam Champion - World Tag Team title - Hardcore title - Intercontinental title - World Heavyweight title	World Wrestling Entertainment	Nov 1, 2001 May 4, 2002 July 7, 2003 July 23, 2006
King of the Ring	World Wrestling	2006

	Entertainment	
Tag Team Award (w/Stevie Ray)	Cauliflower Alley Club	2018
George Tragos/Lou Thesz Pro Wrestling Hall of Fame	National Wrestling Hall of Fame	2018
WWE Hall of Fame	World Wrestling Entertainment	2013
WWE Hall of Fame (w/Stevie Ray)	World Wrestling Entertainment (WWE)	2019

Jazz

Carlene Denise Moore-Begnaud, who wrestles under the name Jazz, was originally an aspiring basketball player. She was attending college on a basketball scholarship but decided higher education was not her calling. She eventually dropped out. However, her athleticism did not go unnoticed and she was asked to consider a career in pro wrestling. After nearly eight months of training under Rod Price at a Louisiana wrestling school, she started her wrestling career with Extreme Championship Wrestling (ECW). She joined ECW under the ring name Jazzmine as a manager/valet for the Impact Players: Lance Storm and Justin Credible along with his manager Jason

Knight. Eventually, the two managers would feud which led to an intergender match. At *Heat Wave* 1999, Jazz defeated Jason Knight. He attempted to powerbomb Jazz onto a steel chair but Jazz reversed it into her Jazz Stinger- a variation of the traditional facebuster finishing move- on the chair. Shortly after her victory, Jazz defeated Steve Corino who was paid by Knight to eliminate her. Jazz remained with the promotion until ECW went bankrupt.

Upon leaving ECW, she joined the World Wrestling Federation in 2001. She initially went to the Ohio Valley Wrestling (OVW) development territory for six months of additional training before joining the main roster as Jazz. Jazz made her presence known quickly by entering a 6-woman tournament for the vacant WWF women's championship at *Survivor Series* 2001. Trish Stratus emerged victorious by pinning Ivory. In early 2002, Jazz defeated former champion Jacqueline to become the top contender for the title and began feuding with Stratus. On February 4, 2002, she became the second black female to win a recognized world championship when she defeated Stratus for the WWF women's world title. Later that year, the WWF changed its name to WWE making her the last WWF women's champion and the first WWE women's champion. She later lost to Stratus in a hardcore-rules match due to a torn ACL. Jazz continued to feud with several top wrestlers and regained the title on April 27, 2003, by again defeating Stratus. She lost the title in a battle royal to Gail Kim due to a dislocated shoulder. Jazz returned as a manager for her husband Rodney Mack but was released from her WWE contract in 2004.

Upon leaving the WWE, she worked with independent promotions and started Down South Championship Wrestling with her husband. She also won the top title in Women's Extreme Championship Wrestling in May 2005. Jazz briefly appeared at the WWE vs. ECW event but only had a small on-screen role. She later worked for Women Superstars Uncensored in New Jersey where she teamed with Marti Belle to win her first tag team championship. After losing the title, Jazz worked for Shine Wrestling where she continued to feud with Mercedes Martinez and Ivelisse, who was the Shine champion. She defeated Ivelisse in a qualifying match in 2013, but never entered the tournament. A year later, Ivelisse successfully defended the title against Jazz. After leaving Shine wrestling, Jazz debuted at the Philadelphia-based Chikara promotion in September 2016. She left after her Original Divas Revolution team was eliminated from the King of Trios tournament.

After spending a few years on the independent circuit, she eventually decided to join the National Wrestling Alliance. Jazz captured the NWA women's world championship on September 16, 2016, from Amber Gallows (Kimberly Davis). Jazz held on to the title until a combination of medical and personal reasons forced her to vacate the title days before she was scheduled to defend it at the Jim Crockett Sr. Memorial Cup Tag Team Tournament against Allysin Kay. Kay defeated Santana Garrett to win the world title. Jazz's historic run as champion lasted 948 days, which is the third longest reign in the NWA's history after Debbie Combs and the Fabulous Moolah.

Jazz appeared in AEW and Southeast Wrestling (SEW) briefly before joining Impact Wrestling. At Impact, she had her final matches before retiring from in-ring competition. The NWA held an in-ring tribute to Jazz at their *Hard Times 2* pay-per-view on December 4, 2021. During the event, Jazz said: "From day one when we met, we said we were gonna make it. We set a goal to become if not the best, but one of the best in this business...Rodney had shoe jobs, we were barely making it. He used to get off from work, come wake me up at 9:30 or 10 o'clock at night to go work out. Boy did I hate it but I knew that's what it took" (A Tribute to Jazz, 2021).

Jazz is the first African American female wrestler to hold the world title in two major promotions. She is the first African American woman to go into *WrestleMania* as a champion. Jazz is the last WWF women's champion and the first WWE women's champion. She is a two-time women's champion in the World Wrestling Federation and is recognized as the third longest reigning women's champion in the National Wrestling Alliance (NWA). She has worked for most of the major promotions including WWF/WWE, NWA, ECW, TNA Impact Wrestling and AEW. She is also among a handful of women who have successfully competed in intergender matches. After more than two decades in the business, "The Female Fighting Phenom" is officially retired from active wrestling competition. She continues to operate her wrestling school and make public appearances at wrestling events.

Major Championships and Accomplishments		
Title	Promotion	Dates
NWA Women's Champion	National Wrestling Alliance	Sept 16, 2016 – 948 days
WSU Tag Team Champion	Women Superstars United	Nov 6, 2010 – 202 days
WWE Women's Champion (2 times)	World Wrestling Entertainment	Feb 4, 2002 – 97 days April 27, 2003 – 63 days

Honors	Sponsor	Year
Texas Wrestling Hall of Fame	Southern Wrestling Hall of Fame	2012
WSU Hall of Fame	Women Superstars Uncensored	2010
Women's Wrestling Award	Cauliflower Alley Club	2020
Women's Wrestling Hall of Fame	Women's Wrestling Hall of Fame (WWHOF)	2022

R-Truth

Ron Aaron Killings is a professional wrestler and rap artist from Charlotte, North Carolina. He holds the distinction of being the first African American male wrestler to hold the NWA world heavyweight championship. He won that title twice when the Total Nonstop Action (TNA) promotion was still affiliated with the National Wrestling Alliance (NWA). Since Killings is also a rap artist, he created his own entrance song "What's Up?" that he has used in both TNA and WWE since 2006.

In high school, Killings excelled in football and track & field. He also developed a love for rap music and breakdancing. Killings received several college scholarships but turned them down to focus on a career in music. Unfortunately, to finance his music career, he began selling drugs. After spending 13 months in prison, Killings changed his life around and ended his involvement in the drug lifestyle. While in a halfway house, he met NWA cameraman Jackie Crockett. Killings was somewhat interested in Crockett's pitch to become a wrestler, but his main focus was on establishing a career in the music industry. After two years of recording and performing, he decided to accept Crockett's offer to learn how to wrestle. He traveled with Crockett to several NWA and Pro Wrestling Federation (PWF) shows before eventually training with Manny Fernandez. In 1997, Killings debuted as a manager traveling with and studying under Fernandez. He joined NWA Wildside in 1999 under the name K-Krush. While in the Wildside promotion, he won the world television championship title in June and held it for 63 days.

Later that year, he signed a developmental contract with the World Wrestling Federation using the ring name K-Kwik. After a title reign as the southern heavyweight champion in the WWF's Memphis territory, Killings was promoted to the main roster. He debuted as a tag team partner with Road Dogg Jessie James. K-Kwik became a singles competitor after Road Dogg was released in 2001 and began competing in the hardcore division. He won the hardcore championship from Raven twice in two days due to the 24/7 rules. As the Invasion angle gained momentum, K-Kwik became more of a background player with little on-screen time. He was released from the WWF in 2001.

After leaving the WWF, Killings joined Total Nonstop Action wrestling in 2002. He established himself as a heel early during his tenure within the promotion. He began using his real name and wrestled as Ron "The Truth" Killings. He is best known for his accomplishments in TNA by winning the NWA world heavyweight championship. Killings' first reign as NWA world champion began on August 7, 2002, when he defeated Ken Shamrock. He won it again a year later in a four-way title match against A.J. Styles, Raven and Chris

Harris. Truth lost the title to Jeff Jarrett due to interference from Vince Russo. He turned heel once again and attacked Jarrett. In May 2003, he began a tag team with Konnan and B.G. James (Road Dogg Jesse James). The trios team became known as the 3 Live Kru. The Kru defeated the team of Simon Diamond, Johnny Swinger and Glenn Gilberti on November 26 to capture the vacant NWA world tag team championship. They lost the titles to Redshirt Security. The Kru later defeated Team Canada to recapture the title. However, Killings and James dropped the titles back to Team Canada after Konnan was injured. Billy Gunn joined TNA and urged his former partner BG James to reform the New Age Outlaws. "The Outlaw" eventually changed his name to Kip James as a psychological tool to lure B.G. He joined the stable and they became the 4 Live Kru. After losing an 8-man tag team match to Team Canada, Killings left the Kru.

Killings returned to the now World Wrestling Entertainment in 2008. His comedic role was increased during this period. In 2009, Truth introduced an invisible character known as Ricky. The character quickly faded. In April 2010, he competed on the Raw brand. R-Truth won the vacant United States championship by defeating The Miz. He lost the title back to The Miz in a fatal four-way match that also included Zack Ryder and John Morrison.

In 2011, R-Truth turned heel and attacked his former partner, John Morrison. R-Truth became a heel and argued that entertaining the fans did not earn him any titles. He attacked Morrison while smoking a cigarette. Fans were screaming "think of the children" at R-Truth for what many perceived as horrible actions. He then used this to develop a fictional character named Little Jimmy. Little Jimmy represented the type of fans Truth was supposed to please when he was a babyface. Truth began to team with The Miz as they attacked other wrestlers and claimed that Triple H was not giving their characters a proper push. They initially formed Awesome Truth during this period. Awesome Truth defeated CM Punk and Triple H in a tag match. Cena and The Rock defeated Awesome Truth at *Survivor Series* and the team dissolved after Cena instigated an argument between them.

After attacking The Miz and turning babyface again, he teamed with Kofi Kingston. They won the WWE tag team titles by defeating Primo and Epico, (cousins Eddie and Orlando Colon). They had a few successful title defenses until finally losing to Kane and Daniel Bryan at the *Night of Champions*. The team dissolved after failing to recapture the titles. After a series of back-and-forth denials, R-Truth reluctantly teamed with Goldust to form the Golden Truth. Goldust initially approached R-Truth after the 2016 *Royal Rumble* and proposed a partnership to which Truth declined. After multiple denials, Truth changed his mind and attempted to form a team with Goldust. This time Goldust declined. After refusing to tag team, R-Truth aligned himself with Tyler Breeze. However, on the May 12 episode of *SmackDown*, R-Truth was paired with Breeze to face Goldust and Fandango. Truth and Goldust refused to fight each other which allowed Breeze to pin Goldust. The next week, R-Truth and Goldust officially became Golden Truth but lost several matches initially. They eventually won a match over Breezango (Breeze and Fandango) at the *Money in the Bank* pay-per-view event. After losing to The Shining Stars and failing at *Battle Royal*, Goldust attacked R-Truth on Raw ending their fragile partnership.

The following year, R-Truth returned to *Smackdown* after recovering from an injury. He formed an alliance with Carmella who agreed to manage Truth in a match against The Miz. They participated in the mixed gender match challenge and defeated Jinder Mahal and Alicia Fox to earn the number 30 spot in the *Royal Rumble*. Truth was attacked by Nia Jax during his *Royal Rumble* entrance and received a United States championship title match as compensation for the offense. He defeated Shinsuke Nakamura for his second US title reign. R-Truth eventually lost to Samoa Joe in a fatal four-way match after only 35 days as champion.

In 2019, Mick Foley announced the creation of the WWE 24/7 championship with its own special belt. Foley said the new belt was designed to be a fun experience by offering the 24/7 rules similar to the hardcore championship but without the violence. Pro wrestling is known for gimmick matches, such as 24/7 rules, because many are proven to be successful entertainment segments. R-Truth has been a major player in the battle for the 24/7 championship since its inception. His charisma and athleticism have given a degree of interest to a relatively meaningless title. R-Truth has won the title a record 54 times and in June 2019 was voted the fan favorite 24/7 champion. The 24/7 title was deactivated in November 2022.

R-Truth returned to action in November 2023 after a yearlong absence. Truth entered a storyline with the Judgement Day claiming to be a member until he was attacked by the group in December. At the January 1, 2024, *Day 1* event, Truth reunited with The Miz. R-Truth and The Miz reformed Awesome Truth and won their first match against Judgment Day members – JD McDonagh and Dominick Mysterio. At *WrestleMania XL*, R-Truth climbed the ladder and captured the tag team title belts. It was his first win at *WrestleMania*. On April 15, the title was renamed the world tag team championship along with newly designed belts. They had four successful title defenses before losing to Judgment Day members McDonagh and Fin Balor.

After losing a non-title match to WWE Champion John Cena on May 24, 2025, R-Truth announced on June 1 that he was released from his WWE contract. However, he returned at the *Money in the Bank* pay-per-view on June 7 to help Cody Rhodes and Jey Uso. On the June 9 edition of Monday Night Raw, R-Truth stood on the announcers table and declared a new direction for his character. After announcing that he is neither a sideshow act nor a gimmick, he cut his hair and said "The truth has set me free. I am Ron Killings. I am the truth, the whole truth, and nothing but the truth so put some respect on my name." (Mrosko, 2025). Whether it's a gimmick or shoot, Killings is a legitimate world champion and has had a stellar career worthy of respect.

Major Championships and Accomplishments

Title	Promotion	Dates
MCW Southern Heavyweight Champion	Memphis Championship Wrestling	April 12, 2000 – 42 days Aug 19, 2000 – 76 days
NWA World Heavyweight Champion	Total Nonstop Action Wrestling	Aug 7, 2002 – 105 days May 19, 2004 – 14 days
NWA World Tag Team Champion	National Wrestling Alliance	Nov 26, 2003 – 63 days Nov 7, 2004 – 28 days
TNA World Tag Team Champion	Total Nonstop Action Wrestling	Sept 9, 2007 – 35 days
WWE United States Champion	World Wrestling Entertainment	May 24, 2010 – 20 days Jan 29, 2019 – 35 days
WWE Hardcore Champion	World Wrestling Federation	Feb 3, 2001 – 0 days Feb 4, 2001 – 0 days
WWE 24/7 Champion (54 times)	World Wrestling Entertainment	May 20, 2019 (first run) June 20, 2022 (last run)

| WWE Tag Team Champion | World Wrestling Entertainment | w/ Kofi Kingston (April 30, 2012) – 138 days |

Honors	Sponsor	Year
Tag Team of the Year (w/Kofi Kingston)	Pro Wrestling Illustrated	2012

Xavier

John Jirus Bedoya was the second person to hold the world heavyweight championship in the Ring of Honor wrestling promotion and its first Black heavyweight champion. Bedoya's title reign was largely overlooked because Ring of Honor (RoH) was a relatively unknown independent promotion during the time when he won the title in 2002. However, the company has endured the test of time and with AFW's acquisition of the company, RoH wrestling champions like Bedoya can get their due respect.

Bedoya debuted in 1995 on the independent circuit in New York City where he soon adopted the ring name Xavier. He wrestled in the first Ring of Honor show on February 23, 2002, where he defeated "The Black Nature Boy" Scoot Andrews. He became the second champion in RoH history on September 21, 2002, with the victory over Low Ki. Xavier successfully defended the title several times before losing to Samoa Joe in March 2003.

He made appearances in the World Wrestling Federation (WWF) in January 2002 and continued to make brief appearances mostly as an extra in the WWE until 2007. He returned to RoH in a losing effort for the world championship against Bryan Danielson in 2006. Xavier also competed in mixed martial arts under the name John

Xavier. He won his first fight in 14 seconds but lost his second fight by decision. Both fights were at the amateur ranks.

In 2010, he wrestled a tryout match for TNA. He lost the untelevised "dark" match to Douglas Williams. After his stint in mixed martial arts, he was attempting a comeback to professional wrestling. In March 2020, Xavier was scheduled to face Jay Lethal in Ring of Honor's *Past vs. Present* event in March 2020, but the show was cancelled due to the COVID-19 pandemic. As an in-ring performer, Xavier was known for his signature moves "Kiss Your X Goodbye" and "X 450." Bedoya died on August 16, 2020, at age 42.

Xavier holding the Ring of Honor championship belt.

Major Championships and Accomplishments		
Title	Promotion	Dates
NEW Heavyweight Champion	Northeast Wrestling	Dec 9, 2006 – 497 days
JAPW Light Heavyweight Champion	Jersey All Pro Wrestling	Aug 8, 2001 – 52 days
ECWA Heavyweight Champion	East Coast Wrestling Association	Nov 2, 2002 – < 1day
ECWA Tag Team Champion	East Coast Wrestling Association	w/Low Ki (April 6, 2002) – 28 days
RoH World Champion	Ring of Honor	Sept 21, 2002 – 182 days

Awesome Kong

Kia Stevens is an actor and retired professional wrestler from Carson, California. According to Stevens, she was inspired by WWE women's legend Lita, to become a wrestler. She was a former contestant on the Discovery channel reality television show *Discovery Healthy Body Challenge* in 2002. In her attempts to lose weight on the show, she was introduced to professional wrestling trainer Jesse Hernandez. Stevens later appeared on the WWE's reality show *Tough Enough 2* in pursuit of a contract with the company. She did not earn a spot with the company but was invited to receive further training with All Japan Women's Pro Wrestling. Debuting in Japan under the ring name Amazing Kong – as a replacement for Japanese wrestler Aja Kong - she quickly found success as an in-ring performer. In 2004, she won the WWWA world singles championship; which is the top singles title in All Japan Pro Wrestling. She later teamed with Aja Kong in the Gaea wrestling promotion to win the AAAW tag team championship.

In 2007, Kong won the AWA Japan world women's championship. She also appeared on the American independent circuit along with her AWA championship. In May, she won the NWA world women's title in a champion versus champion match becoming a double champion. In October 2007, Stevens debuted on Total Nonstop Action (TNA) wrestling's flagship TV show *Impact!* where her name was changed to Awesome Kong. She immediately rose to the top of the women's (referred to in TNA as "Knockouts") division by winning the TNA women's knockout championship. She followed Jackie Moore and Jazz by becoming the third black female to hold a women's world title in a recognized, major North American wrestling promotion.

In December 2010, Stevens signed with the WWE under the ring name Kharma. She made her debut in May 2011 attacking the WWE Divas champion Michelle McCool. Stevens later made a revelation that she was pregnant and took a leave of absence. In her first and only official WWE match, she returned at the 2012 *Royal Rumble* as the 21st entrant. Stevens also made a name for herself by becoming the third female to participate in the men's *Royal Rumble* match after Chyna and Beth Phoenix. In July 2012, she was released from her contract due to not being able to return in the allotted time frame imposed by the company.

Stevens returned to wrestling with the New York based independent promotion Shine as Amazing Kong. She teamed with Jazz to defeat Mercedes Martinez and Rain. She was a contender for the Shine Championship but never captured the title. Kong returned to Japan in 2015 where she retired the name Amazing Kong. On January 7, 2015, she returned to TNA wrestling. Her return to TNA consisted largely of feuds with Gail Kim and Taryn Terrell for the TNA Knockouts championship. Kong had highly entertaining and competitive but unsuccessful matches for the Knockouts title. She was released from her contract in 2016 after a real-life backstage altercation with another female wrestler. Kong made a brief appearance at *Bound for Glory* to induct Gail Kim into the TNA hall of fame.

Her last run was with All Elite Wrestling from 2019-2021. She collaborated with Brandi Rhodes to form the Nightmare Collective. The idea was poorly received by audiences and was dropped in 2020. Stevens took a break to film the television series *GLOW* for Netflix. After not appearing on AEW for over a year, the company decided not to renew her contract in June 2021. She announced her retirement from professional wrestling in August 2021. Two months later, Stevens was inducted into Impact Wrestling's Hall of Fame by Gail Kim.

Major Championships and Accomplishments		
Title	**Promotion**	**Dates**
WWWA World Single Champion	All Japan Women's Pro Wrestling	Jan 4, 2004 – 119 days
WWWA World Tag Team Champion	All Japan Women's Pro Wrestling	w/Aja Kong (Oct 6, 2004) *last champions until belt deactivated April 2005
AWA Japan Women's Champion	AWA Superstars of Wrestling	Jan 14, 2007 – 120 days
AAAW Tag Team Champion	Gaea Japan Women's Pro Wrestling	w/Aja Kong (May 5, 2004) 138 days
NWA World Women's Champion	National Wrestling Alliance	May 5, 2007 – 358 days
TNA Knockouts Champion	Total Nonstop Action Wrestling	Jan 7, 2008 – 169 days Oct 23, 2008 – 178 days
TNA Knockouts World Tag Team Champion	Total Nonstop Action Wrestling	w/Hamada – Jan 4, 2010- 63 days

Honors	Sponsor	Year
Woman of the Year	The Baltimore Sun	2008
Woman of the Year	Pro Wrestling Illustrated	2008
Women's Wrestling Award	Cauliflower Alley Club	2011
TNA Hall of Fame	Total Nonstop Action Wrestling	2021

Vix Crow

In professional wrestling, she's played all of the traditional roles for women wrestlers – singles, tag team competitor, manager and valet. Victoria Crawford was once a fashion model when she was discovered by wrestling executive John Laurinaitis, a brother of Road Warrior Animal. Despite her beauty, Crawford proved she could hold her own within the squared circle.

Crawford started her career with the WWE's developmental territory, Ohio Valley Wrestling (OVW) in 2006 at age 17. Originally, she was a special guest referee before making her in-ring debut in September as Tori. A month later, she won the OVW women's title at a house show on Oct 20, but her victory is not officially recognized by the OVW. The following night, Beth Phoenix regained the title after winning an 8-woman elimination match. After OVW broke away from the WWE, Fox was sent to Florida Championship Wrestling where she worked with future superstars the Bella Twins, Tiffany Stratton and Natalya Neidhart. She formed a tag team with Natalya and feuded with the Bella Twins. Crawford also competed in intergender tag team matches partnering with Sheamus and Tommy Taylor in losing efforts. Later, she started competing against former partner Natalya in singles matches. In her final match with FCW, Crawford competed in the *Queen of FCW* tournament. She lost to inaugural champion Angela Fong before moving up to the WWE's main roster.

At the WWE, she debuted on *Smackdown* in June 2008 using the name Alicia Fox. Fox was the wedding planner for Vicki Guerrero and Edge's storyline marriage. WWE champion Triple H (Paul Levesque) caught Fox kissing Edge at the wedding reception and the feud began. She was off television for three months after failing to help Edge wrestle the title away from WWE champion Triple H. When Fox returned, she appeared on the ECW brand losing a singles match against Katie Lea. After the loss, she partnered with English wrestler DJ Gabriel (Steven Paul Lewington). They were featured in mixed tag team matches against the Burchills (Paul and Katie Lea) and later Tyson Kidd and Natalya. On June 6, 2008, the WWE introduced the WWE Divas championship; a new title for women designed to rival the WWE women's championship which was defended exclusively on *Raw*.

In 2009, Fox was drafted to the *Smackdown* brand. She was the number one contender for the Divas championship. After a year of unsuccessful attempts, Fox pinned Maryse in a fatal four-way match on June 20, 2010, to become the first and only African American Divas champion. After two successful title defenses against Eve Torres, Melina Perez returned from injury and attacked the champion. Fox lost a non-title match to Perez which earned the challenger a title shot. Perez defeated Fox at the *Summer Slam* pay-per-view ending her title reign at 56 days. The divas title was retired on April 3, 2016, after a new women's title was introduced. During its near eight-year existence, Alicia Fox (Victoria Crawford) remained the only African American to hold the title.

Fox continued to compete on various WWE television brands and feuded with other future African American champions such as Naomi, Rich Swann, and Sasha Banks. In 2018, she was scheduled to appear in the first women's *Royal Rumble*. Due to an injury, she was replaced by Damage CTRL's Kairi Sane. Fox made sporadic appearances as both an in-ring performer and manager. She took a break from wrestling for the WWE in 2019. Upon her return to WWE, Fox made a brief appearance at the women's *Royal Rumble* in 2021 where she pinned R-Truth to win the 24/7 title. She was eliminated from the match by Mandy Rose. Once she was outside the ring, R-Truth seized the opportunity and rolled her up to regain the title.

Crawford currently performs under the name Vix Crow on the independent wrestling circuit. She said the new moniker is a shortened version of her full name. In July 2023, she appeared on the Reality of Wrestling promotion owned by Booker T at the *Summer of Champions* show. She continues performing for Reality of Wrestling and other promotions on the independent circuit. Recently, Crawford joined forces with Masters of the Ring Entertainment founder Bambi Weavil to create the virtual Masters of the Ring Accelerator as a resource for new and veteran wrestlers.

According to Crawford, stepping away from the WWE allowed her to grow emotionally and to gain control over her career (Cloete, 2024). She continues to perform primarily with independent wrestling promotions and she uses her social media to promote her new character Vix Crow to existing fans and a growing new fan base. Victoria Crawford has the distinction of being the only African American divas title holder and one of the first African American females to hold a recognized world title. The axe kick and Northern lights suplex were her two go-to finishing moves. Crawford fully embraces her position as a role model for aspiring young women in general and the up-and-coming female wrestlers.

Major Championships and Accomplishments		
Title	Promotion	Dates
WWE Divas Champion	World Wrestling Entertainment	June 20, 2010 – 56 days
WWE 24/7 Champion	World Wrestling Entertainment	Jan 31, 2021 - < 1 day
OVW Women's Champion	Ohio Valley Wrestling	Oct 20, 2006 – 1 day *(not officially recognized by OVW}*

Layla

Women in professional wrestling have always had to play the traditional role of valet to the male wrestlers or simply eye-candy to the male audiences. While Layla had the good looks and sex appeal, she combined those elements with the "mean girl" persona and athleticism to take her to the top of the profession. In fact, she is the last person to hold the coveted women's world championship title. London-born pro wrestler Layla El started acting in England at age 12. At 18, her dancing career started to grow when she joined the Carnival Cruise Line. She traveled throughout the world on the cruise lines. Working for Carnival allowed her to come to the United States. Soon after coming to the US, she joined the Miami Heat NBA basketball team in 2004. She danced for the Heat until a new opportunity presented itself. Her manager encouraged her to answer a casting call to enter the WWE Divas Search. Layla was soon named a finalist and sent to Los Angeles after the NBA finals to appear on the show. "It's a big TV show," she told the *Miami Herald at the time*, "and I think I have a very good chance for making a name for myself" (Eckinger, 2006). Before going to Los Angeles, she celebrated the Heat winning the NBA title and received a championship ring. After the playoffs and dancing for artists like John Legend and Sean "P Diddy" Combs, she flew to LA to compete in the *WWE's Diva Search* contest. She won the competition in August 2006 and made her first television appearance for the WWE during a backstage segment at *SummerSlam*. Her next appearance was a confrontation with Divas Kristal Marshall and Jillian Hall.

Layla made her in-ring debut on *SmackDown* as part of the Divas battle royal in October. The Miz pulled Layla out of the ring allowing Kristal Marshall to win. Layla and Big Vito lost a mixed gender tag match to The Miz and Kristal. Then, she lost her debut singles match to Kristal. She left *SmackDown* by ending her feud in a tag team match with Ashley by defeating Kristal and Jillian. In January, she joined ECW and formed the trio Extreme Expose. Layla choreographed their weekly dance segment. The group eventually dissolved and she was drafted to *Raw* where she became a manager first for Jamie Noble and then William Regal. As his manager, Regal won the Intercontinental championship. Her partnership with Regal ended when she was drafted back to *SmackDown* in April 2009. This time on *SmackDown*, she began by feuding with Eve Torres then, her big break came when she joined forces with WWE Women's Champion Michelle McCool. LayCool, as they were known, were managed by Vickie Guerrero. At *Extreme Rules*, McCool lost the title to Beth Phoenix. After a short reign, Layla and McCool defeated Phoenix in a Texas Tornado handicap match on May 14, 2010, which aired on *SmackDown*. Layla was officially recognized as the champion by the WWE, although they sometimes considered themselves co-champions. LayCool even used the Freebird rules where McCool would sometimes defend the title. At one point, they even split the title in half using a zig-zag "forever friends" design. The idea to split the belts in that style came from former wrestler Dave Batista.[7] At the *Night of Champions*, McCool defeated WWE Divas champion Melina. As a co-women's champion, they used the victory to unify the two titles into the unified Divas championship and retired the Women's championship. As the last recognized champion when the title was retired, Layla remains the lineal women's championship title holder which the WWE dates back to the Fabulous Moolah's NWA World Women's Championship in 1956.

After successfully defeated Natalya in singles competition, Layla won a handicap match at *Survivor Series* to become the new Divas champion. After losing the title, the members of LayCool turned on one another. Layla won a no disqualification match against McCool at *Extreme Rules* on May 1, 2011. As a result, she suffered a legitimate injury and took time off to heal. She returned by starting off in the Florida Championship Wrestling developmental territory in March 2012. After testing the strength of her rehabilitated leg, she returned on April 29, 2012, in a major way by pinning Nikki Bella to win the WWE Divas title. Her championship reign ended on September 16 at *Night of Champions* with a loss to Eve Torres. She defeated Torres in a non-title match but was unsuccessful after a few attempts to regain the Divas championship. She had brief feuds with Tamina, Kaitlyn and Summer Rae. Layla and Rae eventually formed an alliance and called themselves The Slayers. During their brief partnership, The Slayers defeated Natalya and Rosa Mendes on the *Main Event* TV show in September but lost a match at November's *Survivor Series* pay-per-view. In January 2015, she had surgery. Her last in-ring match was a victory over Emma on *Main Event* in April. After nine years in the ring, Layla announced her retirement from WWE. In an interview for the WWE, she said "I am proud that I did make it in the ring and I can truly walk away saying, 'I'm a good wrestler.' I did really well and I was able to break through the negative and definitely prove people wrong." (Tello, 2015).

---

[7] Layla discusses the title on MuscleManMalcolm's podcast - https://www.youtube.com/watch?v=73p3Z7hNkAs

In addition to being a professional cheerleader and dancer during the Miami Heat's championship reign, and a two-time wrestling champion, Layla has also been a featured model in *King*, *Smooth*, *Liquid*, *FHM* and *Flex* magazines. She has also appeared on numerous television programs including *Family Feud*, *Project Runway*, *Celebrity Fit Club* and *Cupcake Wars*. Layla was born and raised in England. She is of Moroccan and Spanish ancestry. Layla is the first Arab woman, British woman and Diva Search winner to capture a WWE championship. She is retired from wrestling but remains an active presence in the professional wrestling industry. She has her own podcast *LayTalks* and continues to make appearances at wrestling conventions and trade shows.

Major Championships and Accomplishments		
Title	Promotion	Dates
WWE Divas Champion	World Wrestling Entertainment	April 29, 2012 - 139 days
WWE Women's Champion	World Wrestling Entertainment	May 11, 2010 - 127 days

Mark Henry

Mark Jerrold Henry is a former Olympian and decorated weightlifter, powerlifter and professional wrestler. Born in 1971, Henry was raised in Silsbee, Texas. Most of the males in Henry's family grew larger than the average man and Mark was no exception. As a freshman at Silsbee High School, he shattered school records with a 600-pound squat. At 300 pounds, Henry lettered in football and basketball. Despite his incredible size and strength, he had enough explosive power to dunk a basketball. As a senior, Henry set world records for teenage powerlifting in the squat at 832 pounds and in the overall combined weight category with 2,033 pounds. He set the Texas state and national records in all four powerlifting categories – squat (832 lbs), bench press (525 lbs), deadlift (815 lbs) and overall (2,033 lbs). The *Los Angeles Times* dubbed him "The World's Strongest Teenager."

At age 19, Henry qualified for the 1992 Summer Olympics held in Barcelona, Spain. He placed 10th in the weightlifting competition for the super-heavyweight division. Later that year, he won the USA Weightlifting American Open and the U.S. National Weightlifting Championships. In 1993 and 1994, he won the U.S. Olympic Festival Championship. At the Pan Am Games in 1995, Henry won the overall silver medal for weightlifting in the super heavyweight division. He won the bronze medal for the clean & jerk and took gold for the snatch. The same year, Henry also won the North American, Central American and Caribbean Athletic Association (NACAC) championship and the U.S. national powerlifting championship by lifting a 1050 kg (2,315 pounds) total. He is also a three-time United States National Champion in weightlifting winning the title in 1993, 1994, and 1996.

Henry's popularity soared during this period. He was frequently featured in the popular news media while preparing for the 1996 Olympics in Atlanta, Georgia. His fame captured the attention of Vince McMahon who signed Henry to a rare 10-year deal with the World Wrestling Federation (WWF). At his prime, Henry stood 6-4 and weighted 415 lbs. He was voted captain of the weightlifting team. Unfortunately, he had to withdraw from the competition due to a back injury after his first attempt at the clean and jerk. This was his last Olympic appearance but he continued to compete winning the USAPL National Powerlifting Championship in 1997.

He started his wrestling career with the WWF in 1996 by feuding with "The King" Jerry Lawler. Henry wore red, white and blue stars and stripes to the ring and defeated Lawler with a backbreaker. After the match, he was attacked by The Rockers and Triple H. In a show of strength, Henry threw Triple H over the top rope into The Rockers. Henry single-handedly defeated Crush, Triple H and Goldust in a tug-of-war match. He was scheduled to tag team with Barry

Windham, Marc Mero and Rocky Maivia at *Survivor Series* but had to withdraw due to injury. Henry returned in November 1997. After a few matches, the WWF decided to turn Henry from babyface into a heal by joining the Nation of Domination in January 1998 with Farooq (Ron Simmons), Kama Mustapha and D'Lo Brown. D'Lo was no stranger to racial polarization in wrestling as he was once a member of Tha Gangstas in Smoky Mountain Wrestling.

The Nation was a dominant force and a threat to other tag teams. Rocky Maivia turned heel by joining the group and took on a new persona as "The Rock." Soon infighting occurred and The Rock emerged as the leader of the group. Henry sided with The Rock over Farooq and became a frequent partner with D'Lo. The Nation feuded with Degenration X and Henry began a romantic storyline with Chyna. When the Nation disbanded, Henry had a signature victory over The Rock at *Judgment Day* pay-per-view with help from D'Lo. After a brief run with The Nation, he fully developed the ladies' man character adopting the nickname "Sexual Chocolate." Henry was awarded the European Championship after helping Jeff Jarrett defeat his former partner D'Lo who at the time held both the Intercontinental and the European championship titles. He would lose the title back to D'Lo after only a month. Henry became a popular babyface again after a brief romantic storyline with the much older veteran wrestler Mae Young. He feuded with Viscera during this period also. The storyline ended after 6"9' 487-pound Viscera splashed Young. In 2000, Henry left the WWE main roster for Ohio Valley Wrestling to hone his skills more. During his time in OVW, Henry's mother died. He took a break from wrestling and decided to pay homage to his mother by entering the Arnold (Schwarzenegger) Strongman Classic in Columbus, Ohio. He competed against the best powerlifters in the world and solidified the "World's Strongest Man" title he used in the ring by winning the inaugural Arnold Classic. At the Classic, he successfully lifted the 172-pound Inch dumbbell with a one-handed clean and press. Henry was the first man in over 100 years to perform the lift. "There was nothing that was gonna stop me from winning that competition and honoring my mom," he said. "Not to mention Vince McMahon had told me that if I lost that I was gonna get fired. So, I had every incentive to go in there and dominate that competition," (Rogers, 2023).

Henry returned to WWE in 2002 with a new angle where he was mostly performing tug of war, arm wrestling and other feats of strength but it was short lived. Over the next six years, he joined Teddy Long's "Thuggin and Buggin' faction and had several main event level feuds with Goldberg, Triple H, the Undertaker, Batista, Rey Mysterio and Booker T. After his memorable feud with the Undertaker where he was victorious at the *Unforgiven* pay-per-view and the subsequent rematch, he took a brief hiatus. Upon returning to action, Henry was drafted to the ECW brand. On June 29, 2008, Henry won the ECW world championship by beating The Big Show and Kane in a triple threat title match. This signature win was his debut match on the ECW brand. While this was considered his first world championship, ECW was a brand owned by World Wrestling Entertainment (WWE) at the time of his title reign. It was at the *Night of Champions* in 2011 when Henry defeated Randy Orton to win the WWE world heavyweight championship. He had several successful title defenses and continued to wrestle despite being plagued with injuries. In 2018, he was inducted into the WWE Hall of Fame.

In 2021, he joined All-Elite Wrestling (AEW) as a commentator. Henry's transition from performer to commentator has had rapid success. As a commentator, he is known for the signature line, "It's time for the main event." While his commentator skills were sharp and a great addition to AEW, perhaps his greatest contribution to the sport was discovering new talent. Henry is credited for discovering Bianca Belair, Braun Strowman, Jade Cargill and WWE ring announcer and classical musician Samantha Irvin. He is also known for the power move dubbed the Mark Henry spot. It's a move where you pick up a wrestler, slam him to the canvas, roll over and stand up all while still holding the opponent. "To create something (unique) in wrestling makes you different." [8] Henry is also working on his autobiography.

---

[8] https://www.youtube.com/shorts/sx9DYvVUk3o

Major Championships and Accomplishments		
Title	Promotion	Dates
ECW Heavyweight Champion	World Wrestling Entertainment	June 29, 2008 – 69 days
World Heavyweight Champion	World Wrestling Entertainment	Sept 18, 2011 – 91 days
WWF European Champion	World Wrestling Federation	Aug 23, 1999 – 33 days
POWERLIFTING		
1st Place -super heavyweight division	National High School Powerlifting Championship	1990
1st Place – super heavyweight division	International Junior (20-23) Powerlifting Championship	1991
1st Place	USA National Powerlifting Championship	1995
1st Place	World Drug-Free Powerlifting Federation	1995
1st Place	USA National Powerlifting Championship	1997
WEIGHTLIFTING		
Silver Medal - overall	Pan American Games	1995
Gold Medal - snatch	Pan American Games	1995
Bronze Medal – clean & jerk	Pam American Games	1995
1at Place	NACAC Championship	1996
1st Place – junior weightlifting	U.S. National Weightlifting Championship	1991

champion		
1st Place – senior weightlifting champion	U.S. National Weightlifting Championship	1993
1st Place – senior weightlifting champion	U.S. National Weightlifting Championship	1994
1st Place – senior weightlifting champion	U.S. National Weightlifting Championship	1996
1st place	U.S. Olympic Festival Championships	1993
1st place	U.S. Olympic Festival Championships	1994
1st Place	USA Weightlifting Am Open Championship	1992

Honors	Sponsor	Year
Arnold Strongman	Arnold Classic	2002
Sports Hall of Fame	International Sports Hall of Fame	2012
Most Improved Wrestler	Pro Wrestling Illustrated	2011
WWE Hall of Fame	World Wrestling Entertainment	2018
Iron Mike Mazurki Award	Cauliflower Alley Club	2019
Frank Gotch Award	George Tragos/Lou Thesz Pro Wrestling Hall of Fame	2021

Mercedes Mone

Once the Boss of WWE and now the CEO of AEW, Mercedes Mone has been a champion in every major wrestling promotion during her era. Mercedes Justine Kaestner-Vernado is an American professional wrestler and actress. She became a household name during her 10-year tenure at the WWE under the ring name Sasha Banks. She currently performs for AEW under the name Mercedes Mone where she is a multiple title holder. Mone is successful because she envisioned being the best female wrestler as a 10-year-old

(Lelinwalla, 2016). At age 17, she joined the Boston-based New England Pro Wrestling Academy fantasy camp and won three free weeks of training. Vernado started her wrestling career in 2010 with the independent promotion Chaotic Wrestling under the name Mercedes KV. After two years of training and one year of in-ring experience, she defeated Alexxis in an "I Quit" match to win Chaotic Wrestling's women's championship. She held the title until she left the promotion in 2012 for the WWE. Vernado made her WWE debut in late 2012. She joined the WWE's developmental territory, NXT, and this is where she took on the name Sasha Banks. Banks lost her debut match to eventual NXT women's champion Paige. Banks teamed up with her one-time foe Summer Rae to become the Beautiful, Fierce Females (BFFs). Banks and Rae defeated tag teams Paige and Emma, then defeated Bayley and Charlotte. With Rae's promotion to the main roster, Charlotte teamed with Banks to eventually face Bayley and Natalya. Banks disbanded the BFFs after Flair turned on her during a match against Bayley and Becky Lynch.

    Banks began feuding with Flair, who was then NXT women's champion. After several attempts, Banks eventually wrestled the title away from Flair in a fatal four-way that also included Bayley and Becky Lynch. Banks lost the title to Bayley after 192 days as champion. Many considered it the match of the year. Bayley retained the title in a rematch before Banks moved up to the main roster. Banks came to the *Raw* brand in July 2015. She teamed with Naomi and Tamina who called themselves Team B.A.D. (Beautiful and Dangerous). However, she continued participating in singles matches; most notably feuding against Paige and Charlotte Flair. After losing in a fatal four-way contest to become number one contender for the Divas championship, she went on a winning streak. Banks later attacked Flair and Becky Lynch in an attempt to challenge for the Divas title. Banks announced her intentions to leave Team B.A.D. and she was attacked by her former teammates during a match with Lynch. Banks later teamed with Lynch to defeat Tamina and Naomi becoming fan favorites in the process. When the Divas title was retired and replaced with the women's championship, Banks unsuccessfully challenged for the new title at her *WrestleMania* debut. However, Banks later defeated Flair at *SummerSlam* on July 25, 2016, for her first reign as women's champion. She feuded with Flair trading the title two more times. Their feud ended with Banks losing to Flair in a 30-minute iron woman match at the *Roadblock* pay-per-view. Eventually, Banks would bury the hatchet and help Bailey take the title away from Flair. It was her feuds with Flair that is credited with elevating the competitiveness in women's wrestling in the modern era. "NXT treated its women wrestlers as legitimate competitors, while the main roster treated them as accessories or a 'bathroom break' sideshow" (Harkulich, 2018, p. 158). Banks, along with Flair, Becky Lynch and Bailey were dubbed the Four Horsewomen of wrestling and they revolutionized the sport with their competitive matches. The fan reaction to serious wrestling from the women led to all four women being called up to the main roster.

When Banks and Bayley settled their differences, they formed the tag team dubbed Boss 'n' Hug Connection. They won the inaugural WWE women's tag team championship by defeating Mandy Rose and Sonya Deville in the *Elimination Chamber* match. They would go on to lose the titles at *WrestleMania* to the IIconics (Billie Kay and Peyton Royce). Banks and Bailey won the tag team titles again on June 5, 2020. Additionally, Banks defeated Asuka for the women's championship. With the win, Banks and Bailey became the first female tag team to hold singles titles and the tag team titles at the same time. In August, Banks lost her women's championship to Asuka and a week later, she and Bailey lost the tag team titles to Shayna Baszler and Nia Jax. Banks became a triple crown champion by defeating Bayley for the women's world championship on *Smackdown*. Banks would go on to face Bianca Belair to headline *WrestleMania* 37. The historic match was the first time two African

American wrestlers were the main event match-up at *WrestleMania*. Belair defeated Banks to win her first world championship.

In February 2022, Banks reunited with Naomi to challenge for the women's tag team titles. The duo won the belts which was a first for Naomi and a third for Banks. On the May 16, 2022, episode of *Raw*, Banks and Naomi walked out of the arena and left the WWE due to creative differences with management. They were suspended indefinitely and the titles declared vacant. Banks would later say that she left because of the treatment she received from the company.

On *The Breakfast Club* morning radio show, Vernado said:

> "I left for many different reasons. A lot of personal stuff happened with myself and the chairman (Vince McMahon) at the time. I didn't like how he talked to me and how I was talked down to and I was like 'you know what. It's time to legit listen to your soul and your heart. There was a light that came to me one day and I just left WWE. My guides told me and I'm guided to being a two-time champion at AEW."

After leaving the WWE, Vernado re-emerged in New Japan Pro Wrestling and the all-women's promotion, World Wonder Ring Stardom on January 4, 2023. She dropped the name Sasha Banks and assumed the new, more personal identity Mercedes Mone. She immediately attacked IWGP women's champion Kairi. Mone defeated Kairi for the title a month later at *Battle in the Valley*. Mone dropped the title to Mayu Iwatani after a 64-day reign as champion.

In August 2023, Mone made a cameo appearance with All Elite Wrestling. She made her in-ring debut May 26 at the *Double or Nothing* pay-per-view defeating Willow Nightingale to win AEW's TBS championship. In June, she beat Stephanie Vaquer in a winner-takes-all match to obtain the Strong women's championship – making her a double champion. Mone defeated Jamie Hayter by pinfall to win the 2025 Owen Hart Cup. She earned a title shot against AEW women's world champion "Timeless" Toni Storm. In March 2025, she returned to the independent circuit and swept through the competition. In her first match on the independent circuit since 2012, she won a non-title match against Renegades of Wrestling women's champion Indi Hartwell by submission (Carey, 2025). The match was held at House of Glory which was founded by wrestler and promoter Amazing Red in 2012. Rap artist and entrepreneur Master P bought the New York-based wrestling promotion and school in 2019. She added the European Wrestling Association's women championship to her collection by winning a triple threat match involving EWA women's champion Lexa Valo and Mila Smidt. Along with the EWA championship, she currently holds the AEW TBS women's championship, Revolution Pro Wrestling's undisputed British women's championship and the Consejo Mundial de Lucha Libre (CMLL) world women's championship.

Mone said that she is happy in AEW and wants to help the company continue to grow. Vernado is truly a world women's champion by holding belts in the United States and Japanese based promotions. She is the only female wrestler to hold major titles in WWE, AEW and New Japan Pro Wrestling. Her acting credits include the 2023 film *The Collective* and she has a recurring role as Koska Reeves in the *Disney+* series *The Mandalorian*. Vernado is also a cousin of rapper Snoop Dogg and sibling singers Brandy and Ray J Norwood.

Major Championships and Accomplishments		
Title	Promotion	Dates
Women's Champion	Chaotic Wrestling	Dec 2, 2011 – 378 days
NXT Women's Champion	World Wrestling Entertainment	Feb 11, 2015 – 192 days
WWE Women's Champion	World Wrestling Entertainment	July 25, 2016 – 26 days Oct 3, 2016 – 27 days Nov 28, 2016 – 20 days Aug 20, 2017 – 8 days July 20, 2020 – 34 days
WWE Women's World Champion	World Wrestling Entertainment	Oct 25, 2020 – 167 days
Women's Tag Team Champion	World Wrestling Entertainment	Feb 17, 2019 (w/Bayley) – 49 days May 20, 2020 (w/Bayley) – 85 days April 3, 2022 (w/Naomi) – 46 days
IWGP Women's Championship	New Japan Pro Wrestling	Feb 18, 2023 – 64 days

Strong Women's Championship	New Japan Pro Wrestling	June 30, 2024 – 313 days
TBS Champion	All Elite Wrestling	May 26, 2024 -
Undisputed British Women's Champion	Revolution Pro Wrestling	Jan. 5, 2025 – 155 + days
EWA Women's Champion	European Wrestling Association	June 6, 2025 -
CMLL World Women's Champion	Consejo Mundial de Lucha Libre (CMLL)	June 18, 2025 -

Honors	Sponsor	Year
Match of the Year (vs. Bayley)	Pro Wrestling Illustrated	2015
Woman of the Year	Pro Wrestling Illustrated	2015
Feud of the Year (vs Charlotte Flair)	Pro Wrestling Illustrated	2016
Feud of the Year (vs. Bayley)	Pro Wrestling Illustrated	2020
Future Diva of the Year	Rolling Stone	2015
NXT Match of the Year	Rolling Stone	2015
Tag Team of the Year (w/ Bayley)	Pro Wrestling Illustrated	2020
Wrestler of the Year	Sirius XM Busted Open Radio	2020
Tag Team of the Year (w/ Bayley)	Sirius XM Busted Open Radio	2020
Tag Team of the Year (w/ Bayley)	CBS Sports	2020
Best WWE Moment	ESPY Award	2021
Wrestler of the Year	Sports Illustrated	2020
Triple Crown Champion - Women's Champion	World Wrestling Entertainment	July 25, 2016

- Women's Tag Team Champion (w/Bayley) - Women's World Champion		Feb 17, 2019 Oct 25, 2020
Grand Slam Champion - NXT Champion - Women's Champion - Women's Tag Team Champion (w/Bayley) - Women's World Champion	World Wrestling Entertainment	 Feb 11, 2015 July 25, 2016 Feb 17, 2019 Oct 25, 2020

Naomi

Trinity Fatu aka WWE Superstar Naomi, is a world women's champion both as a singles and tag team competitor. Fatu, born Trinity McCray in Sanford, Florida, is a former dancer for the NBA's Orlando Magic and the rap artist Flo Rida. Her professional wrestling career started in 2009 with the WWE's developmental territory, Florida Championship Wrestling. She defeated Serena Deeb on June 20, 2010, to become the inaugural FCW divas champion. Naomi appeared on the third season of NXT in 2010. She finished in second place. Naomi lost the FCW championship in 2011 and joined the main roster in January 2012.

On the *Raw* brand, Naomi debuted along with *Tough Enough* alum Cameron as the Funkadactyls. They served as valets for Broadus Clay (Tyrus). During this time, she competed with the cast of *Total Divas* and feuded with Divas champions AJ Lee and Paige. In December 2014, Naomi joined her husband Jimmy and his brother Jey Uso and competed in mixed gender tag team matches. Naomi fought for the Divas championship against Nikki Bella and Paige but was unsuccessful each time. Before leaving Raw, she teamed with then-NXT women's champion Sasha Banks and Tamina briefly forming Team B.A.D. After recovering from a torn ankle tendon, Naomi returned to television on *Smackdown* in July 2016. She became a babyface with the new gimmick called "The Glow."

On February 12, 2017, Naomi defeated Alexa Bliss to win the women's world championship (known as the *Smackdown* women's championship at the time). She became the first African American to win the title. Eight days later, she was forced to relinquish the title due to an injury. She returned from injury in April and regained the title from Bliss. She eventually lost the title to Natalya after a 140-day reign. Naomi went on to win the inaugural *WrestleMania* women's battle royal by eliminating Bayley. On the second night of *WrestleMania 38*, Naomi teamed with Sasha Banks in a four-way tag team match. They won the WWE women's tag team titles from Carmella and Queen Zelina. After only a month as champions, Naomi and Banks walked out of the arena during an episode of *Raw* due to creative differences with CEO Vince McMahon. They were stripped of the titles and suspended from the company indefinitely.

On April 28, 2023, she debuted at Impact/TNA Wrestling using her given name Trinity. She immediately confronted TNA Knockouts world champion Deonna Purrazzo. In her first pay-per-view match since leaving WWE, Trinity defeated Gisele Shaw at *Under Siege*. On July 15, Trinity defeated Purrazzo with a submission hold to win the Knockouts world title at *Slammiversary*. After a few successful title defenses, she lost the title to Jordynne Grace ending her 182-day reign as champion. Her last match was February 8 episode of *Impact* where she and Grace partnered to defeat Gisele Shaw and Savannah Evans.

After two years away from the company, Fatu made a surprise return to WWE at the *Royal Rumble*. She resumed using the ring name Naomi and entered the *Rumble* at number two. She lasted over an hour before being eliminated by Jade Cargill. At *WrestleMania XL*, Naomi, Cargill and Bianca Belair teamed up to defeat Damage CTRL. Naomi recently shared a part of the WWE women's tag team championship with Bianca Belair. Belair and Cargill won the titles on August 31, 2024. After Cargill was mysteriously attacked and unable to compete, Belair was allowed to choose a partner. She chose Naomi on December 20, 2024. Although Naomi was chosen to replace Cargill, the WWE considers this as one continuous title run. They defended the titles until losing to Liv Morgan and Raquel Rodriguez on February 24, 2025. Naomi was later revealed as Cargill's mysterious attacker. Most recently, she has turned heel and feuded with Cargill and Belair. Naomi's heel character is a significant change from the positive "glow" image she is known for. However, the change has increased her visibility and sparked a lot of interest in her character's new angle. Naomi has started wearing yellow caution tape on her outfits. She lost a match to Jade Cargill at *WrestleMania 41*. In May, she won a triple threat match against Cargill and Nia Jax. At *Money in the Bank*, Naomi won the women's ladder match earning the contract to face the champion of her choice. The victory puts her in line for another potential championship run.

By marriage to Jimmy Uso, Trinity is a member of the famed Anoa'i Samoan wrestling dynasty, also known as The Bloodline. The couple married January 16, 2014. In May 2014, she released the single "Dance All Night." In 2017, she starred in the WWE film *The Marine 5: Battleground*. Trinity also modeled along with Mercedes Vernado (Sasha Banks) at the New York Fashion Week in 2022.

Major Championships and Accomplishments		
Title	Promotion	Dates
Women's World Championship	World Wrestling Entertainment	Feb 12, 2017 – 8 days April 2, 2017 – 139 days
Women's World Tag Team Champion	World Wrestling Entertainment	w/Sasha Banks (April 3, 2022) – 47 days w/Bianca Belair and Jade Cargill (Aug 31, 2024) – 177 days
Inaugural WrestleMania Women's Battle Royal winner	World Wrestling Entertainment	April 8, 2018
TNA Knockouts World Champion	Total Nonstop Action (TNA) Wrestling	July 15, 2023 – 182 days
FCW Divas Champion	Florida Championship Wrestling	June 10, 2010 – 189 days

Honors	Sponsor	Year
Most Welcome Heel Turn (tied w/ Sheamus)	Rolling Stone	2015
Comeback of the Year	Pro Wrestling Illustrated	2023
Knockout of the Year	Impact/Total Nonstop Action Wrestling	2023

Kofi Kingston

Kofi Nahaje Sarkodie-Mensah was born in Kumasi, Ghana. When he was young, his family moved to the United States. He graduated from Winchester High School in Massachusetts and later Boston College. He started wrestling in 2005 with organizations in the New England territories including the NWA- New England, Chaotic Wrestling, Millennium Wrestling and New England Championship Wrestling. In 2006, he signed with the WWE and was billed as a Jamaican wrestler using the name Kofi Kingston.

In September 2006, Kingston signed with the WWE and worked his way through the developmental ranks in the Georgia-based Deep South Wrestling and Ohio Valley Wrestling. He mostly worked dark matches - untelevised "house" shows that primed the crowd before the televised *Monday Night Raw* went live on air. He joined Florida Championship Wrestling in June 2006 and wrestled with the promotion until the end of the year. Kingston debuted on ECW in January 2008 as a babyface. He was undefeated in ECW until losing to Shelton Benjamin. He avenged his loss to Benjamin with a victory before moving on to the *Raw* brand.

In June 2008, Kingston made an impressive debut on *Raw*. In his first match, he defeated Chris Jericho for the intercontinental championship. The win made Kingston the first African-born champion in the WWE. Kingston and women's champion Mickie James lost a winner-take-all intergender tag team match at *SummerSlam* to Santino Marella and Beth Phoenix. After losing the title, he began a partnership with then WWE champion CM Punk. The duo went on to win the world tag team titles. After losing the titles to John Morrison and The Miz in December, Kingston returned to singles wrestling. In 2009, he defeated Montel Vontavious Porter (MVP) to win the United States championship. He successfully defended the title for 126 days until losing on Oct 5 to The Miz. On October 19, he stopped using the Jamaican gimmick and started being billed as a Ghanaian. Kingston was receiving a push toward main event status until he mishandled the finish of a match with Randy Orton and John Cena. Orton put a stiff RKO on Kingston and complained to management. Kingston's push to main event status was halted.

Despite the setback, Kingston continued to fight his way back up the ranks. In May, he won the intercontinental championship from Drew McIntyre. However, he lost it to Dolph Ziggler (Nic Nemeth) on August 8. In January 2011, he won back the title from Ziggler and began a feud with Alberto Del Rio and Wade Barrett. He lost the belt to Barrett on March 25. The next week, he won the rematch by disqualification. In April, he was drafted back to *Raw* where he defeated Sheamus for his second reign as United States champion. After a successful defense against Jack Swagger, he lost the belt to

Dolph Ziggler. Kingston won the rematch, but this victory was also by disqualification so Ziggler retained the title. On August 22, 2011, Kingston and Evan Bourne defeated David Otunga and Michael McGillicutty to win the WWE tag team championship. Known as "Air Boom," Kingston and Bourne had a string of successful title defenses before losing to Primo & Epico. After Bourne was suspended for violating company rules, Kingston started teaming with R-Truth. The new tag team successfully wrestled the titles away from Primo & Epico. They lost the title to Kane and Daniel Bryan at the *Night of Champions* pay-per view and soon dissolved the team after being eliminated early in the tournament ending their quest to regain the belts. On October 17, 2012, Kingston won the intercontinental championship for the fourth time by defeating The Miz. He lost the title to Wade Barrett on December 31. On April 15, he won the United States championship for the third time with a win over Antonio Cesaro.

A major move changed the trajectory of Kingston's WWE career in 2014 when he was paired with Big E and manager/wrestler Xavier Woods. The new team known as The New Day, were victorious over Curtis Axel, Heath Slater and Titus O'Neil in their debut. After a few months of teaming together, the duo defeated Tyson Kidd and Cesaro to win the WWE world tag team championship. They lost the titles to The Prime Time Players at *Money in the Bank* but regained the belts at *SummerSlam*. The New Day became the longest reigning WWE tag team champions on July 22, 2016, by surpassing the 331-day mark. During their reign, the WWE split the championship and created a separate tag team title for *Raw* and another for *Smackdown*. The New Day's title was renamed the Raw tag team championship. Their title reign ended at 483 days after losing the belts to Cesaro and Sheamus at *Roadblock: End of the Line*. At *Battleground* on July 23, 2017, the duo of Kingston and Woods won the SmackDown tag team titles from The Usos. With the victory, Kingston became the first wrestler to hold the Raw, SmackDown and original world tag team championship. The team of Big E and Woods lost the titles to the Usos after 28 days. Then, Kingston and Big E won the titles back from the Usos but lost to them at *Hell in a Cell*. The New Day captured the titles for a third time by defeating the Bludgeon Brothers. They would eventually lose the titles to The Bar.

On February 12, 2019, Kingston replaced an injured Mustafa Ali in the *Elimination Chamber*. His superb performance led to a major push dubbed KofiMania, where Kingston was on a quest to become WWE champion leading up to *WrestleMania*. However, he faced continuous obstacles place in his path by WWE chairman Vince McMahon. Kingston was first put in a handicap match against both members of The Bar which he lost. Then, he faced five men in a gauntlet match. Seemingly victorious, a weakened Kingston lost when Daniel Bryan entered and defeated him. The final title shot for Kingston was at the hands of his partners in The New Day as Big E and Xavier Woods defeated five teams in a gauntlet match which finally granting Kingston a title shot. On April 7, 2019, he became the first African-born WWE champion by defeating Bryan at *WrestleMania 35*. Kingston's reign looked promising as he had a string of successful title defenses against Bryan, Kevin Owens and Dolph Ziggler. In July at *Extreme Rules*, he successfully defended the title against Samoa Joe and became a double champion as Big E and Woods captured the tag team titles. Kingston continued his reign as world champion defeating Ziggler and Samoa Joe in a triple threat match. Later, he retained the title against Randy Orton first in a double count-out and then a rematch. In October, Kingston's reign ended rather unceremoniously after losing the title match in 10-seconds to Brock Lesnar.

He returned to tag team matches and teamed with Big E to win the SmackDown tag team titles against The Revival. In February, 2020, they lost the titles to John Morrison and The Miz. Big E won the tag titles back in April. But he and Kingston would not only lose the titles at July's *Extreme Rules* but Kingston suffered a legitimate back injury after being power bombed through a table. When Kingston returned, he and Woods won the titles back from Cesaro and Shinsuke Nakamura. In December, they lost the Raw tag titles to The Hurt Business (Cedric Alexander and Shelton Benjamin). In March, The New Day captured their 11th championship by winning back the titles from Alexander and Benjamin. They held the titles until *WrestleMania* in a losing effort to AJ Styles and Omos. Kingston and Woods would continue to challenge for the tag team titles and reignited their feud with The Usos. They were unsuccessful most of 2022 until December when they invaded NXT and captured the NXT tag team titles. The win made Kingston a double triple crown champion as both a singles and tag team wrestler. Their reign ended after 56-days in a losing effort to the Scottish tag team Gallus (Mark Coffey and Wolfgang) at NXT *Vengeance Day*. With Big E out of in-ring competition due to what could be a career-ending injury, The New Day is being represented by Woods and Kingston. On the first day of *WrestleMania 41*, they won the world tag team titles for the fifth time.

Kofi Kingston is a triple crown singles, tag team and grand slam champion in WWE. Throughout his career, he has won the intercontinental title four times, the United States championship three times and he is a 15-time tag team champion in addition to his reign as world heavyweight champion. His other accolades include being named *Pro Wrestling Illustrated'*s Tag Team of the Year (2012, with R. Truth), Tag Team of the Year (2015 & 2016, with The New Day) and Best Gimmick by the *Wrestling Observer Newsletter*. Kingston continues to compete in singles competition and tag team with The New Day.

Major Championships and Accomplishments		
Title	Promotion	Dates
WWE Champion	World Wrestling Entertainment	April 7, 2019 – 180 days
WWE Intercontinental Champion	World Wrestling Entertainment	June 29, 2008 – 48 days May 23, 2010 – 74 days Jan 4, 2011 – 76 days Oct 16, 2012 – 76 days
World Tag Team Champion	World Wrestling Entertainment	w/CM Punk (Oct 27, 2008) – 47 days
Raw Tag Team Champion	World Wrestling Entertainment	w/Evan Bourne (Aug 22, 2011) – 145 days w/R-Truth (April 30, 2012) – 138 days w/Big E (April 26, 2015) – 49 days w/Big E & Xavier Woods (Aug 23, 2015) – 483 days w/Xavier Woods (Oct 12, 2020) – 69 days w/Xavier Woods

		(March 15, 2021) – 26 days
Smackdown Tag Team Champion	World Wrestling Entertainment	w/Xavier Woods & Big E (July 23, 2017) – 27 days
		w/Big E and Xavier Woods (Sept 12, 2017) – 25 days
		w/Xavier Woods & Big E (Aug 21, 2018) – 55 days
		w/The New Day (July 14, 2019) – 62 days
		w/Big E & Xavier Woods (Nov 8, 2019) 110 days
		w/Big E & Xavier Woods (April 17, 2020) 92 days
		w/Xavier Woods & Big E (Oct 9, 2020) – 2 Days
NXT Tag Team Champion	World Wrestling Entertainment	w/Xavier Woods (Dec 10, 2022) – 56 days

Honors	Sponsor	Year
Grand Slam Champion - Intercontinental title - United States title - Raw Tag Team title - Smackdown Tag Team title - WWE Heavyweight title	World Wrestling Entertainment	June 29, 2008 June 1, 2009 Aug 22, 2011 July 23, 2017 April 7, 2019
Tag Team of the Year (w/R Truth) Tag Team of the Year (w/The New Day)	Pro Wrestling Illustrated	2012 2015, 2016
Best Moment/Angle of the Year (winning WWE title)	CBS Sports	2019
Best Gimmick	Wrestling Observer Newsletter	2015

Bobby Lashley

    Franklin Roberto Lashley, known professionally as Bobby Lashley, is a champion amateur wrestler, professional wrestler and mixed martial artist. "The Almighty" Bobby Lashley is the fifth Black male to win the world title in the WWE and by some accounts, the first to win the title in three different promotions. He is an eight-time world title holder. Lashley is a four-time Impact Wrestling champion, two-time WWE champion, two-time ECW champion and current AEW tag team champion. Despite his success thus far, the desire to dominate the squared circle is still burning strong.

The Kansas native, was introduced to wrestling in junior high school primarily to train and stay in shape during football's offseason. He was a National Association of Intercollegiate Athletics (NAIA) national wrestling champion for three years (1996, 1997, 1998) in the 177-pound weight class while attending Missouri Valley College.[9] Already an accomplished amateur wrestler, he continued to compete while serving in the U.S. Army under the World Class Athlete Program. The WCAP allows active-duty soldiers to train and compete in national and international athletic competitions. While in the Army, Lashley won a silver and gold medal from the International Military Sports Council. While training for the 2004 Olympics, Lashley suffered a knee injury that ended his amateur wrestling career.

He exploded onto the professional wrestling scene in 2005 in the WWE's Ohio Valley developmental territory. He wrestled in four dark matches under the name Blaster Lashley before making his *Smackdown* debut in 2005. He won his first singles title by defeating John "Bradshaw" Layfield (JBL) for the United States championship on May 26, 2006. He lost the title in July to Fit Finlay. After a brief leave, Lashley returned to action under the ECW brand. At the *December of Dismember* pay-per-view, he pinned The Big Show to capture the ECW world heavyweight championship. By the time Lashley appeared in ECW, it was not the original independent promotion under the creative direction of Paul Heyman. Lashley had several high-profile title defenses against Big Show, Test, Rob Van Dam and others. A highlight of his title reign was becoming the first and only person to break the Master-lock hold; a swinging full nelson which was the finishing hold by wrestler Chris Masters. This move later became one of Lashley's finishing moves, which he calls the hurt-lock.

---

[9] A brief history of Missouri Valley College wrestling champions is archived here:
https://web.archive.org/web/20070928044529/http://www.moval.edu/athletics/wrestlingm/Misc/allamerican.asp

Another memorable moment during Lashley's first reign as ECW champion was the celebrity gimmick match called the Battle of the Billionaires. At *WrestleMania 23*, future US president Donald Trump chose Lashley to represent him against Vince McMahon's chosen representative Umaga in a hair vs. hair match. Stone Cold Steve Austin was the special guest referee. Lashley defeated Umaga and helped Trump and Austin shave McMahon's head. McMahon sought revenge against Lashley by booking him in a handicap match against Umaga, Mr. McMahon and Shane McMahon. After two high-flying splashes from Umaga, Mr. McMahon pinned Lashley to win the title. At *One Night Stand*, Lashley would regain the title by defeating Mr. McMahon in a street fight. Lashley is the first African American wrestler to hold that version of the ECW world championship and the first to win it twice under the WWE. Lashley was drafted to the *Raw* brand and subsequently stripped of the ECW title. He was injured in a losing effort against WWE champion John Cena at the *Great American Bash*. Lashley took time off for surgery and after six months away from action, he was released from his contract.

In 2008, he wrestled on the independent circuit taking matches in Puerto Rico and Japan. In April 2009, he made a brief appearance on Total Nonstop Action (TNA) Wrestling. Three months later, he was introduced by Kurt Angle as a member of the Main Event Mafia. However, he turned on Angle and helped Mick Foley against the Mafia. Lashley's in-ring debut for TNA was on June 30 in a tag team match. He helped Foley pin Kevin Nash and become the TNA legends champion. In January 2010, Lashley turned heel and attacked several wrestlers claiming he wanted to be released from his contract. In February, he was released by Eric Bischoff in order to legitimately focus on his mixed martial arts (MMA) career. He again wrestled on the independent circuit and in Japan before returning to TNA in 2014. On June 19, 2014, Lashley defeated Eric Young on an episode of Impact Wrestling to become the first African American to win the TNA world heavyweight championship. Throughout his tenure with the company, Lashley won the title four times.

Lashley eventually returned to the WWE after an 11-year hiatus. His initial quest for the universal championship was ended by a loss to Roman Reigns. However, Lashley did win gold by capturing the intercontinental championship in a triple-threat match against Dean Ambrose and Seth Rollins. Lashley had notable feuds with The Shield, Braun Strowman, and Rusev before joining forces with MVP. The two were joined by Shelton Benjamin and together they formed the Hurt Business. Lashley defeated Apollo Crews for the United States championship and later defeated Sami Zayn in a champion vs champion match to win the intercontinental championship. Lashley won the WWE world heavyweight title in March 2021 when he defeated The Miz on *Raw*. He successfully defended the title against McIntyre, Strowman, Kofi Kingston, Goldberg and Randy Orton. After the match with Orton, Big E cashed in his *Money in the Bank* guarantee and defeated an exhausted Lashley. At the 2022 *Royal Rumble*, Lashley defeated Brock Lesnar to win the championship for a second time. However, he lost the rematch at the following *Elimination Chamber* match in February.

Lashley returned to form and at *WrestleMania 38*, he ended the undefeated streak of Nigerian giant Omos. MVP turned on Lashley and started managing Omos. Lashley ended their feud when he defeated MVP and Omos in a handicap match. He now turned his attention to United States heavyweight champion Austin Theory. Lashley defeated Theory for the title at *Money in the Bank*. He lost the title to Seth Rollins after interference from Brock Lesnar. He defeated Lesnar by disqualification at *Elimination Chamber* ending their feud. He was drafted to Smackdown but was unsuccessful in regaining the US championship and lost in the tournament to crown the newly created world heavyweight champion.

On *Smackdown*, Lashley formed an alliance with the Street Profits. They had a brief feud with the Latino World Order (LWO) and the Final Testament. Lashley's last appearance in WWE was on May 3, 2024, when he confronted Carmelo Hayes backstage. His contract with WWE expired in August. In September, he signed with All Elite Wrestling (AEW) and made his debut on October 30 at Friday night *Dynamite*. After Shelton Benjamin, with MVP in his corner, lost a match to Swerve Strickland, Lashley made a surprise appearance attacking Strickland. Lashley, Benjamin and MVP reformed the Hurt Business in AEW as the Hurt Syndicate.

Mixed Martial Arts (MMA)

In addition to professional wrestling, Bobby Lashley has had a successful mixed martial arts career as well. He started in 2008 with the Mixed Fighting Alliance. His debut fight was December 13, 2008, against Joshua Franklin. Lashley won in 41 seconds by technical knockout after a cut prevented Franklin from continuing. His next fight was originally supposed to be against MMA legend Ken Shamrock. Shamrock tested positive for a performance enhancement drug and was replaced by Jason Guida. Lashley won a unanimous decision over the Bellator veteran fighter. His next fight was a 21-second destruction of Mike Cook. Lashley took offense to Cook entering the cage wearing a Lucha Libre mask. Afterwards, Lashley said:

> *"I'm here for business," Lashley said. "I'm here and everyone wants to and tries to make fun of the wrestling thing. I'm real. If they want to play around, I'll knock them out or choke them out. And that's what I did. I choked him out and made him pay. Now he can go put the mask back on and have fun with himself."* (Cofield, 2009).

Lashley then defeated Bob Sapp by technical knock-out. He later joined Strikeforce with a 4-0 record. His opponent changed twice before the promotion settled on UFC veteran Wes Sims. Lashley defeated Sims in the first round by TKO. His first loss was a second round TKO to Chad Griggs. After the fight, Lashley was diagnosed with mono and couldn't train for four months. He signed with Titan Fighting Championship in February 2011. He won a unanimous decision over John Ott and defeated Kevin Asplund via submission. In 2011, he joined Shark fights. Lashley's first three opponents pulled out due to various reasons. He captured the promotion's heavyweight title by defeating Karl Knothe by a first round submission. After winning the title, he competed in the India-based Super Fight League. He lost a unanimous decision to James Thompson. His next fight was a victory over Matthew Larson using a rear choke submission hold in the first round. He later defeated Tony "The Rock" Melton by unanimous decision.

Lashley fought for Bellator MMA from 2014-2018. In his debut, he defeated Josh Burns with a rear-naked choke in the second round. In his second fight, he defeated Karl Etherington in the first round with punches and strikes. Next, he defeated Dan Charles with a second round TKO. In his long-awaited rematch against James Thompson, Lashley avenged his earlier loss with a first round TKO. His last fight for Bellator was on October 21, 2016. He defeated Josh Appelt with a rear-naked choke submission. Lashley announced his retirement in February 2022 via an interview with award-winning Canadian MMA journalist Ariel Helwani on *The MMA Hour*.

Bobby Lashley operates several businesses including a gym, smoothie shop, and several websites. Lashley has two children with former WWE wrestler Kristal Marshall. His MMA overall mixed martial arts record is 15 wins with 2 losses. He captured two heavyweight championships while competing in mixed martial arts. In wrestling, Lashley is a grand slam champion in WWE. He has held the following titles on multiple occasions: WWE championship, ECW world title, WWE intercontinental title and the WWE United States championship. He is a four-time TNA world champion and currently the world tag team champion with Shelton Benjamin in All Elite Wrestling.

Major Championships and Accomplishments

Title	Promotion	Dates
World Heavyweight Champion	Total Nonstop Action/Impact Wrestling	June 19, 2014 – 91 days Jan 7, 2015 – 24 days June 12, 2016 – 113 days Jan 8, 2017 – 175 days
King of the Mountain / Television Champion	Total Nonstop Action/Impact Wrestling	Aug 11, 2016 – 1 day
TNA X Division Champion	Total Nonstop Action/ Impact Wrestling	July 13, 2016
ECW World Champion	World Wrestling Entertainment	Dec 3, 2006 – 146 days June 3, 2007 – 7 days
WWE Champion	World Wrestling Entertainment	March 1, 2021 – 195 days Jan 29, 2022 – 20 days
Intercontinental Champion	World Wrestling Entertainment	Jan 14, 2019 – 33 days March 11, 2019 – 27 days
United States Champion	World Wrestling Entertainment	May 23, 2006 – 48 days Aug 30, 2020 –

		175 days July 2, 2022 – 100 days

Honors	Sponsor	Year
Rookie of the Year	Pro Wrestling Illustrated	2005
Most Improved Wrestler of the Year	Pro Wrestling Illustrated	2006
Andre the Giant Memorial Battle Royal winner	World Wrestling Entertainment	2023

Bianca Belair

Bianca Belair is an accomplished athlete in track & field, fitness and professional wrestling. Belair is a rare women's triple crown champion and only the second African American after Sasha Banks. She is also star of Love & WWE: Bianca & Montez. In 2021, she and Sasha Banks were the first Black women to headline WrestleMania.

Bianca Nicole Blair was born and raised in Knoxville, Tennessee. She was an outstanding athlete at Austin-East Magnet High School. As a young girl, she excelled in both track & field and tumbling or floor gymnastics. Blair was an outstanding athlete at Austin-East Magnet High School setting records in both the 100 and 300- meter hurdles. She won a Tennessee State championship during her senior year. After high school, Blair received a full scholarship to the University of South Carolina. After one year, she transferred to Texas A&M. Feeling homesick, Blair decided to return home and attend the University of Tennessee. She joined the Lady Volunteer track team first as a walk-on and later earned a full scholarship. Blair felt her athletic prowess return and she ended her track career with the Vols. After college, she still had the competitive spirit. Her next goal was to compete in the *CrossFit Games*.

Blair was making progress through the ranks but soon developed intercostal chondritis, or shifting rib syndrome. While she was forced to quit, Mark Henry saw her compete back in 2015 and was impressed by her athleticism. He asked her to consider wrestling and offered a tryout. Blair signed with the WWE in 2016 and trained at the WWE Performance Center in Orlando, Florida. In 2017, she made her television debut as Bianca Belair in a battle royal to determine the top contender for the NXT women's championship. After compiling a series of victories, she made her *WrestleMania* debut as a participant in the women's *Battle Royal* on April 2018. She was eliminated by Becky Lynch. In January 2020, Belair was dominant in the *Royal Rumble* where she lasted 33 minutes and eliminated a record eight opponents before losing to Charlotte Flair. Belair unsuccessfully challenged Rhea Ripley for the NXT women's championship and in February ended her run in the developmental ranks losing her final match to Flair.

In the 2020 draft, she went on to the *Smackdown* brand. Her first major victory on the main roster was winning the 2021 women's *Royal Rumble*. By eliminating Rhea Ripley, she became the second African American to win the *Royal Rumble*. Belair teamed with Sasha Banks to challenge Nya Jax and Shayna Baszler for the women's tag team championship. Their bid was unsuccessful and Belair challenged Banks for her Smackdown women's title at *WrestleMania*. On April 10, 2021, Belair won her first major singles title by defeating Banks for the Smackdown women's championship (now known as the women's world championship). After a 133-day reign, she lost the title to Becky Lynch.

Belair avenged the loss by defeating Lynch for *Raw's* WWE women's champion at *WrestleMania 38*. She successfully defended the title against Sonya Deville, Asuka, Becky Lynch, Bayley, Alexa Bliss, Iyo Sky before finally losing the title to Asuka at the *Night of Champions* on May 27, 2023, held in Jeddah, Saudi Arabia. The lost ended her record shattering 420 days as champion. Belair's reign as WWE women's champion made her the longest reigning African American world champion male or female and the longest reigning women's WWE champion. Belair teamed with African American wrestlers Jade Cargill and Naomi to defeat Damage CTRL (pronounced "control") at *WrestleMania XL*. She later teamed with Cargill to win the WWE women's tag team titles against the Kabuki Warriors at *Backlash* held in Lyon, France. They lost the titles to Alba Fyre and Isla Dawn, known as The Unholy Union in a triple threat match. Belair and Cargill became two-time champions by regaining the tag team belts at the inaugural *Bash in Berlin* pay-per-view.

Known as the EST of the WWE, she is the ninth female recognized as a triple crown champion. Her signature move, the K.O.D. (Kiss of Death) is where she lifts her opponents up into a torture rack and slams them to the mat with a face-buster. Belair has shown glimpses of her tremendous strength by putting the KOD finishing move on Piper Niven (Doudrop) and picking up 330-pound male wrestler Otis. She's known for her chiseled physique and long ponytail that is sometimes used as a weapon. Bianca is also married to fellow WWE superstar Montez Ford (Kenneth Crawford).

Major Championships and Accomplishments		
Title	Promotion	Dates
Smackdown Women's Championship/ World Women's Championship	World Wrestling Entertainment (WWE)	April 10, 2021 – 133 days
Raw Women's Championship / WWE Women's Championship (2 times)	World Wrestling Entertainment (WWE)	April 2, 2022 – 420 days Aug 5, 2023 - < 1 day
Women's Tag Team Champion (2 times)	World Wrestling Entertainment (WWE)	w/ Jade Cargill (May 4, 2024) – 42 days w/ Jade Cargill and Naomi (Aug 31, 2024) – 177 days

Honors	Sponsor	Year
Division I All-American Track and Field	NCAA	2011, 2012
All-SEC Track and Field	Southeastern Conference	2011, 2012
ESPY Award	ESPN	2021
Female Wrestler of the Year	ESPN	2022
Female Wrestler of the Year	New York Post	2022
Woman of the Year	Pro Wrestling Illustrated	2022
Best WWE Female	Slam Wrestling	2022
1st place Wellness Class	World Beauty Fitness & Fashion (WBFF)	2022
2nd Place Fitness Class	World Beauty Fitness & Fashion (WBFF)	2022
Triple Crown Champion - Women's World Champion - WWE Women's Champion - Women's Tag Team Champion	World Wrestling Entertainment	April 10, 2021 April 2, 2022 May 4, 2024

Big E

Big E is the sixth Black male to hold the WWE's world heavyweight championship title. He has the distinction of being the first Black wrestler to win the WWE's *Money in the Bank* ladder match – which afforded him the opportunity to challenge for the title. Big E is also considered a triple crown champion in the WWE and a nationally recognized powerlifter.

Ettore Ewen started wrestling in Tampa, Florida, where he won a state wrestling championship at Tampa Preparatory School. He transferred to Wharton High School for his senior year to play football. After he graduated, Ewen played one season for the Iowa Buckeyes.

After an injury ended his football career, he turned to powerlifting. Ewen's powerlifting career was brief but significant. He 2010, he competed in the USA Powerlifting Championships in Florida. He broke all four Florida state raw records in the 275-pound class. His lifts were 611 pounds (squat) 490 pounds (bench press) 749 pounds (deadlift) for a raw total of 1,850 pounds. In 2011, he competed in the USAPL super heavyweight division and set an American and national raw record with a 799-pound deadlift and 2.039-pound overall total.

While continuing to train and compete as a powerlifter, he was introduced to professional wrestling. He made his wrestling debut as Big E Langston in Florida Championship Wrestling (FCW) in 2009. In the Florida developmental territory, Langston notably teamed with Calvin Raines to win the FCW tag team championship from Seth Rollins and Richie Steamboat. After WWE rebranded FCW as NXT, Langston debuted on August 1, 2012, with a win over Adam Mercer. He continued his winning streak which caught the attention of Vicki Guerrero. After refusing to allow Guerrero to manage him, she put a bounty on Langston. He defeated all attempts by other wrestlers to claim the bounty until Dusty Rhodes made it null and void. Langston then started a feud with The Shield. On January 9, 2013, he won the NXT championship from Shield member Seth Rollins. He held the title until June 12 when he lost to Bo Dallas. Langston appeared on the *Raw* roster in an angle with AJ Lee and Dolph Ziggler. He and Ziggler were unsuccessful in their attempt to gain the WWE tag team championship from Daniel Bryan and Kane. In October, Langston lost a match to CM Punk but earned the veteran's respect and assistance in the ring. The unlikely pair teamed up to defeat Axel and Ryback further elevating Langston's status. He was given a push for the intercontinental championship but Axel withdrew due to a legitimate hip injury. Instead, Langston won the United States championship from Dean Ambrose. In November, he received his chance to fight Axel and successfully won the intercontinental championship title. On February 23, 2014, at *Elimination Chamber*, his name was officially shortened to Big E. He held the title for 167 days after losing to Bad News Barrett at *Extreme Rules*.

The New Day

Big E was teamed up with Kofi Kingston and Xavier Woods served as the manager during the summer of 2014 to form The New Day. The team debuted on November 28, 2014, and defeated the trio consisting of Axel, Heath Slater and Titus O'Neil. They went on a brief winning streak earning a title shot at *WrestleMania 31*. The New Day failed to capture the title in a fatal four-way match. After a negative response from the audience, The New Day turned heel. The heel turn resulted in the beneficial push the group needed. At 2015's *Extreme Rules* pay-per-view, Big E and Kofi Kingston defeated Cesaro and Tyson Kidd to win their first WWE tag team championship. They lost the titles on June 14 at *Money in the Bank* against Darren Young and Titus O'Neil who formed The Prime Time Players. However, they regained the titles two months later at *SummerSlam*. On July 22, 2016, three days after being drafted to *Raw*, The New Day became the longest reigning tag team champions at that time by breaking the previous record of 331 days. When the WWE SmackDown tag team championship was established, The New Day's title was renamed the Raw tag team championship. At *Roadblock: End of the Line*, The New Day lost the titles to Cesaro and Sheamus. In April 2017, The New Day members were drafted to *SmackDown*. The team of Kingston and Woods won the SmackDown tag team titles from The Usos. They traded the titles back and forth with The Usos. At *WrestleMania 34*, The New Day lost the titles in a triple threat match against The Usos and new champions, the Bludgeon Brothers. The New Day failed to win the titles at *SummerSlam* but regained them from the Bludgeon Brothers days later on *SmackDown*. On July 14, Big E and Xavier Woods won the title in a triple threat match. On September 15, The Revival won the titles but The New Day regain the titles for the fifth time on November 8 episode of *SmackDown*. Big E and Kofi Kingston lost the titles to John Morrison and The Miz at the 2020 Super ShowDown. On April 17, The New Day – represented by Big E who fought against Morrison and Jey Uso in a singles triple threat match– became the six-time SmackDown tag team champions. They lost the titles on July 19 to Cesaro and Shinsuke Nakamura. In October 2020, Kingston and Woods were drafted to *Raw* while Big E remained on *SmackDown* which reignited his solo career.

On December 25, Big E defeated Sami Zayn to capture his second intercontinental title reign. On the second night of *WrestleMania*, Big E lost the title to Apollo Crews after interference from Commander Azeez. Big E avenged his loss to Crews and on July 18, he won the men's *Money in the Bank* ladder match. On September 13, Big E cashed in his contract and defeated Bobby Lashley for the WWE championship. He successfully defended the title until losing to Brock Lesnar in a fatal five-way match on January 1, 2022. In his attempts to regain the title, Big E lost to Lashley and later to Seth Rollins. Big E's championship reign lasted for only 110 days. While he appreciated the push, he felt his reign was too short to make the sort of positive impact The New Day members represented at the time. "I wish it would have lasted longer and we would have had that period to produce more dynamic things. It's difficult to latch on to a new champion when, within the first month, they have multiple losses on TV" (Lambert, 2022). Brock Lesnar ended the title runs of both Kofi and Big E. However, Big E credit's Kingston's reign as champion for providing an example of leadership. "I was able to see the way he handled things with his title run and the way things ended. It's interesting how our runs weren't too drastically different. That falling off of a cliff feeling at the hands of one Brock Lesnar and then suddenly, it feels like you woke up a year prior and you're back to doing what you were doing before" (Lambert, 2022).

Big E's in-ring career came to an end on March 11, 2022. During a match against Ridge Holland and Sheamus, he was at the receiving end of an overhead belly-to-belly suplex at ringside. Big E landed on his head which caused a broken neck. Since recovering from the injury, he only makes appearances on WWE shows as an announcer or panelist in non-wrestling roles.

Major Championships and Accomplishments		
Title	Promotion	Dates
FCW Tag Team Champion	Florida Championship Wrestling	w/Calvin Raines (May 12, 2011) – 70 days
NXT Champion	World Wrestling Entertainment	Dec 6, 2012 – 153 days
Intercontinental Champion (2 times)	World Wrestling Entertainment	Nov 18, 2013 – 167 days Dec 22, 2020 – 107 days
WWE Champion	World Wrestling Entertainment	Sept 13, 2021 – 110 days
Raw Tag Team Champion	World Wrestling Entertainment	w/The New Day (April 26, 2015) – 49 days w/The New day – (Aug 23, 2015) – 483 days w/The New Day – (Oct 12, 2020) – 69 days w/The New Day (March 15, 2021) – 26 days
Smackdown Tag Team Champion	World Wrestling Entertainment	w/The New Day (July 23, 2017) – 27 days w/The New Day (Sept 12, 2017) –

		25 days
		w/The New Day (Aug 21, 2018) – 55 days
		w/The New Day (July 14, 2019) – 62 days
		w/The New Day (Nov 8, 2019) – 110 days
		w/The New Day (April 17, 2020) 92 days
		w/The New Day (Oct 9, 2020) – 2 days

Honors	Sponsor	Year
Best Gimmick	Wrestling Observer Newsletter	2015
Shad Gaspard/Jon Huber Memorial Award	Wrestling Observer Newsletter	2020
Tag Team of the Year	Pro Wrestling Illustrated	2015 & 2016
Men's Money in the Bank	World Wrestling Entertainment	2021
Triple Crown Champion - Intercontinental title - Raw Tag Team title - WWE Heavyweight title	World Wrestling Entertainment	Nov 18, 2013 April 26, 2015 Sept 13, 2021

Nyla Rose

As a youth, Nyla Rose was an up-and-coming performer with a dream of becoming a pro wrestler. She wrestled on the independent circuit on the East Coast and in Japan. During her training at the dojo for the Japanese wrestling promotion Marvelous, she earned the nickname "Kenny Omega Hair" because her natural curls resembled the popular AEW Canadian wrestling star. Rose would impersonate Omega's signature catchphrase "good bye (kiss) and good night, bang." It should not have come as a surprise when Omega reached out to her on social media. Omega, who at the time was New Japan Pro Wrestling's IWGP heavyweight champion, invited Rose to try out for a new wrestling promotion that he along with Cody Rhodes and the Young Bucks were helping to start called All Elite Wrestling.

Rose is a professional wrestler and actor of both African American and Native American heritage. She is the first Black women's world champion in All Elite Wrestling (AEW) and the first transgender woman to win a world title in a major wrestling company. Rose trained at the KYDA pro wrestling school and began her career in 2013 on the independent circuit mostly performing with the New Jersey-based Women Superstars Uncensored. Rose performed under the moniker "Native Beast," which was an ode to her Native American heritage. Rose is a member of the Oneida tribe. She also wrestled with Japanese independent promotions before signing with AEW after it launched in 2019.

After signing with All Elite Wrestling (AEW), Rose debuted in the promotion's inaugural pay-per-view show *Double or Nothing*. She lost the fatal four-way match but made a grand introduction by spearing legendary wrestler Awesome Kong into the ring steps. She won the right to compete against Riho on the debut of *Dynamite* on October 2, 2019. Rose was unsuccessful as Riho became the inaugural champion. However, she established herself as a bona fide heel when she attacked both Yuka Sakazaki and women's champion Riho after losing a triple threat match. Rose eventually defeated Riho on February 12, 2020, to win the women's title. She lost the title on May 23, 2020 to Hikaru Shida. Shortly after losing the title, she hired Vicki Guerrero as her manager. She continues to wrestle in main event title matches in AEW and Ring of Honor. Rose also co-host AEW's *Unrestricted* podcast

Major Championships and Accomplishments		
Title	Promotion	Dates
WOW Women's Champion	Warriors of Wrestling	April 14, 2018 – 113 days Oct 9, 2019 – 218 days
UPWA Women's Champion	United Pro Wrestling Association	April 7, 2013 – 198 days
WDWA West Virginia Champion	World Domination Wrestling Alliance	Aug 19, 2017 – 112 days
CP Women's Champion	Covey Promotions	Aug 17, 2013 – 56 days Nov 8, 2014 – 84 days Oct 17, 2015 – 56 days
AEW Women's World Champion	All Elite Wrestling	Feb 12, 2020 – 101 days

Big Ryck

He's body slammed The Big Show and put the Great Khali in the torture rack. Despite taking down giants throughout his career, ninety-seconds was the length of his reign as ECW world champion. Rycklon Edward Stephens is a wrestler, bodybuilder and personal trainer who was born in Guyana. As a youth, he moved to the United States and graduated from the University of Buffalo. Stephens became a household name when he wrestled in the WWE under the name Ezekiel Jackson. Stephens started his career in 2007 with Ultimate Pro Wrestling in California as Big Ryck Hytz. Ultimate Pro was a school and development company that scouted several wrestlers for the WWE before closing in 2007. Later that year, Stephens signed with the WWE's Florida Championship Wrestling (now NXT) first using the name Rycklon. He debuted in FCW on the July 18, 2008, edition of *SmackDown* under the name Ezekiel. He first appeared as the bodyguard for Brian Kendrick. The following month, he appeared on *SmackDown* again but this time as the advisor to Kendrick and "Jackson" was added as his last name.

Jackson started interfering in matches and eventually started teaming with Kendrick. His official in-ring debut in October resulted in a victory over Super Crazy. He and Kendrick unsuccessfully challenged Carlito and Primo Colon for the WWE tag team titles. In 2009, Jackson was drafted to the ECW brand. After a few weeks of one-upmanship squash match challenges with Vladimir Kozlov, Jackson tag teamed with Christian in place of Tommy Dreamer against Kozlov and William Regal (Battle, 2009). Jackson turned on Christian and helped Regal in his feud against ECW champion Christian. However, Regal failed to win the title. Jackson went on to win a battle royal earning a title shot. On January 31, 2010, he faced Christian at the *Royal Rumble* in a losing effort. However, on February 16 – the last episode of ECW – Jackson defeated Christian for the world title in an Extreme Rules match. After his victory, the ECW title was retired.

In January 2011, he helped Wade Barrett, Justin Gabriel and Heath Slater attack Big Show. The four men formed an alliance that became known as The Corre. In a show of his strength, Jackson defeated Big Show in a singles match. When the other members of the Corre celebrated his victory, Jackson refused to join in and was attacked by his former teammates. Jackson fought Barrett for the intercontinental championship in May at *Over the Limit* and won by disqualification. At *Capital Punishment* on June 19, 2011, he won the intercontinental title from Barrett. Jackson successfully defended the title in a rematch against Barrett and Ted DiBiase before dropping the title to Cody Rhodes. In 2014, Jackson made his TNA debut using the name Rycklon again. After a brief stint with TNA and the Lucha Underground, Jackson joined the German-based Westside Xtreme

Wrestling (wXw) in 2015. After unsuccessfully challenging for the promotion's Unified World Wrestling title, he took a 10-year hiatus to focus on his personal training business. Jackson returned to the ring in March 2025 as Big Ryck at Fortitude Wrestling Entertainment's *Full Throttle* in a triple-threat match for the Sylvan's FWE heavyweight title. Big Ryck did not get the win but had a successful return to the ring.

Big Ryck is the third black and final ECW world champion. In addition to his wrestling career, he once owned a wrestling school. He still continues to train many up-and-coming athletes and has reignited his own wrestling career on the independent circuit.

Major Championships and Accomplishments		
Title	Promotion	Dates
ECW World Champion	World Wrestling Entertainment	Feb 16, 2010 – <1 day
WWE Intercontinental Champion	World Wrestling Entertainment	June 19, 2011 – 53 days

Jay Lethal

Jamar Shipman, who wrestles under the ring name Jay Lethal, is perhaps the most decorated wrestler in the history of the Ring of Honor (RoH) promotion. He is a two-time RoH world heavyweight champion and is known as "The Franchise" in the promotion. He is also known for his championship title runs in Total NonStop Action (TNA) wrestling.

Shipman was born in Elizabeth, New Jersey. He started his career at age 16 in 2001 when he won a lifetime of free training sessions with Jersey All Pro Wrestling (JAPW) professional wrestling school. He spent 6 months in the wrestling school until it closed.

Shipman debuted on December 7, 2001, under the ring name Jay Lethal. On September 13, 2002, he won his first title, the JAPW television championship in a three-way match against Rain and the champion Ghost Shadow. He held the belt for 11 months. Next, Lethal defeated Azrieal to capture the JAPW light heavyweight Championship. Lethal fended off Azrieal for 8 months until finally dropping the title back to him at December 2004's *Seasons Beatings*. In January 2005, Lethal defeated Dan Maff for the JAPW heavyweight championship but the decision was overturned. Maff retired in March vacating the title. It was awarded to Lethal but he refused to accept. Lethal won the title in May by pinning Homicide in a fatal four-way match that also included Kevin Steen and Samoa Joe. He lost the title to Rhino on November 12, 2005, and failed to regain it after two attempts. On October 28, 2006, Lethal teamed with former rival Azrieal to win the JAPW tag team champions. They lost the titles on June 9, 2007, to Homicide and Hernandez at *Back to Business*. Lethal pinned Kenny Omega in 2009 to win the JAPW heavyweight championship for a second time. He lost the title to Dan Maff in July at *Caged Destiny* which was his last appearance in the promotion. He is a triple crown champion in JAPW, winning the television championship, light heavyweight championship and the heavyweight championship twice.

In 2003, he debuted in Ring of Honor (RoH) wrestling as a member of Special K using the name Hydro. The following year, at the advice of Samoa Joe, he left Special K and reverted back to using the name Jay Lethal. During this run in RoH, he feuded with The Embassy. Despite being attacked at the Trios Tournament in March 2005, Lethal won the Pure championship. This was his first title in RoH. He would later lose the title to his mentor Samoa Joe in May. His last match was a clean loss to Samoa Joe in February 2006. After the loss to Samoa Joe, he would make sporadic appearances in one-night only matches and losing each time.

He left the promotion in December to join Total Nonstop Action (TNA) Wrestling. After a few matches, Lethal participated in the Paparazzi Championship Series. In February 2007, TNA's *Impact!* ran a segment called "Paparazzi Idol." At the suggestion of Kevin Nash, who served as a judge, Lethal did a spot-on impersonation of Randy "Macho Man" Savage and began using the Black Machismo gimmick. In 2009, he won the X Division championship. In January 2009, Lethal teamed with Consequences Creed, to form Lethal Consequences. They defeated Beer Money, Inc to win the TNA world tag team championship on January 8, 2009, but lost in a rematch three days later at *Genesis*. On March 29, 2010, TNA released Creed from his contract and the team dissolved.

After a brief hiatus from television, Lethal returned to *Impact!* In March 2010 with another successful imitation. After reminiscing with Hulk Hogan about the Mega Powers tag team, Hogan gave Lethal Ric Flair's stolen Hall of Fame ring. Similar to his Black Machismo impersonation, Lethal would come to the ring and impersonate Nature Boy Ric Flair, which led to a feud with Flair's group Fortune. Lethal went on to defeat Fortune member and X Division Champion Douglas Williams for his fourth title reign. He lost the title to Amazing Red but regained it two days later. Lethal lost the title on an episode of *Impact!* to Robbie E. He regained the title from Robbie E in December. At the January 9, 2011, *Genesis* pay-per-view, Lethal dropped the title to Kazarian, another member of Fortune. He left the promotion in April.

Lethal returned to Ring of Honor (RoH) in June 2011. He won the world television championship two times before eventually capturing the world heavyweight title. His campaign for the world title began in April 2015. He first declared himself as "the champion" in Ring of Honor. Next, he had a new television championship belt made. It said RoH champion instead of television champion. These maneuvers eventually led to a champion versus champion match. In the winner-take-all match, Lethal defeated Jay Briscoe to claim both the world television and world heavyweight titles. He lost the world title to Adam Cole on August 19, 2016, after 427 days. Lethal is credited as being the first black wrestler to hold the Ring of Honor world title and the longest reigning television champion. He is also a RoH grand slam champion having held the world heavyweight championship twice, world television championship twice, Pure championship and the world tag team championship with Jonathan

Gresham, also a world heavyweight title holder. Lethal made his debut for All Elite Wrestling (AEW) in November 2021. He is currently active in both AEW and RoH.

Major Championships and Accomplishments		
Title	Promotion	Dates
RoH Pure Champion	Ring of Honor	March 5, 2005 – 63 days
RoH World Champion	Ring of Honor	June 19, 2015 – 427 days June 30, 2018 – 280 days
RoH World Tag Team Champion	Ring of Honor	w/Jonathan Gresham (Dec 13, 2019) -?
RoH World Television Champion	Ring of Honor	Aug 13, 2011 – 231 days April 4, 2014 – 567 days
TNA World Tag Team Champion	Total Nonstop Action (TNA)	w/ Consequences Creed (Dec 16, 2008) – 26 days
TNA X Division Champion	Total Nonstop Action (TNA)	June 17, 2007 – 2 days

Honors	Sponsor	Year
Grand Slam Champion	Ring of Honor	
- Pure title		March 5, 2005
- World Television title		Aug 13, 2011
- World Heavyweight title		June 19, 2015
- World Tag Team title		Dec 13, 2019

Jonathan Gresham

He's been called one of the best wrestlers in the world. With a strong amateur wrestling background, it is hard to deny the technical skills of Jonathan Gresham. Gresham is a former world heavyweight champion and a triple crown champion in Ring of Honor (RoH) wrestling. He has wrestled in more than 15 different countries for major and independent promotions. A native of Atlanta, Georgia, Gresham had his first match at age 16. His professional career started in 2006. He trained under Mr. Hughes (Curtis Hughes) and Jay Fury at the World Wrestling Alliance Pro Wrestling School in Atlanta. Gresham debuted in the National Wrestling Alliance independent promotion in 2006 as Jonathan Davis. Like many new wrestlers, he honed his skill by competing on the independent circuit. In 2008, he appeared in Pro Wrestling Alliance (now Reality of Wrestling) owned by Booker T as Hero Tiger. In 2010, he joined Combat Zone Wrestling. Gresham debuted for Westside Xtreme Wrestling in 2011. He and Jay Skillet became RockSkillet in 2012. In August 2012, they won the wXw world tag team championship. He won the CZW heavyweight title in 2016. During this period, Gresham went back and forth wrestling for a few different promotions. In 2014, he started using his name Jonathan Gresham.

After continuing to wrestle for different promotions, Gresham signed with Ring of Honor (RoH) in 2017. In 2019, Gresham teamed with Jay Lethal to win the RoH world tag team championship by defeating the Briscoe Brothers. In 2020, Gresham emerged victorious from a 16-man tournament to win the Pure Championship. After losing the Pure championship, Gresham went on to win the vacant RoH world heavyweight championship in December 2021 at the *Final Battle* pay-per-view. He won the title by defeating his former partner Jay Lethal. In March 2022, Gresham also won the Progress Wrestling world title from the British wrestling promotion. He competed in TNA wrestling but did not achieve the same level of success. He competed for the X Division title and the TNA world heavyweight championship but failed to win either title. Despite his 5'4" height, Gresham has a solid muscular build. His technical skills combined with high-flying, aerial moves makes Gresham a formidable professional wrestler.

While being considered one of the best wrestlers in the industry, Gresham remains humble and appreciative of the recognition he receives from fans. On the *Fightful Wrestling with Sean Ross Sapp* podcast, he said: "The more I thought about it to be honest, I'm more so happy that people are looking at someone that looks like me as someone that can be best in the world. For years, Black people-people that look like me have not been considered or in the conversations of being best in the world...I'm just happy that people of color are actually getting looked at in a different way now" (Sapp, 2021).

Gresham is also known for wearing masks to the ring. In similar fashion to Lucha Libre wrestling, the mask has strong visual imagery and is part of his wrestling character. Gresham's unique face mask resembles an octopus. On the King Nebuchadnezzar promo for TNA, Gresham said he wears three masks – one he presents to the general public, one he only shows to close friends and family and the third mask that no one has ever seen. In the promo, Gresham said it's necessary to keep the third mask hidden. "I've been embarrassed. I've gone for years unheard and it's gotten to the point where I am ashamed. I'm ashamed that it took me this long to realize that life is a costume party and the entire time I've been attending it. I've been showing up with my real face."[10] Gresham is known for three finishing moves – the figure-four leglock, shooting star press and the octopus hold. Gresham is currently a free agent as of January 2025. He still competes sporadically for Impact Wresting and on the independent circuit. In late 2024, he signed a deal with Memphis Wrestling as both an in-ring performer and mentor/coach for WrestleCenter Starrs of Tomorrow. Gresham also operates Octopus University where he offers personal training in different wrestling styles including Pure, Lucha Libre and overall ring fitness. He is married to fellow wrestler and powerlifter Jordynne Grace who is a three-time Impact/TNA Knockouts world champion.

---

[10] (*Jonathan Gresham: King Nebuchadnezzar | The Complete Story* 2024) https://www.youtube.com/watch?v=8hNOL0k1aeo

Major Championships and Accomplishments		
Title	Promotion	Dates
CZW World Heavyweight Champion	Combat Zone Wrestling	Sept 10, 2016 – 91 days
RoH Pure Champion	Ring of Honor	Oct 30, 2020 – 317 days
RoH World Champion	Ring of Honor	Dec 11, 2021 – 224 days
RoH World Tag Team Champion	Ring of Honor	Dec 13, 2019
Progress World Champion	Progress Wrestling	March 20, 2022 – 56 days
The Crash Cruiserweight Champion	The Crash Lucha Libre	March 23, 2019 – 223 days
wXw World Tag Team Champion	Westside Xtreme Wrestling	w/Jay Skillet (Aug 12, 2012) – 203 days

Honors	Sponsor	Year
Triple Crown Champion - World Tag Team title - Pure title - World Heavyweight title	Ring of Honor	Dec 19, 2019 Oct 30, 2020 Dec 11, 2021

Athena

    She was trained by wrestling legends. She can deadlift 400 pounds. And she has a strong, analytical mind along with a high-flying unpredictable style. Female wrestler Athena possesses an air of mystery and intrigue that intimidates opponents and excites crowds. She earned the nickname "forever champion" due to being the longest reigning women's world champion and the longest reigning overall title holder in Ring of Honor. As a young girl, Adrienne Reese used to read comics and play video games. She grew up in Garland, Texas and attended Lakeview Centennial High School where she participated in tennis, soccer and was a member of the chess club. Her introduction to professional wrestling came from her grandfather (Saxton, 2016). However, her motivation to take the sport seriously came from being bullied by other teens because she was considered a nerd. Her career began in 2007 at age 19 when she started training under General Skandor Akbar. The old school training under Akbar gave her discipline and conditioning. When his school closed, she learned power moves and how to strike opponents from Vance Archer. Then, she learned high-flying moves from Booker T at his Reality of Wrestling promotion in Houston. She later trained at Houston-based Pro Wrestling Alliance under the names Trouble and Athena. Her first years in the industry were spent wrestling for other independent promotions, including Chicago's Shimmer Women Athletes and Women Superstars Uncensored in New Jersey. Her most successful independent run was with Anarchy Championship Wrestling in Austin, Texas where she was a three-time women's champion and also held the television title.

Athena first joined Ring of Honor in 2013. She performed in singles matches and was a member of Team R&B who later became known as Adrenaline Rush. In 2015, Palmer left RoH and signed a developmental contract with the WWE. She made her debut in NXT under her real name Adrienne Reese. In June 2016, the company gave her the name Ember Moon. She built and impressive resume winning in tag team and singles matches until finally losing to NXT Champion Asuka. Moon won the NXT championship in a fatal four-way match. She held on to the title for 140 days before losing to Shayna Baszler. She was promoted to the main roster after dropping the title.

Her first appearance was at the 2018 women's *Royal Rumble* match. She was later drafted to *SmackDown* where she feuded with Mandy Rose and Sonya Deville. She teamed with women's champion Bayley to defeat Rose and Deville but later lost a title match to Bayley leading to a losing streak. An ankle injury caused her to be inactive and she was reassigned to NXT. At NXT, she partnered with Shotzi Blackheart in the inaugural Dusty Rhodes Tag Team Classic. They lost to Dakota Kai and Raquel Gonzalez at the classic, but later defeated them to win the tag team titles. After 55 days, they lost the belts to The Way (Candice LeRae and Indi Hartwell). Moon unsuccessfully challenged Gonzalez for the championship and was later released from her contract.

Moon returned to the independent circuit using the name Athena. She challenged Thunder Rosa for the Warrior Wrestling women's championship in February 2022. The 30-minute time limit match ended in a draw. On May 22, 2022, she made her surprise debut for All Elite Wrestling appearing at the end of Jade Cargill's match. Athena challenged Cargill for the TBS championship but lost. She also challenged for but did not win the AEW women's championship in a fatal four-way where Toni Storm maintained the title. On an episode of *Rampage*, Athena turned heel by attacking the referee Aubrey Edwards after pinning Madison Rayne. Ring of Honor champion Mercedes Martinez, made the save which earned Athena a title shot. On December 10, 2022, Athena won the RoH women's world championship from Martinez at the *Final Battle* pay-per-view. At *Death Before Dishonor*, Athena retained her title against Willow Nightingale while making history as the first woman's match to headline a RoH pay-per-view. Athena currently holds the record for the longest title reign in RoH history surpassing Samoa Joe's 644 days. "I've wrestled in one-night, in tournaments, main events, in thumbtacks, in TLC matches and even competed against men. I had no limits because I wanted to be the best, and that's what got me here" (Saxton, 2016).

Major Championships and Accomplishments		
Title	Promotion	Dates
NXT Women's Champion	NXT/World Wrestling Entertainment	Nov 18, 2017 – 139 days
NXT Women's Tag Team Champion	NXT/World Wrestling Entertainment	w/ Shotzi Blackheart (March 10, 2021) – 55 days
RoH Women's World Champion	Ring of Honor	Dec 10, 2022 – 900+ days
Warrior Wrestling Women's Champion	Warrior Wrestling	April 23, 2022 – 531 days

Rich Swann

Richard Anthony Swann was born in Baltimore, Maryland in 1991. He began training as a wrestler at age 14 in York, Pennsylvania under Adam Flash and Darren Wyse. In 2009, he joined Combat Zone Wrestling. He was known as a member of the Irish Driveby and The Blackout. He challenged for the CZW junior heavyweight title, Wired television title and world heavyweight title but was unsuccessful at each attempt. In 2010, he wrestled for Dragon Gate USA and Evolve. Swann made several tours in Japan under the parent company Dragon

Gate. He won the Open the Owarai Gate championship title, which is more of a playful championship. The word "owarai" means comedy in Japanese. The competition uses over-the-top, even slapstick humor in presentation and storyline unlike the more serious competition. Regardless, it's still a recognized title. Upon returning to the United States, Swann competed in Maryland Championship Wrestling and Jersey All Pro Championship Wrestling in 2009. Swann won his first wrestling title, the inaugural Real Championship Wrestling cruiserweight title, on January 16, 2010. He would lose the title on his second defense in a three-way ladder match.

Swann would later join forces with Ricochet to form the tag team called the Inner City Machine Guns. They would compete as a team in several independent promotions including Dragon Gate Japan Pro Wrestling, Evolve, Pro Wrestling Guerrilla, London's RevPro and the German promotion Westside Xtreme Wrestling. The duo briefly held the wXw tag team titles and they won Pro Wrestling Guerilla's 2014 Battle of Los Angeles tournament. They competed for belts in the other promotions but overall, they achieved moderate success as a tag team. Swann would remain on the independent circuit until an unlikely tweet from rap artist Wale in 2014 caught the attention of Mark Henry. Henry secured a tryout for him and Swann later signed with NXT in October 2015. Swann participated in the Cruiserweight Classic tournament but lost to the eventual winner T.J. Perkins. On the premiere of *205 Live*, WWE's streaming program for cruiserweight wrestlers, Swann defeated Brian Kendrick for the cruiserweight championship. He lost the title to Neville shortly after. Swann was suspended from the WWE following an arrest in December. On February 15, 2018, he was officially released from his contract.

Following his release from WWE, Swann returned to the independents and also joined Impact Wrestling. On June 21, 2018, Swann debuted in TNA Impact Wrestling. At December's *Homecoming*, Swann won the vacant X Division title in a fatal four-way match. Swann eventually lost the title on July 19 to Jake Crist after 194 days as champion. On July 18, 2020, Swann returned from an injury and competed for the Impact world championship at *Slammiversary*. After eliminating Eric Young, Young attacked Swann's injured knee with a steel chair. He later avenged the attack by defeating Young to win the world title at *Bound for Glory*. At *Sacrifice,* Swann united the Impact world championship and the TNA world heavyweight championship becoming a double champion by defeating Moose. Swann lost to AEW World Champion Kenny Omega ending his title reign as world champion. On May 28, Swann defeated Matt Cardona to become the Impact digital media champion. Cardona refused to give the belt to Swann but he couldn't compete. Instead, he decided to give the belt to his tag team partner Brian Myers. In a fashion similar to his feud with Moose, Myers challenged Swann to a match to decide who was the real champion. Swann defeated Myers at *Slammiversary* but lost the title to Myers at *Against All Odds*. He continued to wrestle for the promotion until August 29, 2004. In June, he was arrested for public intoxication and suspended by TNA. He decided to enter rehab. Speaking out about the incident on a podcast[11], Swann admitted to being so drunk he tried to enter a neighbor's apartment thinking it was his own. He said a lady saw him heavily intoxicated, assumed he did not live in the gated community and called the police. Swann has said the experience turned out to be a defining moment because he is now sober and in his best physical shape (Mukherjee, 2025). Swann has left TNA and currently competes only on the independent circuit.

      Rich Swann is a grand slam champion in TNA/Impact Wrestling having won four major titles. He is also a former British tag team champion with Ricochet and a WWE cruiserweight champion. Swann is married to pro wrestler Vannarah Riggs who uses the ring name Su Yung.

---

[11] Swann discusses his release from TNA on the Keepin' It Real podcast - https://www.youtube.com/watch?v=UTyRJjDXe4s

Major Championships and Accomplishments		
Title	Promotion	Dates
NXT Cruiserweight Champion	World Wrestling Entertainment	Nov. 29, 2016 – 60 days
British Tag Team Champion	Revolution Pro Wrestling	w/Ricochet (Mar 15, 2014) – 1 day
FIP World Heavyweight Champion (2 times)	Full Impact Pro/ World Wrestling Network	Nov 14, 2014 – 98 days April 18, 2015 – 76 days
TNA Digital Media Champion	TNA/Impact Wrestling	May 28, 2022 – 34 days
TNA X Division Champion	TNA/Impact Wrestling	Jan 6, 2019 – 194 days
TNA Impact World Champion	TNA/Impact Wrestling	Oct. 24, 2020 – 183 days
TNA World Heavyweight Champion	TNA/Impact Wrestling	Mar 13, 2021 - < 1 day

Honors	Sponsor	Year
Grand Slam Champion	TNA/Impact Wrestling	
- Digital Media Champion		May 28, 2022
- X Division Champion		Jan 6, 2019
- Impact World Champion		Oct 24, 2020
- TNA World Heavyweight Champion		Mar 13, 2021

Moose Ojinnaka

Quinn "Moose" Ojinnaka is a former professional football player and two-time world heavyweight champion in Total Nonstop Wrestling (TNA). Ojinnaka has Nigerian ancestry but he was born in Seabrook, Maryland. Growing up, he was an All-Prince George's County offensive lineman at DeMatha Catholic High School. Ojinnaka was a starting offensive lineman his senior year at Syracuse University and played in the Las Vegas All-American Classic. In 2006, he was drafted in the fifth round by the Atlanta Falcons. He played with the Falcons for three years. In 2010, he was traded to the New England Patriots serving as an active reserve for the season. He had a brief stint with the St. Louis Rams and the Indianapolis Colts in 2011 before re-signing with the Rams in March 2012. However, he was released in October.

In 2012, Ojinnaka began training as a pro wrestler at the World Wrestling Alliance training facilities in Atlanta. In February,

2014, he debuted for Dragon Gate USA and in May 2015 he wrestled dark matches only for Global Force Wrestling (GFW). He could only wrestle house shows and non-televised matches because he was under contract to Ring of Honor. Ojinnaka took the name Moose in RoH. Due to their partnership, he regularly wrestled in both RoH and New Japan Pro Wrestling from 2014-2016. Moose made his TNA debut on July 12, 2016, by interfering with the main event match against TNA Heavyweight Champion Bobby Lashley and X Division Champion Eddie Edwards. Moose defeated Aron Rex on December 1 for the Impact Grand championship. He lost the title to Drew Galloway then regained it in March. He had successful title defenses until the August 3 episode of *Impact* where he lost to Ethan Carter III.

On April 28, 2020, Moose won a triple threat match that was originally scheduled to be a world title match but Impact World Champion Tessa Blanchard did not participate in the match due to the Covid-19 pandemic. Blanchard, the first female to hold the world title, was eventually stripped due to not defending the title during the pandemic. Moose declared himself "Mr. TNA" and the new TNA world heavyweight champion. He even wore the original TNA title belt that was used before the company changed its name to Impact Wrestling in 2017. TNA did not recognize the championship; however, Moose made several unofficial "title" defenses. On the February 23, 2021, episode of *Impact!*, TNA sanctioned the title as a separate championship from the Impact world championship. The TNA world heavyweight championship held the lineage of the original TNA world championship (Terry, 2021). Moose began calling himself the "real" world champion and challenged Rich Swann. A unification match between Moose and Impact Champion Rich Swann was held on March 13 at *Sacrifice*. Swann was victorious and briefly carried both championship belts until the TNA world heavyweight championship was deactivated and retired by Christian Cage on August 19, 2021. At *Bound for Glory* on October 23, 2021, Moose earned the Call Your Shot gauntlet match. Later that evening he defeated Josh Alexander for his first Impact world championship. After 182 days as champion, Moose lost the title to Alexander at *Rebellion*.

At *Hard To Kill*, Moose used a low blow and appeared to defeat Joe Hendry for Impact Digital Media championship. However, the match was restarted and Hendry pinned Moose to win and maintain the title. After failing to win the Digital Media title in a rematch, Moose participated in the Feast or Fired match on September 9, 2023, at *Impact 1000,* which celebrated the company's 1000 episode. As a result, he grabbed one of the four briefcases which contained a contract to have a world championship title match. In the countdown preview show before the *Hard to Kill* pay-per-view, Moose was joined by Brian Myers, Eddie Edward, Alisha Edward and former NFL running back DeAngelo Williams. The group became known as The System. During the main event, Moose defeated Alex Shelley to capture the renamed TNA world championship. He held the title for 189 days before losing a six-way elimination match in which Nic Nemeth emerged victorious. Although he was eliminated by Joe Hendry, Moose failed to win the title in a one-on-one rematch against Nemeth. However, he won the X Division title from "Speedball" Mike Bailey on the November 7, 2024, episode of *Impact*. In March 2025, Moose challenged Oba Femi for the NXT championship but was pinned after Femi's "fall from grace" powerbomb. Moose retained his TNA X Division title.

In 2023, he signed the longest contract in TNA's history. Moose said he made the decision to stay long term with TNA instead of going to another promotion because he has a great relationship with Executive Vice President Scott D'Amore and he wanted a chance to perform at the highest level of the professional wrestling business (Van Vliet, 2024). Moose is a triple crown champion in TNA/Impact Wrestling and is the fourth African American to hold the world heavyweight title after Ron Killings, Bobby Lashley and Rich Swann.

Major Championships and Accomplishments		
Title	**Promotion**	**Dates**
TNA X Division Champion	TNA/Impact Wrestling	Oct. 27, 2024 – 230+ days
GWF Heavyweight Champion	German Wrestling Federation	March 6, 2017 – 70 days
IPW UK World Champion	International Pro Wrestling: United Kingdom	Oct. 11, 2017 – 42 days
TNA World Champion	TNA/Impact Wrestling	Oct 23, 2021 – 182 days Jan. 13, 2024 – 189 days
TNA World Heavyweight Champion	TNA/Impact Wrestling	Apr 28, 2020 – 301 days Feb 23, 2021 – 18 days
Impact Grand Champion	TNA/Impact Wrestling	Oct 9, 2016 – 90 days Jan 12, 2017 – 174 days

Honors	Sponsor	Year
Triple Crown Champion - Impact Grand Champion - X Division Champion - World Champion	TNA/Impact Wrestling	Oct. 9, 2016 Oct 27, 2024 Feb. 23, 2021
Rookie of the Year	Pro Wrestling Illustrated	2015

Tyrus

Tyrus is the second person of African American descent to hold the NWA world heavyweight championship after R-Truth. Born George Murdoch in Boston, Massachusetts, he became a champion professional wrestler who parlayed his wrestling career into acting and eventually becoming a regular television personality on cable news. Murdoch, who is biracial, left home when he was young and lived in a foster home with his brother before returning to live with their mother. At 15, he left home again. After graduating high school, he first attended Antelope Valley College. He later studied education and played football at the University of Nebraska.

Murdoch signed with the WWE in 2006 and worked in the developmental territories. He started with Deep South Wrestling playing the character of a street thug named G-Rilla. In 2007, he was re-assigned to Florida Championship Wrestling. He had a title match but lost due to disqualification. He was released from his contract in 2008. He resigned with the company in 2010 and started using the name Brodus Clay. This was a play on Snoop Dogg's given name Calvin Broadus. Murdoch once served as Snoop Dogg's bodyguard. Brodus Clay appeared on the fourth season of *NXT* where he teamed with Ted DiBiase, to defeat Byron Saxton and Chris Masters. Clay won a four-way elimination match and chose Alberto Del Rio on *Raw* as his new mentor. He debuted as Del Rio's bodyguard. They were eventually split as Del Rio remained on *Raw* and Clay went to *Smackdown*.

Clay took a three-month leave to appear in the film *No One Lives*. He returned to competition on WWE Superstars where he mostly defeated jobbers. When he returned to action on the main roster in 2012, his new gimmick was a dancing babyface (good guy) called "The Funkasaurus." This character was also accompanied by female backup dancers Cameron and future women's champion Naomi known as the Funkadactyls. The gimmick was well received from a management standpoint as Clay went on a 24-match winning streak. The streak ended after he lost to the Big Show who had turned heel. Clay soon formed a partnership with Tensai (Matt Bloom) calling themselves the "Tons of Funk." They teamed with the Funkadactyls to defeat Team Rhodes Scholars (Cody Rhodes and Damien Sandow) and the Bella Twins. When Xavier Woods debuted in November 2013, Clay attacked him accusing Woods of stealing his music and the Funkadactyls for his ring entrance. He defeated Woods in a match and assaulted Wood's partner R-Truth. Clay taunted and toyed with R-Truth during a match he could have easily won, but his relentless assault caused Tensai and the Funkadactyls to leave his corner. In their next tag team match, Clay abandoned Tensai causing them to lose a match which completed his heel turn. He went on to lose singles matches to Woods and R-Truth. His final match with WWE was a loss to NXT champion Adrian Neville.

In September 2014, Clay joined Total Nonstop Action (TNA) using the name Tyrus. He competed for the TNA world heavyweight championship on April 26, 2016, at *Sacrifice*, but lost to Drew Galloway (McIntyre). He also competed with Eli Drake for the TNA world tag team champions but lost to Matt and Jeff Hardy. He disagreed with the booking decisions and left the company in 2018.

Tyrus had a brief stint on the independent circuit joining Tommy Dreamer's House of Hardcore before signing with the National Wrestling Alliance (NWA) in 2021. Tyrus had his sights on winning the NWA world television championship. He fought the champion "The Pope" (Elijah Burke) to a draw and defeated The Pope in a non-title match. Tyrus accomplished his goal on August 6, 2021, when he defeated The Pope for the title. After a few successful title defenses, he vacated the title to challenge Trevor Murdoch for the NWA worlds heavyweight championship. Tyrus pinned Murdoch at *NWA Hard Times 3* on November 12, 2022, to win the world title. As NWA worlds heavyweight champion, Tyrus was featured during a Super Bowl commercial for The Fox News Channel Talk Show *Gutfeld!* At the NWA's two day 75th Anniversary Show, Tyrus faced EC3 (Ethan Carter III) in a bull rope match on day two, August 27, 2023. Tyrus retired from wrestling after losing the world title to EC3.

Murdoch first appeared on *The Greg Gutfeld Show* in 2016 as a guest commentator. His appearance was well received and he was invited to appear twice a month using his wrestling name Tyrus. He became a regular contributor on a few Fox News programs including *The Five*, *Un-PC* and *The Daily Briefing*. He has been a regular panelist on Gutfeld's new program *Gutfeld!* since April 2021. He also hosted the premiere episode of *Fox News Saturday Night* and in February 2024, Murdoch debuted the series *Maintaining with Tyrus* on the *OutKick* streaming service.

Major Championships and Accomplishments		
Title	Promotion	Dates
NWA World Television Champion	National Wrestling Alliance	June 5-7, 2021 – 474 days
NWA World's Heavyweight Champion	National Wrestling Alliance	Nov 12, 2022 – 288 days

Swerve Strickland

Stephon "Swerve" Strickland is the first black male world champion in All Elite Wrestling. Performing under the name Swerve Strickland, he is a former world singles champion and world tag team champion. He is currently one of the highest paid performers in the wrestling business and resolute in his commitment to promoting excellence among African American athletes. However, Strickland's humble beginnings in the business helped him realize his future potential. Strickland's unwavering confidence comes from years of hard work and understanding his value.

Strickland was born in Tacoma, Washington in 1990. Because his father was a U.S. Army sergeant stationed in Frankfurt, he grew up on a military base in Germany for seven years. The family eventually moved to Pennsylvania where he played basketball, football and track & field at Donegal High School. After graduating, he joined the U.S. Army Reserves. While in the reserves, Strickland started training as a pro wrestler at Ground Xero (pronounced Zero) Academy in 2008. During the early stages of his career, he wrestled for several independent promotions including the NWA, East Coast Wrestling Association and World Xtreme Wrestling. On February 4, 2012, he debuted for Combat Zone Wrestling in a dark match. He wrestled in a few main events over the next two years. His break came in March 2014 when he defeated Devon Moore to win the CZW wired championship. Strickland lost the title later that year and wrestled for Westside Xtreme Wrestling in Germany. In July 2017, he won the CZW world heavyweight championship in a fatal four-way match. He lost the title in November. In 2018, he won the Evolve Wrestling championship with a victory over Matt Riddle. He captured the PCW ultra-light heavyweight championship in March 2018. Strickland became a double champion on December 7, 2018, by winning the PCW ultra heavyweight championship. He relinquished the light heavyweight title. In 2019, he lost the heavyweight title to Mil Muertes after a farewell speech he made earlier indicating his plans to sign with a major promotion. He started working for the WWE in April 2019 under the name Isaiah "Swerve" Scott on NXT. In May 2021, after turning heel, he was joined by Top Dolla (A.J. Francis), Ashante "Thee" Adonis (Tehuti Miles) and B-Fab (Briana Brandy) to form Hit Row. On June 29, he won the NXT North American championship by defeating Bronson Reed. After a 105-day reign, he lost the title to Carmelo Hayes. In November, all four members of Hit Row were released from the company.

In March 2022, he signed with AEW under the name Swerve Strickland. He teamed with Keith Lee to fight Powerhouse Hobbs and Ricky Starks, known as Team Taz and also debuted for Ring of Honor. Strickland and Lee as a duo became known as Swerve In Our Glory. They defeated The Young Bucks and Team Taz to win the AEW world tag team championship at the July 2022 *Fyter Fest*. They lost the belts to The Acclaimed in September. Lee and Strickland eventually broke up. Strickland formed the Mogul Affiliates which included hip-hop star Rick Ross. Strickland would go on to feud with "Hangman" Adam Page, making a push to become the first Black world champion in AEW. Strickland's dream was realized on April 21, 2024, at *Dynasty* when he defeated Samoa Joe for the title. He lost the title after 126 days to Brian Danielson at *All In*.

Outside of the ring, Strickland is a solo hip-hop artist, known as Swerve the Realest and a member of the group Swerve City. From 2014-2018, he appeared on Lucha Underground, a professional wrestling television series on the *El Rey* Network. He portrayed the character Lt. Jermaine Strickland. The character wore dog tags in memory of his fellow soldiers. He also wore a mask and wrestled as Killshot. He is a cousin of Fred Strickland, a former NFL linebacker.

Swerve celebrates after winning the AEW world title from Samoa Joe.

Major Championships and Accomplishments		
Title	Promotion	Dates
CZW Wired Television Champion	Combat Zone Wrestling	March 8, 2014 – 144 days Aug 13, 2014 – 122 days
CZW World Heavyweight Champion	Combat Zone Wrestling	July 8, 2017 – 126 days.
NXT North American Champion	World Wrestling Entertainment	June 29, 2021 – 105 days
AEW World Tag Team Champion	All Elite Wrestling	w/Keith Lee (July 13, 2022) – 70 days
AEW World Heavyweight Champion	All Elite Wrestling	April 21, 2024 – 126 days

Trick Williams

Before "*Whoop That Trick!*" became a viral catchphrase at wrestling arenas, Matrick Belton was an aspiring football player. The Columbia, South Carolina native earned a full scholarship to play college football for Hampton University. After suffering a pulled hamstring his sophomore year, he left the Pirates and walked on at his hometown team, the University of South Carolina. His father played fullback for legendary head coach Willie Jeffries at South Carolina State University. When Belton decided to leave Hampton, he also played for a legendary football coach – the head ball coach Steve Spurrier and later Will Muschamp. After graduating and coaching football at Airport High School, he went to the Philadelphia Eagles training camp but was cut. Next, he tried out for the XFL which was owned by WWE Chairman Vince McMahon. The XFL ended after one season but he was contacted by the WWE to give wrestling a try. He went to train at Philadelphia's Combat Zone Wrestling and lived with his great uncle. His character was inspired by his uncle's nickname Sweet Daddy Trick. After a brief stay, he moved out of his uncle's home and settled in Los Angeles to train at KnokX Pro Wrestling Academy. In 2021, he signed a developmental contract with WWE as Trick Williams.

Williams' first appearance on camera was inconspicuous. He portrayed a "Nigerian" elite guard protecting Apollo Crews. In September, he appeared on NXT as a friend and partner of Carmelo Hayes. They established themselves as a heel faction called the Trick Melo Gang. After an attack from Bron Breakker in April 2023, The Trick Melo Gang turned babyface. In August, Williams left the group to pursue a singles career. At *NXT No Mercy*, he defeated Dominik Mysterio to win the North American title. Three days later, he lost the title in a rematch with Mysterio after interference from the Judgment Day. Williams and Hayes began a feud as they both challenged for the NXT championship. Williams attacked Hayes at *Halloween Havoc* costing him the title. Williams and Hayes teamed up again in 2024 to compete in the Dusty Rhodes Tag Team Classic. At *Vengeance Day*, they lost to Breakker and Baron Corbin in the finals. Later that night, Williams lost an NXT title shot against Dragunov. Hayes attacked Williams after the match. He also revealed that he attacked Williams back in October. Williams got his revenge by defeating Hayes in a steel cage match at *Stand & Deliver*. The feud was called one of the most compelling in pro wrestling due to their three-year friendship turned sour due to betrayal (Barrasso, 2024). Then at *Spring Breakin*, he won the NXT championship from Dragunov. On July 7, at *Heatwave*, Williams lost the championship to Ethan Page. Williams regained the title from Page on October 1, when NXT premiered on the *CW Network*. During his second title reign, he successfully defended against Ridge Holland and Eddy Thorpe in a controversial double count out. He lost the title to Oba Femi in a triple threat match that also included Thorpe on January 7, 2025. After failing to regain the title from Femi, Williams turned heel. He insulted Femi and continued to feud with Thorpe. He lost a strap match at *Vengeance Day* but was victorious at *NXT Underground* in March. Williams faced Femi and Je'Von Evans in a triple threat match but Femi retained the title. At *WrestleMania 41*, TNA World Champion Joe Hendry answered Randy Orton's open challenge. He lost after an RKO. Williams insulted and attacked Hendry a week later. Then, at *Battleground* on May 25, he defeated Hendry to become the first active WWE wrestler to hold a TNA championship.

In January 2025, WWE and TNA signed a multi-year collaboration deal where wrestlers from NXT and TNA would appear on each other's weekly programs and pay-per-view events (Mahjouri et al, 2025). At *Battleground*, Williams won his first world title by defeating Hendry. Outside of the ring, he was an extra on the sports drama *All American*. Williams also released a rap song called "Average Joe." The WWE is giving Williams the platform to showcase his various talents in music and acting. For Williams, the different roles are a natural part of who he is in real life. "I'm actually very, very fortunate that Matrick Belton and Trick Williams are the same person," he said (Titus, 2024).

Major Championships and Accomplishments		
Title	Promotion	Dates
NXT Champion	World Wrestling Entertainment	April 23, 2024 – 74 days Oct 1, 2014 – 98 days
NXT North American Champion	World Wrestling Entertainment	Sept 30, 2023 – 3 days
TNA World Champion	Total Nonstop Action Wrestling	May 25, 2025 – ? days

BLACK TAG TEAM WORLD CHAMPIONS

Soul Patrol

Rocky Johnson and Tony Atlas were two successful singles competitors who joined forces to become the Soul Patrol. As the Soul Patrol, Johnson and Atlas became the first black tag team to win the world tag team championship in the World Wrestling Federation. After feuding with the Wild Samoans (Afa and Sika) who were managed by Captain Lou Albino, they demanded a no disqualification match to which the champions agreed. On November 15, 1983, they defeated the Wild Samoans to win the titles. They successful retained the titles in a rematch. But the historic title reign would come to end too soon. At their next title defense on April 17, 1984, they lost the titles to

Adrian Adonis and Dick Murdoch, known as the North/South Connection. In an interview with Hannibal TV, Johnson said their title reign could have last much longer but Atlas was difficult to work with. According to Johnson, Atlas would pick and choose the shows he wanted to appear on despite the duo drawing large crowds. In a separate interview, Atlas said he and Johnson were never friends and that Johnson was the real culprit causing him to miss shows. "We got into a fist fight the day before they took the belts off of us," Atlas said. "I jumped Rocky in the dressing room. He used to leave me at hotels. Make me miss shows and say to (Vince McMahon Sr.) it was me."[12]

Both Atlas and Johnson were physically imposing and possessed tremendous strength and agility. While their physical appearances were strikingly similar, Johnson was 10 years older than Atlas. The age difference perhaps contributed to ideological differences which led the partners to have a rather contentious relationship. Their unlikely pairing led to their only title reign ending prematurely with a 1-1 record. Still, the Soul Patrol coming together was a significant and historical moment for black tag team wrestlers.

Soul Patrol - Major Championships and Accomplishments		
Title	Promotion	Dates
WWF World Tag Team Champions	World Wrestling Federation	Nov 15, 1983 – 154 days

---

[12] https://www.youtube.com/watch?v=uuK4y5Ha14Q

ROCKY JOHNSON

Johnson was born Wade Bowles in Nova Scotia, Canada in 1944. He grew up in Toronto where he was trained at first to be a boxer. He once sparred with heavyweight boxing champions George Foreman and Muhammad Ali. Johnson later converted to professional wrestling where he was known as "The Soul Man."

In 1964, Bowles made his wrestling debut in Ontario using the ring name Rocky Johnson. The name was homage to his favorite boxers Rocky Marciano and Jack Johnson. He liked the moniker so much, shortly after debuting he legally changed his name to Rocky Johnson. As a 20-year-old rookie, he was strong and had a chiseled physique. In 1967, after only three years as a professional, he had his first taste of championship gold winning the NWA Canadian (Vancouver) tag team title with partner Don Leo. Johnson went on to win numerous singles and tag team titles throughout the territories including Los Angeles, San Francisco, Georgia and Florida. Johnson became a major draw and a main event talent in the NWA during the 1970s. He never won the world championship, but had world title matches against Harley Race, Terry Funk and Jack Brisco. Johnson also held the NWA television title in the Mid-Atlantic region wrestling under a mask as Sweet Ebony Diamond. In the 1980s, Johnson joined the World Wrestling Federation. He was soon paired with Tony Atlas. After winning the world tag teams titles from the Wild Samoans (Afa and Sika), and losing them to Adrian Adonis and "Dirty" Dick Murdoch, Johnson left the WWE in 1985 for the independent circuit.

Johnson met his second wife Ata, while wrestling in tag team matches with her father "High Chief" Peter Maivia. Johnson and Ata Maivia's friendship soon turned romantic and they had a son Dwayne in 1972. Upon his retirement in 1991, Johnson along with Pat Patterson, reluctantly trained his son, Dwayne "The Rock" Johnson who has transcended wrestling to become a major Hollywood celebrity. In retirement, Johnson was a trainer for the WWE's developmental territories including Ohio Valley Wrestling (OVW). He stepped in the ring for the last time going back to his roots in a boxing match against Mabel (Big Daddy V) in Memphis. Rocky Johnson's finishing move was the dropkick. In addition to his historic tag team run with Atlas, Johnson broke racial barriers by becoming the first African American wrestler to win the NWA Southern (Memphis), Georgia and Florida heavyweight titles. In 2008, The Rock inducted both his father and grandfather Peter Maivia into the WWE Hall of Fame. Rocky Johnson died on January 15, 2020, at his home in Florida. He was 75.

Rocky Johnson - Major Championships and Accomplishments		
Title	Promotion	Dates
WWF World Tag Team Champion	World Wrestling Federation	w/Tony Atlas (Nov 15, 1983) – 154 days
NWA World Tag Team Champion (Detroit)	Big Time Wrestling	w/Ben Justice (Jan 18, 1969)
NWA Florida Heavyweight Champion	Championship Wrestling from Florida	July 1975 Dec 23, 1975 – 8 days Mar 8, 1978 – 5 days
NWA Georgia Heavyweight Champion	Georgia Championship Wrestling	Dec 6, 1974
NWA Television Champion	Mid-Atlantic Championship Wrestling	April 29, 1981 – 7 days May 30, 1981 – 15 days
NWA Canadian Tag Team Champion	NWA All-Star Wrestling (Vancouver)	w/Don Leo Jonathan (Apr 3, 1967) – 21 days
NWA Texas Heavyweight Champion	NWA Big Time Wrestling	Aug 11, 1976 – 9 days

Honors	Sponsor	Year
St. Louis Wrestling Hall of Fame	St. Louis Wrestling Club	2008
WWE Hall of Fame	World Wrestling Entertainment	2008
Memphis Wrestling Hall of Fame	United States Wrestling Association (USWA)	2022

TONY ATLAS

"Wrestling gives us the opportunity to be who we really are."

Tony Atlas, born Anthony White in 1954 in Clifton, Virginia, is a former champion pro wrestler, powerlifter and bodybuilder. Known as "Mr. USA" for his bodybuilding prowess, Atlas won several singles and tag team championships throughout his legendary career. According to his autobiography *Too Much, Too Soon*, Atlas was raised in a single parent home by his mother Beatrice James. His mother worked from 7:00am until 11:00pm every day. She worked 16-hour days but only brought home no more than $30 a week as both a cook at the Hotel Roanoke and a maid at a hospital. He was the youngest of nine children. As a child, he grew up poor and had to fight for a living. In fact, his father encouraged him to fight for money. As a teenager, his father would take him to a local hangout spot in Low Moor that was called Scrappers Corner and fist fight against men for money. Age differences would sometimes pit young boys against men 15 years their senior. "The only road to success for poor black men was through fighting, sports, singing, or dancing. That was just about it. None of us had any thought or hope of going to college. The idea never crossed our minds." Because of their extreme poverty, Atlas and one of his brothers were sent to live in the Virginia Negro Baptist Children's

Home. Living in the orphanage gave him structure. Atlas later spent six months in a reform school where he developed a passion for weightlifting. Atlas eventually found himself in a detention center and realized he had to change his life. Atlas was already in great shape and a good fighter. At age 19, Atlas won Teenage Mr. Virginia and was the state champion in weightlifting, powerlifting and arm wrestling. Atlas soon received a try-out in professional wrestling. Although he had no experience, he was being paid to train in Charlotte. He was initially under the tutelage of Larry Sharpe, and Gene and Ole Anderson. After training at Larry Sharpe's Monster Factory wrestling school, Atlas made his official wrestling debut in 1976 in Atlanta as the Black Atlas.

Atlas had an incredible physique standing at 6'2" and weighing 250 pounds. In 1979, he won the World Bodybuilding Guild's (WBBG) Pro Mr. USA contest.[13] He also won the USPF Atlanta Open in 1979 with a raw bench press of 540 pounds. As a show of strength, his signature moves in wrestling were the bearhug and the Gorilla Press Slam. Atlas was so popular in the early 1980s, he feuded with Hulk Hogan. He was one of only a few men to apply the Gorilla Press Slam on Hogan. In March 1981 at Madison Square Garden, Atlas defeated Hogan by pinfall; although the referee didn't see Hogan's foot on the ropes. However, Atlas pinned Hogan again, in April 1981 in Philadelphia. "By booking Atlas to beat Hogan, the WWWF showed that they thought Atlas was a budding superstar as well." (Klein, p. 56). Hogan, of course, would go on to win the WWF Championship resulting in the Hulkamania craze that catapulted him into major celebrity status.

Atlas even pinned NWA Champion Harley Race in November 1980 but the belt didn't change due to a botched finish. According to Atlas, Race wanted to drop the belt to Atlas while he was on tour in Japan. After the tour, he would win the title back. This would have made Atlas the first Black world heavyweight champion, but booker Ole Anderson didn't think he was ready for the title. From 1979 to 1984, Atlas worked for several different promotions including New

---

[13] https://musclememory.com/show.php?c=Pro+Mr+USA+-+WBBG&y=1979

Japan Pro, the Universal Wrestling Federation, Georgia Championship Wrestling and the World Wrestling Federation. He teamed with Rocky Johnson in 1983 to create the trailblazing duo, the Soul Patrol. They defeated the Wild Samoans for the tag team titles making them the first black tag team world champions. When they lost the titles, Atlas was becoming addicted to drugs and left the WWF in 1984. Atlas admittedly hit rock bottom due to the choices he made. He was struggling financially and reached out to Vince McMahon. To help Atlas out of a bind, the WWF offered him a role portraying an African named Saba Simba. The character was dressed in traditional African attire but instead of a proud African warrior, he portrayed a character that Westerners identified as an uncivilized savage. Black audiences in particular were offended by the stereotypical character. In a shoot interview, Atlas confessed to not liking the role initially, but accepted it because he needed the money. "I didn't like it at first but then I thought about 'Tony you just left the frickin' city park brother. Be thankful that you got a job.' So that's how I looked at it from that point on. Once you hit rock bottom, it humbles you. So maybe years ago him dressing me up like an African and bouncing around the ring like a monkey, would have upset me. But after coming from where I come from being homeless and being without and I saw an opportunity to make money."

On March 25, 2003, Atlas teamed with "Cowboy" Bob Orton, father of WWE's Randy Orton, to defeat the LA Hustlers (Bradley Diggs and Lamonte Potts) for the Southern Illinois Championship Wrestling (SICW) tag team belts. Their title reign lasted 105 days before they lost the belts back to the LA Hustlers. Atlas was inducted into the WWE Hall of Fame in 2006. In July 2008, Atlas made another brief return to the WWE. He appeared as a special ring announcer during the match where ECW Champion Mark Henry faced Tommy Dreamer with Colin Delaney in his corner. Atlas attacked Delaney which distracted Dreamer. The match was officially a double count out but Atlas declared Henry the winner and became his manager. In December 2008, he wrestled a tag team match with Henry and they defeated Finlay and Hornswoggle. In June 2009, Henry was drafted to *Raw* which officially ended their partnership. ECW's last television broadcast was February 2010. Atlas was released in April. In 2010, he released his autobiography Too Much, Too Soon. In 2014, Atlas was a regular on the *Legend's House* reality show on the WWE Network. He is no longer active in the ring but continues to do interviews and make personal appearances.

Tony Atlas - Major Championships and Accomplishments		
Title	Promotion	Dates
NWA Georgia Heavyweight Champion	Georgia Championship Wrestling	Oct 24, 1980 - ?
NWA Georgia Tag Team Champion (4 times)	Georgia Championship Wrestling	w/Tommy Rich (Sept 9, 1977) – 6 days w/Tommy Rich (Nov 15, 1977) – 29 days w/Mr. Wrestling II (Feb 7, 1978) – 20 days w/Kevin Sullivan (April 21, 1980) – 3 days
NWA Mid-Atlantic Heavyweight Champion	Mid-Atlantic Championship Wrestling	Sept 17, 1978 – 28 days
WWF World Tag Team Champion	World Wrestling Entertainment	w/Rocky Johnson (Nov 15, 1983) – 154 days

Honors	Sponsor	Year
New England Pro Wrestling Hall of Fame	New England Pro Wrestling	2008
WBBG Hall of Fame	World Body Building Guild	2007
WWE Hall of Fame	World Wrestling Entertainment	2006

Doom

After The Soul Patrol's groundbreaking title run, it would be nearly seven years before another black tag team would wear championship gold. Ron Simmons and Hacksaw Butch Reed came together to wreak havoc on the NWA tag team division and were appropriately known as Doom. Both were former stand-out college football players before turning to professional wrestling. Simmons and Reed formed the team Doom in late 1989.

In early 1989, Rick Steiner decided to tag team with his young brother Scott in World Championship Wrestling. At that time, the Steiner Brothers were managed by Missy Hyatt. As they began to rise through the tag team ranks, a (kayfabe) "fan" using the name Robin Green started following the team with her eyes on Rick Steiner. He soon found himself being stalked. The fan started to subtlety interfere in their matches. During one such interference, she "accidentally" tripped up Scott costing them the NWA world tag team titles in a match against the Fabulous Freebirds. After several attempts at breaking the bond between the brothers proved unsuccessful, the "fan" adopted a new look and began using the moniker "Woman." After being rejected, she told Rick that he and his brother would meet their doom at 1989's *Halloween Havoc* pay-per-view. Simmons and Reed made their tag team debut as Doom and were victorious over the brothers. Doom's win over the Steiner's was followed up with a victory at *Clash of the Champions IX* over Eddie Gilbert and Tommy Rich.

Simmons and Reed appeared in all black outfits and wearing black masks covering their faces. Although wearing face masks, their identity was hardly a secret due to their physiques and the limited number of black male wrestlers in the promotion. Things began to decline when Doom lost to the Steiner brothers at the February *Clash of the Champions X* and were forced to unmask. Woman left the group and started managing the Four Horsemen. This allowed Doom to rebuild including taking on former referee Teddy Long as their new manager. Long noted the personality differences between Simmons and Reed but still felt the duo split up too soon. In a shoot interview for Title Match Wrestling, he said Doom was his favorite group to manage in WCW. "It was a lot of fun with Butch and Ron," he said. "It was more fun with them because they were just two characters." Doom feuded with the Four Horsemen, specifically Flair and Arn Anderson, and again with Rick and Scott Steiner. They ended up dropping the titles to the Fabulous Freebirds with Diamond Dallas Paige as their manager. Long said the Freebirds were a hot new group and the company needed a big win to help get them over with the WCW fan base. Butch Reed and Ron Simmons went on to have successful wrestling careers after their brief but historic title run.

Doom - Major Championships and Accomplishments		
Title	Promotion	Dates
NWA/WCW World Tag Team Champions	National Wrestling Alliance / World Championship Wrestling	May 19, 1990 – 281 days

RON SIMMONS

Ron Simmons is a former football player and professional wrestler. He is known for his prowess as a college football player at Florida State University. After playing professional football, he started wrestling. Simmons is recognized as the first African American wrestler to win a world heavyweight title from a major wrestling promotion.

Simmons and Reed wearing the masks along with original manager Woman.

BUTCH REED

Bruce Franklin "Butch" Reed was a college football player and professional wrestler known by his ring name Butch Reed. Reed played linebacker for the University of Central Missouri. In 1976, he signed as a free agent with the Kansas City Chiefs but was cut before the season started. Reed trained to wrestle under the tutelage of Ronnie Etchison, a former wrestler and referee in the Central States territory. Two years after his debut, he saw his first taste of gold as a tag team champion in the Central States with partner Jerry Roberts. Later, Reed teamed with Sweet Brown Sugar to win Florida's version of the NWA Florida North American tag team championship. Reed had a competitive match against Ric Flair for the NWA world heavyweight title in 1982 before moving on to the Mid-South Wrestling territory under "Cowboy" Bill Watts.

Reed became a household name during his time in Mid-South. He adopted the nickname "Hacksaw" and started off in the promotion as a tag team partner with the Junkyard Dog. He also began a feud with Jim Duggan over the name Hacksaw. He later feuded with his former partner Junkyard Dog which was a major draw throughout the Mid-South territory. Reed was once a double champion in Mid-South holding both the North American heavyweight title and the tag team championship along with partner Jim Neidhart. As Reed's feud with Junkyard Dog reached a climax, JYD unexpectedly left the company and joined the World Wrestling Federation. Reed continued to have high profile matches until meeting up with Kamala. After failing to beat the "Ugandan Giant," Reed left Mid-South for the American Wrestling Association (AWA). After a short stint with the AWA, he returned to Mid-South and recaptured the North American title. Reed challenged Ric Flair for the NWA world title on April 7, 1982, and again in 1985. The 1982 match which took place in Florida was dubbed a five-star match for Reed and earned him huge notoriety and respect among wrestling insiders. Despite having great matches against Flair, including pinning the champion at the Municipal Auditorium in New

Orleans, Reed was unsuccessful in winning the world title.[14] Reed lost his North American title to Dick Slater who helped Flair retain the world title in one of their one-hour "iron man" matches. Reed again left Mid-South this time for the Central States territory where he was managed by Slick. When Reed lost a "loser leaves town" match to Bruiser Brody in 1986, he and Slick decided to join the World Wrestling Federation.

Doom with manager Teddy Long being interviewed by Paul Heyman.

The World Wrestling Federation gave him a new gimmick. Reed dyed his hair blonde and became known as "The Natural" Butch Reed. He competed in the first *Royal Rumble* in January 1988. Unfortunately, he has the distinction of being the first man eliminated. A couple of months later, he was eliminated in the first round of the *WrestleMania* championship tournament that was held to crown the eventual champion Randy Savage. Reed left the company after this

---

[14] Butch Reed vs. Ric Flair - https://www.youtube.com/watch?v=7LP9m8g-Jy0

loss and returned to the NWA under the flourishing Jim Crockett Promotions. Reed was paired with Ron Simmons to form Doom. The duo enjoyed a brief but dominant run as world tag team champions. After losing to the Fabulous Freebirds in 1991, Reed turned on his partner Simmons. Their feud ended at *SuperBrawl* in May with Simmons defeating Reed in a steel cage match. Reed and Teddy Long left WCW shortly after. He made a brief return in 1992 but left later that year for the United States Wrestling Association where he resumed his popular feud with Junkyard Dog. Reed defeated JYD for the USWA world title in October 1992. He held the title for one week before losing to Todd Champion. He left the USWA for the Global Wrestling Federation. He became the GWF North American champion and held the title for a month before losing to "Gentleman" Chris Adams. The promotion closed and Reed returned to wrestling with the independent promotions. Outside of wrestling, Reed was a cowboy. Once GWF closed, he decided to become a part time wrestler to devote more time to participate in Kansas City's rodeo circuit.

Reed was semi-retired from wrestling but had a short stint with Mid States Wrestling in 2005. He participated in the Legends of Wrestling tour in 2006 and 2007. Reed made a cameo appearance in WWE on September 9, 2007, in a backstage segment with his former manager and then *SmackDown* general manager Theodore Long. May 18, 2013, was Reed's last match. He partnered with Cowboy Bob Orton, Jr in a losing effort against Ron Powers and Flash Flanagan in SICW. On February 5, 2021, Reed's official Instagram account announced his death resulting from two heart attacks. He also tested positive for COVID-19 in January 2021. He was inducted into the St. Louis Wrestling Hall of Fame in 2025.

Butch Reed - Major Championships and Accomplishments		
Title	Promotion	Dates
NWA/WCW World Tag Team Champion	National Wrestling Alliance / World Championship Wrestling	May 19, 1990 – 281 days
NWA North American Heavyweight Champion	Mid-South Wrestling Association	April 16, 1983 – 30 days Oct 24, 1983 – 2 days Oct 14, 1985 – 79 days
Mid-South Television Champion	Mid-South Wrestling Association	July 22, 1985 – 84 days
Mid-South Tag Team Champion	Mid-South Wrestling Association	w/Jim Neidhard (Oct 12, 1983) – 74 days
GWF North American Heavyweight Champion	Global Wrestling Federation	June 4, 1994 – 27 days
USWA World Heavyweight Champion	United States Wrestling Association	Oct 12, 1992 – 5 days
WLW Heavyweight Champion	World League Wrestling	March 31, 2001 – 300 days

Honors	Sponsor	Year
Strongest Wrestler	Wrestling Observer Newsletter	1984
St. Louis Wrestling Hall of Fame	St. Louis Wrestling	2025

Sasha Banks & Naomi

It was *WrestleMania 38*. The location was the Dallas Cowboys' stadium in Arlington, Texas. It was the third *WrestleMania* to take place over two nights (April 2-3, 2022) since the COVID-19 pandemic forced the 2020 event to be filmed over two days. And it was a defining moment for both the female participants and the sport of women's professional wrestling. In a fatal four-way match, champions Queen Zelina and Carmella faced challengers Sasha Banks and Naomi, Rhea Ripley & Liv Morgan, and Natalya & Shayna Bazler. On April 3, 2022, which was the second night of *WrestleMania*, Sasha and Naomi made history by becoming the first black females to win the WWE women's tag team titles. "These titles did not exist five years ago because we wanted more," Banks said in an interview after their victory. "We demanded more and we have more. And now we're gonna create more opportunities for so many more women and I just can't wait."[15]

"Oh my gosh, this has been a dream of mine," Naomi said. "We got these titles to make history, open doors and so that this becomes something we see more often and not a first. There are still many more doors that are not open (that need) to be knocked down. And we just continuing to blaze that trail that the women before us started and hope to inspire more."

In an interview with *TNT Sports*, at the time Banks credited her "best friend" Vince McMahon for putting the team together (Helwani, 2022). It was also Sasha's first *WrestleMania* victory. Then something happened. The tag team champions walked out of a live television appearance on May 16, 2022, just over a month into their reign. According to an official statement from the WWE:

> "When Sasha Banks and Naomi arrived at the arena this afternoon, they were informed of their participation in the main event of tonight's *Monday Night Raw*. During the broadcast, they walked into WWE Head of Talent Relations John Laurinaitis' office with their suitcases in hand, placed their tag team championship belts on his desk and walked out. They claimed they weren't respected enough as tag team champions. And even though they had eight hours to rehearse and construct their match, they claimed they were uncomfortable in the ring with two of their opponents even though they'd had matches with those individuals in the past with no consequence. *Monday Night Raw* is a scripted live TV show, whose characters are expected to perform the requirements of their contract."

---

[15] https://www.youtube.com/watch?v=bZocsATPKQ8

According to wrestling insiders, the new tag team champions were going to be used as merely tools to help bring further respect to the other *Raw* and *Smackdown* female champions. While most people will agree that walking out of the job should not go unpunished, "WWE, however, has seemingly gone out of its way to paint Banks and Naomi as the bad actors in this situation where they were not only standing up for themselves, but the consistently poor creative around the women's tag team division they appear to care more about than WWE does" (Staszewski, 2022).

Their last television appearance was a title defense on the May 13 episode of *Smackdown* and a live event on May 15 was their last official match as champions. As a result of their suspension, Banks and Naomi left the WWE. They both moved on to compete in other federations and each had individual success. Nearly a year after walking out and being stripped of the titles, Naomi reemerged in Impact Wrestling on April 28, 2023, using her given name Trinity. She wasted little time making an impact. She won her first pay-per-view match with the company on May 26 by defeating Gisele Shaw. Then, on July 15 at *Slammiversary*, she defeated Deonna Purrazzo to win the Impact Knockouts world title. The company rebranded itself back to TNA Wrestling in 2024 and the title was renamed the TNA Knockouts World Championship. Trinity lost the title after 182 days to her tag team partner Jordynne Grace. In her last match with the company, she again tagged with Grace to defeat Gisele Shaw and Savannah Evans. She returned to the WWE at the January 27, 2024 *Royal Rumble.*

Sasha Banks decided to explore more than one option. On January 4, 2023, Sasha Banks made her debut at New Japan Pro Wrestling's *Wrestle Kingdom 17* using the name Mercedes Mone. She won the IWGP Women's championship from Kairi in February. After 64 days, she lost the title to Mayu Iwatani. She teased a U.S. comeback by appearing in the audience at AEW's *All In* pay-per-view in August 2023. At the May 2024 *Double or Nothing* pay-per-view, Mone made her AEW in-ring debut by defeating Willow Nightingale for the TBS championship. She became a double champion a month later by defeating Stephanie Vaquer for the Strong Women's championship. At the *Wrestle Dynasty* pay-per-view on January 5, 2025, Mone defeated

Mina Shirakawa in a winner-takes-all match to capture the undisputed British Women's championship. Thus, making Mone a triple champion. Both women have moved on and revived their careers. Mone is collecting championship titles in AEW and Naomi held the tag team title and as the *Money in the Bank* winner, she is a contender for the belt of her choice.

Major Championships and Accomplishments		
Title	Promotion	Dates
WWE Women's Tag Team Champions	World Wrestling Entertainment	April 3, 2002 – 46 days

Lethal Consequences

Lethal Consequences was a tag team that competed in Total Nonstop Action (TNA) Wrestling in the late 2000s. The team's name blends together the two members Jay Lethal (Jamar Shipman) and Consequences Creed (Austin Watson). They started working together in August 7, 2008, but officially became a team in November as members of the stable called TNA Front Line. TNA Front Line was formed to challenge the Main Event Mafia (Kurt Angle, Booker T, Sting and Kevin Nash), a major heel faction at the time with the goal of teaching the young wrestlers how to show respect to the elders of the wrestling industry.

After winning one of the Feast or Fired briefcases at the *Final Resolution* pay-per-view in December 2008, Lethal was granted a title shot for the world tag team championship. He teamed with Creed to defeat *Beer Money* (Bobby Roode and James Storm) and claim the belts. At the following *Genesis* pay-per-view (Jan 11, 2009), they lost the titles to *Beer Money* in a three-way match that also included Matt Morgan teaming with Abyss (Chris Park). In February, Lethal Consequences would challenge Beer Money again but lost due to a shoulder injury Creed suffered a week before their match. Lethal Consequences continued to participate in tag team matches until 2010 mostly as jobbers for the X-Division. TNA released Creed from his contract in March and the group disbanded.

Major Championships and Accomplishments		
Title	Promotion	Dates
TNA World Tag Team Champions	Total Nonstop Action Wrestling (TNA)	Dec 16, 2008 – 26 days

CONSEQUENCES CREED

Austin Watson was born in Columbus, Georgia. He attended Furman University. In addition to the independent promotions, Watson has worked for TNA and WWE. As Consequences Creed he was a TNA world tag team champion. As Xavier Woods, he is a member of The New Day and a triple crown tag team champion winning the NXT, Raw and Smackdown tag titles.

JAY LETHAL

Jamar Shipman was born in Elizabeth, New Jersey. Known professionally as Jay Lethal, he is a former champion in Ring of Honor (RoH) and Total Nonstop Action Wrestling (TNA). Lethal has been called "The Franchise" in Ring of Honor because he is the longest reigning world champion and world television champion. He has been a world tag team champion in both RoH and TNA wrestling. Lethal currently wrestles for All Elite Wrestling (AEW).

Men On A Mission

Before The New Day infused crowds with a dose of positive energy, Men on a Mission broke stereotypes with their carnivalesque appearance and power of positivity through music. However, before they were WWF superstars entering the ring with positive rap lyrics from Oscar, Nelson Frazier, Jr and Robert Horne started wrestling as a duo in the early 1990s. The tag team was originally known as The Harlem Knights with Frazier as Nelson Knight and Horne as his storyline brother Bobby Knight. They started out on the independent circuit with the Charlotte, North Carolina based Pro Wrestling Federation and later the United States Wrestling Association based in Memphis, Tennessee. Around August 1992, the Harlem Knights won the PWF Tag Team championship. They lost the titles in December to Cruel Connection. They would later return in 1996 to win the title for a second time but now they would be known as Men on a Mission. After leaving PWF, they competed in the USWA. While they did not win the title in the USWA, their work as major heels feuding against Jerry Lawler and Jeff Jarrett caught the attention of the World Wrestling Federation. In 1993, they signed with the WWF and were renamed Men on A Mission.

Frazier and Knight made their WWF debut in June 1993 as babyfaces instead of heels. They wore bright colors and paired with a manager named Oscar who rapped as they entered the ring. Frazier became Mabel and Horne was renamed Mo. All three were collectively known as Men on a Mission - for Mabel, Oscar and Mo. Their babyface gimmick included being a positive force and trying to make the black and poor neighborhoods a better place to live. The group was over with the fans quickly due to their persona and Mabel's imposing size. They won the WWF world tag team championship from the Quebecers at a London house show on March 29, 1994. However, they lost the titles two days later in a rematch. Men on a Mission competed for the titles again in a tournament but were eliminated in the first round. Their next attempt to regain the titles resulted in a loss to the Smoking Gunns. After the match, Mabel and Mo attacked Billy and Bart Gunn turning heel in the process. Oscar objected to the sneak attack and was subsequently attacked by Mabel and Mo. Shortly afterwards, he left the group. Oscar was supposed to remain in the group but he objected to the heel turn because he really wanted to project a positive image outside of the ring, not just as a television show gimmick. In a 2009 interview with *Pro Wrestling Insider*, he explained.

> "I did not want to be a heel because I've always had this thing where – and I know it's wrestling and everything like that – but one of my strong convictions in my entertainment career, I've always talked to kids about saying no to drugs, yes to

education and things like that. I was never gonna be a gangsta rapper in my career. I did not want a stigma of being on television in a negative light."

After the feud with the Smoking Gunns, Mabel returned to singles action. He was crowned King of the Ring in 1995 and knighted his partner now known as Sir Mo. King Mabel's next feud was with WWF Champion Diesel. However, he accidentally injured the champion cancelling their planned match at *SummerSlam*. Mabel was then placed in a feud with The Undertaker. In similar fashion, Mabel injured The Undertaker and quickly ended their feud. The group left the WWF in January and returned to the United States Wrestling Association. In the USWA, they feuded with The Moondogs, Brian Christopher and Doug Gilbert. Mo joined forces with the USWA's version of the Nation of Domination and turned against Mabel. He and Mo were put in a tournament and Mabel won their match. The duo broke up in June. The two fought again on January 4, 1997, with Mabel again emerging victorious. Mabel eventually returned to the WWF while Mo remained on the independent circuit. Men on a Mission made an appearance together in 2003 for Memphis Wrestling. Mo retired from wrestling in 2007. However, he made his return to the ring in 2014. He also runs an independent promotion called SOAR Championship Wrestling in Dallas, Texas.

Major Championships and Accomplishments		
Title	Promotion	Dates
WWF World Tag Team Champions	World Wrestling Federation	March 29, 1984 – 2 days
PWF Tag Team Champions	Pro Wrestling Federation	As Harlem Knights (Aug. 1982) Dec 15, 1996 – 16 days?

Honors	Sponsor	Year
New England Pro Wrestling Hall of Fame	New England Pro Wrestling Hall of Fame and Fan Fest	2013

SIR MO

Sir Mo (Horne) and Frazier returned to the USWA as Men on a Mission after leaving the WWF. Mo joined the promotion's version of the Nation of Domination that was in existence prior to the WWF. Mo was known as Sir Mohammad in the group that included PG-13, Ice Wolfie D, Shaquille Ali (Tracy Smothers) and Queen Moishe (Jacqueline). When the group broke up, Mo wrestled as Rob Harlem. In 1997, the USWA closed and Horne joined Southern Extreme Wrestling. While he was in Power Pro Wrestling, he teamed with Deon Harlem to win the promotion's tag team championship. They held the titles until the promotion closed in April 2001.

After a brief hiatus, Mo returned to Memphis Wrestling in 2003 as a manager using the name Marley Pride. After chiding Mabel about his size, Pride attacked Mabel and revealed his true identity as his former partner Mo. The feud with Mabel was short lived. Mo wrestled matches for Ohio Valley Wrestling until April 2007. He retired from professional wrestling and resumed his former career as a truck driver until 2014. Like most pro wrestlers, Mo came out of retirement and performed as "Sir Mo" for Ultimate Championship Wrestling in Nova Scotia, Canada. He teamed with Lord Deon Johnson to capture the UCW tag team tiles. He wrestled as Rob Harlem and teamed with Deon Harlem as The Regulators in Power Pro Wrestling. They held the tag team titles from April 8, 2000, until the promotion folded on March 17, 2001. He now operates SOAR Championship Wrestling with his wife. Since 2018, Mo has struggled with serious health issues including having both a kidney and liver transplant.

Sir Mo - Major Championships and Accomplishments		
Title	Promotion	Dates
PPW Tag Team Champion	Power Pro Wrestling	w/Deon Harlem (April 8, 2000) – 343 days
WWC Universal Heavyweight Championship	World Wrestling Council	w/Nelson Knight (Aug 1992) – 60 days? w/Mabel (Dec 15, 1996) – 15 days? w/Black Angel (July 31, 1998) – 29 days w/Black Angel (Sept 12, 1998) – 21 days
UCW Tag Team Champion	Ultimate Championship Wrestling	w/Deon Johnson (July 30, 2015) – 42 days
SOAR Tag Team Champion	SOAR Championship Wrestling	w/Nate Lawson (Feb 13, 2020) – 67 days
WWF World Tag Team Champions	World Wrestling Federation	March 29, 1984 – 2 days

Honors	Sponsor	Year
New England Pro Wrestling Hall of Fame	New England Pro Wrestling Hall of Fame and Fan Fest	2013
Memphis Wrestling Hall of Fame	United States Wrestling Association	2024

OSCAR

Greg Garard was born in Harlem, New York. He is best known for his role as Oscar, the manager for Men on a Mission. Garard is also a professional rap artist, author and producer. In 1993, he became a WWF superstar by happenstance when one night he was performing at a casino in Las Vegas and he saw "Macho Man" Randy Savage. Garard approached Savage who agreed to listen to him rhyme on the spot freestyle.

"I approached Randy, who was really nice about it, and said I had a singing telegram for him. I didn't know Vince McMahon was with him until he told me to go ahead, and I did a Macho Man Randy Savage rap for about thirty seconds," he said. "They were all flabbergasted and amazed because, on the spot, I could include other wrestlers such as Jerry Lawler and Mr. Perfect (Curt Hening) who were also there. After this, Vince McMahon told me to call him on Monday" (Ojst, 2025). Oscar was signed to a three-year deal with the WWF. He was given the red-carpet treatment as a guest at *WrestleMania 9*.

When Oscar joined the group there was friction at first. He was performing on shows with Andrew Dice Clay and other big-name comedians, while Mabel and Mo were considered country bumpkins from Tennessee. Oscar brought his real personality into the wrestling business. Despite the fictional nature of professional wrestling, Oscar refused to take part in the heel turn. He was a positive hip hop artist and did not want to be portrayed in a negative light. However, Mabel and Mo had been heels for the majority of their career and never fully embraced the babyface role. "They started as heels in wrestling and they knew that better and were experts at it," Oscar said. "So once the opportunity came up to become heels once again, they grabbed on one hundred percent. No matter the situation, there was no way I would allow myself to be perceived as a bad guy. I couldn't bring myself to do it" (Ojst, 2025).

Oscar left the company in February 1995. After leaving the WWF, he joined Mancow's Morning Madhouse radio show in Chicago. He also started his own podcast and leveraged his history in radio, wrestling and hip-hop to earn his living after an active career in professional wrestling. He continues to travel and make appearances at wrestling conventions and shows around the country.

Honors	Sponsor	Year
New England Pro Wrestling Hall of Fame	New England Pro Wrestling Hall of Fame and Fan Fest	2013
Best Entertainer	WWF Slammy Award	1994

KING MABEL

Nelson Frazier, Jr. was the first black and final world heavyweight champion in the short-lived Xcitement Wrestling Federation (XWF). He is primarily known for his time in the WWF/WWE where he was a world tag team champion, hardcore champion and King of the Ring. Frazier used several popular in-ring names throughout his career including Mabel, King Mabel, Viscera and Big Daddy V.

Frazier, a native of Goldsboro, NC, made his professional wrestling debut using the ring name Nelson Knight. He was a member of the tag team "The Harlem Knights" along with his storyline brother Bobby Knight. They wrestled in the United States Wrestling Association, and won the Pro Wrestling Federation's tag team championship before joining the World Wrestling Federation (WWF) in 1993. The duo was renamed Men on a Mission and Frazier renamed Mabel while "Bobby" (Robert Horne) became Mo. When Mabel turned heel, he received a push and won the 1995 King of the Ring tournament. After the victory, he was known as King Mabel and his tag team partner became Sir Mo. Mabel is the only wrestler in history awarded a King of the Ring championship belt. The belt was never seen on WWF television. If the WWF officially adopted and recognized the belt, he would have been a Triple Crown champion.

The only King of the Ring belt (above) was made for King Mabel.

Mabel was inexplicitly downgraded to mid-card status allegedly for his reckless style. As a superheavyweight, he weighed over 500 pounds. His signature move, the sit-down splash, injured several wrestlers. Mabel briefly wrestled on the independent circuit before returning to the WWF. In 1999, he joined the Undertaker's Ministry of Darkness as the enforcer Viscera. When the Ministry disbanded, he joined the hardcore division and won the hardcore championship.

Upon being released from his contract, he returned to the Memphis Wrestling promotion (formerly USWA) and joined the upstart Xcitement Wrestling Federation. Wrestling as Mabel he won the XWF world heavyweight title in Puerto Rico in July 2003. While wrestling in Memphis he lost a boxing match to Rocky Johnson in 2003. However, on March 6, 2004, he won the Southern heavyweight title. After winning the title in Memphis, he was stripped of the XWF title. He also made a brief appearance in Total Nonstop Action (TNA) in 2003 under his original ring name Nelson Knight. Then, he returned again to the WWE in 2004 as Viscera before transforming into the "world's largest love machine." He was paired with Trish Stratus, and became smitten first with ring announcer Lilian Garcia and later *Raw* bikini contest winner Candice Michelle. In 2007, he was drafted to the ECW brand and renamed Big Daddy V. After leaving the WWE for the final time, he wrestled in the National Wrestling Alliance (NWA) and All Japan Pro Wrestling until 2011. His final match as Big Daddy V was in 2013 with Qatar Pro Wrestling. Frazier died of a heart attack on February 18, 2014.

King Mabel - Major Championships and Accomplishments

Title	Promotion	Dates
Southern Heavyweight Championship (Memphis)	United States Wrestling Association / Memphis Championship Wrestling	March 16, 1996 – 65 days March 6, 2004 – 390 days?
WWC Universal Heavyweight Championship	World Wrestling Council	Jan 7, 1996 – 34 days
WWF Hardcore Champion	World Wrestling Federation	April 2, 2000 - <1 day
WWF World Tag Team Champion	World Wrestling Federation	March 29, 1994 – 2 days
XWF Heavyweight Champion	Xcitement Wrestling Federation	July 5, 2003 – 245 days
All Asia Tag Team Champion	All Japan Pro Wrestling	April 29, 2010 – 122 days

Honors	Sponsor	Year
New England Pro Wrestling Hall of Fame	New England Pro Wrestling Hall of Fame and Fan Fest	2013

Swerve In Our Glory

Keith Lee and Shane (Swerve) Strickland entered professional wrestling as a tag team in October 2017 for All American Wrestling (AAW) in Illinois. The duo competed for the tag team titles in the AAW but were not successful. They both signed with All Elite Wrestling in

2022. Lee made his television debut in February and Strickland followed in March at the *Revolution* pay-per-view. The two teamed up in the new promotion to take on Team Taz. They lost that match to Ricky Starks and Powerhouse Hobbs (Team Taz) after Taz interfered. The duo went on a winning streak and quickly became one of the top tag teams. They won the AEW world tag team titles on July 13 in a "triple or nothing" match against The Young Bucks and Team Taz. Swerve In Our Glory beat The Acclaimed initially, but lost the titles to them in September at *Grand Slam*. Lee and Strickland feuded with each other and the team eventually broke up. Lee and Strickland teamed up again May 7, 2023, for the Blind Eliminator Tag Team tournament. They lost in the quarter finals to Darby Allin and Orange Cassidy.

Major Championships and Accomplishments		
Title	Promotion	Dates
AEW World Tag Team Champions	All Elite Wrestling	July 13, 2022 – 70 days

SWERVE STRICKLAND

Stephon Strickland was born in Tacoma, Washington. He is a former 3-sport star athlete in high school. Strickland is also a professional rap artist. He is a former AEW world heavyweight champion and AEW world tag team champion.

KEITH LEE

Keith Gerald Lee Jr. was born in Wichita Falls, Texas. He played football at Texas A&M University. Lee debuted in 2005 using the ring name Kevin Paine. He started using his real name in 2008. Lee wrestled on the independent circuit until signing with the WWE in 2018. Before officially signing with the WWE, he first appeared as a security guard on an episode of *Raw* and later he won an untelevised NXT "dark" match against Kassius Ohno. He officially signed with the company on May 1, 2018, and competed in NXT. On January 22, 2020, he won the NXT North American title. On July 8, at the Great American Bash, he defeated Adam Cole to win the NXT championship making Lee the first person to hold both the NXT championship and NXT North American championship at the same time. Lee relinquished the North American title and feuded with Karrion Kross for the NXT championship. He lost the title to Kross on August 22 which was his last NXT match.

He moved up to the main roster and unsuccessfully challenged Drew McIntyre for the WWE championship. After being sidelined due to COVID-19, Lee returned using the gimmick Keith "Bearcat" Lee as a way of honoring legendary wrestler Bearcat Wright. On November 4, he was released from his contract with the WWE. On February 9, 2022, he made a surprise appearance on AEW. He became a tag team partner with Swerve Strickland. In July 2023, Swerve In Our Glory, won the AEW world tag team titles from the Young Bucks. They lost the titles to The Acclaimed in November and Lee returned to Ring of Honor. In February 2023, Lee joined forces with Dustin Rhodes and they called themselves "Naturally Limitless." Lee challenged Samoa Joe for the RoH world television title on November 8, 2023, but was unsuccessful. He defeated former tag team partner Shane Taylor at *Final Battle*. Lee had double surgeries in January 2024 and took a break to heal.

Keith Lee - Major Championships and Accomplishments		
Title	Promotion	Dates
AEW World Tag Team Champions	All Elite Wrestling	w/Swerve (July 13, 2022) – 70 days
NXT Champion	World Wrestling Entertainment	July 1, 2020 – 44 days
NXT North American Champion	World Wrestling Entertainment	Jan 22, 2020 – 181 days
WWN Champion	World Wrestling Network	Oct 14, 2017 – 174 days

The Acclaimed

The tag team known as The Acclaimed consists of wrestlers Max Caster, Anthony Bowens and manager/wrestler Billy Gunn. Gunn only competes in six-man or trios matches. They are currently signed to All Elite Wrestling (AEW). Bowens and Caster debuted as a team on October 27, 2020. The team was formed by AEW owner Tony Khan who offered them an initial 5-year contract. The Acclaimed's quest for the tag team titles started in December 2020 with a loss to the reigning champions, The Young Bucks. They continued to challenge for the titles throughout the next year. In 2022, The Acclaimed became close allies with The Gunn Club. By August, their alliance ended with The Acclaimed emerging victorious from a dumpster match. After the match, Billy Gunn's sons turned on him and he became the manager for The Acclaimed.

After securing the managerial services of Billy Gunn, The Acclaimed challenged Swerve in our Glory for the tag team titles. At *All*

Out, the champions retained the titles; however, they lost to The Acclaimed in a rematch two weeks later on the Sept 21, 2022, episode of *Dynamite*. After a few successful defenses, they lost the titles to the Gunn Club. In 2023, all three members won the AEW World Trios Championship by defeating House of Black in a no-holds barred match. A record-setting 238 days, The Acclaimed lost the trios titles to Ring of Honor (RoH) Six-Man champions Bullet Club Gold in a unification match.

Major Championships and Accomplishments		
Title	Promotion	Dates
AEW World Tag Team Champions	All Elite Wrestling	Sept 21, 2002 – 140 days
AEW World Trios Champions (w/Billy Gunn)	All Elite Wrestling	Aug 27, 2023 – 238 days

ANTHONY BOWENS

Bowens started training to become a pro wrestler in 2012. He would debut in 2013 and soon started wrestling for the WWE's developmental territory. In 2016, his career was halted after suffering a concussion during a match for NXT. Upon his return to the ring, he worked on the independent circuit. He held the Wrestle Pro Gold Championship from 2016-2020. In November 2020, he signed with AEW and became tag team partners with Max Caster. Bowens was out for several months following knee surgery in May 2022. He returned in September and helped his team win the AEW tag team titles at *Grand Slam*. He is the first openly gay champion in AEW. Bowens was previously a baseball player in college for Seton Hall University and his alma mater Montclair State University. Like his partner Caster, he also trained to become a wrestler under Pat Buck.

MAX CASTER

Max Caster started training to become a professional wrestler in 2015 at Create A Pro Wrestling Academy in Hicksville, New York. According Cagematch.net, Caster was a two-time CAP Champion. He graduated from the wrestling school in 2016. Caster wrestled on the independent circuit before signing with AEW in 2020. He first appeared on *AEW Dark* on June 23, 2020, teaming with Luther and Serpentico. They fought against AEW Tag Team Champions Jurassic Express. His next appearance on *AEW Dark* was another tag match this time with Anthony Bowens against Best Friends. Caster and Bowens first appeared as The Acclaimed in a winning effort against SoCal Uncensored. He is also a rap artist. Caster released his debut album *Critically Acclaimed, Vol 1* under the pseudonym Platinum Max in May 2021. Caster is the son of American football great Richard C. Caster. The elder Caster, a graduate of Jackson State University, played tight end for 13 seasons in the National Football League. He is the NFL's career receptions leader by a tight end averaging 17.3 yards per reception.

Tha Gangstas

In 1994, New Jack and Mustafa Saed formed Tha Gangstas in Atlanta's North Georgia Wrestling Alliance. In only a few months, they won the promotion's tag team titles. Soon after, they moved on to Smoky Mountain Wrestling where they first made a name for themselves. In Smoky Mountain, they added D'Lo Brown and later Killer Kyle into the fold. They were known to incite the predominantly white Tennessee crowds with racially charged rhetoric about civil rights issues and even support for O.J. Simpson during his murder trial (Djeljosevic, 2003). Besides using a Black nationalist gimmick, they were known for feuding with The Rock & Roll Express (Ricky Morton and Robert Gibson). New Jack and Mustafa won the tag team championship from Morton and Gibson but dropped the belts to them after a couple of months. As their popularity began to skyrocket, New Jack and Mustafa left SMW in June 1995 and joined Extreme Championship Wrestling (ECW) which appeared to be the perfect fit. Their head of security Downtown D'Lo Brown, left and joined the WWF.

While in ECW, Tha Gangstas were over with audiences and grew to become babyfaces more so than heels. They were known to bring weapons including barbwire, staple guns and trash cans into the ring. The hip hop song "Natural Born Killaz" by Dr. Dre and Ice Cube would play throughout their matches – not just during the introduction. They would go on to win the ECW World Tag Team Championship twice. The duo split when Mustafa left ECW in 1997. In 2008, they would reunite for Xtreme Pro Wrestling's *Cold Day in Hell* match against the Westside NGZ (Bigg Rott and Chronic) and again, on August 8, 2010, at *Hardcore Justice*, the ECW reunion show produced by TNA wrestling.

Major Championships and Accomplishments		
Title	Promotion	Dates
SMW Tag Team Champions	Smoky Mountain Wrestling	Oct 3, 1994 – 83 days
ECW World Tag Team Champions	Extreme Championship Wrestling	Aug 3, 1996 – 139 days July 19, 1997 – 29 days

MUSTAFA SAED

Jamal Mustafa, also known by his ring names Mustafa Saed and birth name Terrance Blalock, is best known for his partnership with New Jack. He was trained by wrestling legend Gene Anderson. Saed started wrestling in 1990 for World Championship Wrestling (WCW). He was mostly used as a jobber and left the company in 1993. Saed joined Smoky Mountain Wrestling from 1994-95 and wrestled for ECW from 1995-97. He left ECW after Tha Gangstas lost the tag team titles. He then joined the independent circuit.

Saed briefly returned to ECW to reunite with New Jack in February 1999 but it was a ruse and he turned on New Jack. His feud ended at *Living Dangerously* in March in a losing effort to New Jack. Saed left the company again in May. Since 1997, he mostly wrestled for the World Wrestling Council in Puerto Rico where he is a triple crown champion. He has held the WWC's Puerto Rican heavyweight championship, world television championship and world tag team title.

Mustafa Saed - Major Championships and Accomplishments		
Title	Promotion	Dates
Puerto Rico Heavyweight Champion	World Wrestling Council	Sept 11, 1999 – 42 days
WWC World Tag Team Champion	World Wrestling Council	w/Rastaman (June 30, 2001) – 15 days
WWC World Television Champion	World Wrestling Council	Aug 14, 1999 – 36 days
APW Tag Team Champion	All Pro Wrestling	w/Boyce LeGrande (Oct 26, 2013) – 140 days

NEW JACK

Jerome Young, better known by his ring name New Jack, was groomed from childhood to be hardcore. He adopted the name from the popular 1991 movie *New Jack City*. In an interview with Boston Wrestling, New Jack credited the Rock & Roll Express for mentoring both him and Mustafa when they entered the promotion as rookies. "Ricky and Robert taught me a lot. Ricky would have to remind me sometimes that my job as a heel was to piss people off. But the fans in Smoky Mountain was calling us Nigger, coon, go back to Africa; they was on some crazy shit. And I wasn't quite used to that. Ricky said 'when they boo you, they are cheering me. You're doing your job.' And that took some getting used to. But once I figured out what he was talking about, I took the ball and ran with it."

New Jack went to jail for armed robbery and assault during his senior year in high school. After serving two years in prison, he was released to attend Clark Atlanta University where he played football and had his own apartment. Since going to school was a condition of his parole, once he had served time, he dropped out of school and became a truck driver and eventually a bounty hunter. He left the bounty hunting business because a friend who was wrestling for WCW suggested he give it a try. Initially, he refused but later decided to explore the opportunity to earn more money. He met Ray Candy and received formal pro wrestling training.

After their second ECW title reign as The Gangstas ended, New Jack found an unlikely partner in former rival John Kronus from the Eliminators when his partner left the promotion. As the Gangstanators, New Jack and Kronus defeated the Dudley Boyz for the tag team titles at September's *As Good As it Gets* pay-per-view. They lost the titles to the Full-Blooded Italians on Nov 1 but continued to feud with the Dudley Boyz. During the feud, he teamed with Spike Dudley against his "brothers" and New Jack and Kronus quietly disbanded the Gangstanators. During his time as a singles competitor, New Jack starting dragging a trash can full of weapons to the ring. At one point during his life, he used to lay carpet with a friend. He decided to bring the staple gun to the ring also. Stapling an opponent's head became one of his signature moves. New Jack had a long rivalry with Angel to claim the title "King of the Streets." During one of their bloody matches, Angel took New Jack's staple gun and stapled his eye causing him to be out of action for several months. In March 2000 at *Living Dangerously*, New Jack and Vic Grimes fell 15 feet off a scaffold (as planned) but missed the tables below which were designed to help break their fall. They landed on the concrete floor with Grimes on top of New Jack's head. New Jack suffered a fractured skull, broken leg and became blind in one eye. In his last match with the company, he defeated Angel on December 17. The company closed in January.

Hardcore matches

New Jack joined the independent circuit when ECW went bankrupt. In February 2000, he again fought Vic Grimes in a scaffold match. New Jack shocked Grimes with a taser and threw him 40 feet below. Grimes nearly missed the mat and broke his fall on the ring ropes. In April 2003, New Jack fought 69-year-old Gypsy Joe in a hardcore match. Joe refused to sell any of New Jack's moves, so he starting giving legitimate bumps with weapons including a baseball bat covered with barbwire. The crowd became furious and called New Jack the "n-word" and others left the arena. New Jack also wrestled for Thunder Wrestling Federation on the independent circuit. In October 2004, he was scheduled to have a match against William Jason Lane. According to New Jack, Lane started punching him in the face. To retaliate, he pulled out a metal blade that was planned but he stabbed Lane multiple times in the head. This led to felony charges against New Jack including aggravated assault to commit murder. During 2003, he wrestled mostly tag matches for TNA wrestling. His last match was in July 2003 but he returned for the reunion show with Mustafa in 2010. His final match was for VIP Wrestling where he teamed with other former ECW Wrestlers including The Sandman, Justin Credible, C.W. Anderson and Shane Douglas. Jerome Young died of a heart attack on May 14, 2021, at his home in Greensboro, N.C.

New Jack - Major Championships and Accomplishments		
Title	Promotion	Dates
SMW Tag Team Champion	Smoky Mountain Wrestling	Oct 3, 1994 – 83 days
ECW World Tag Team Champion	Extreme Championship Wrestling	Aug 3, 1996 – 139 days July 19, 1997 – 29 days w/Kronus (Sept 20, 1997) – 28 days
USWA World Tag Team Champion	United States Wrestling Association	w/Homeboy (June 21, 1993) – 14 days

Street Profits

When a skilled wrestler and a former Marine decide to join forces, the result is guaranteed money in the bank. Gary Gordon and Kenneth Crawford, known professionally as Angelo Dawkins and Montez Ford, have made a big impact on the WWE's tag team division collectively known as The Street Profits. Dawkins and Ford became a team in 2016. Crawford's debut match was a losing effort to the Hype Bros on March 16. Crawford was renamed Montez Ford the following year. He and Dawkins started making promos on NXT introducing the team as The Street Profits. The Street Profits defeated the Metro Brothers in their triumphant return to NXT television. They went on a winning streak on their quest for the NXT tag team titles; eventually losing to the Authors of Pain in January 2018. The Street Profits lost again to the Authors of Pain at the Dusty Rhodes Tag Team Classic in the semifinal round. On May 1, 2019, the Viking Raiders relinquished the tag team titles.

The Street Profits won the titles for the first time on June 1, 2019, at NXT *TakeOver XXV*. In August, they lost the titles to The Undisputed Era (Bobby Fish and Kyle O'Reilly). In October, they were drafted to the Raw roster. After a few unsuccessful attempts, The Street Profits won the Raw tag team titles in a "last chance match' on the March 2, 2020, episode of *Raw*. The Street Profits continued to feud with The Viking Raiders in several non-wrestling competitions including axe-throwing, bowling and golf. They ended the feud with a victory over The Viking Raiders in June. In the October 2020 draft, The Street Profits were sent to *SmackDown*. They traded their *Raw* titles with The New Day to acquire the SmackDown tag team titles. As members of *SmackDown*, they feuded with Dolph Ziggler and Robert Roode; eventually losing the titles on January 8, 2021. Dawkins and Ford feuded with The Usos but failed to regain the titles before being drafted back to the *Raw* brand. While on the *Raw* roster, Dawkins and Ford failed to win titles in both singles matches and as a duo. They were drafted back to *SmackDown* in 2023.

In July, Bobby Lashley recruited The Street Profits along with manager B-Fab (Briana Brandy) to form a collective known as The Pride. They joined Lashley in a 6-man contest between the Latino World Order (LWO) at October's *Fastlane* pay-per-view. The Street Profits challenged The Judgement Day for the undisputed WWE tag team championship but lost due to interference from Rhea Ripley. The Pride turned babyface after Lashley was attached by The Final Testament at *New Year's Revolution*. The Pride ended their feud with a victory over The Final Testament at *WrestleMania XL*. Lashley left the WWE in August 2024 and The Pride disbanded. Dawkins and Ford continue to compete as a tag team along with B-Fab as their manager. They are currently the WWE tag team champions for the second time.

The Street Profits are the fastest duo to become triple crown champions in WWE.

Major Championships and Accomplishments		
Title	Promotion	Dates
Evolve Tag Team Champions	Evolve Wrestling	Oct. 28, 2018 – 138 days
NXT Tag Team Champions	World Wrestling Entertainment	June 1, 2019 – 88 days
Raw Tag Team Champions	World Wrestling Entertainment	March 2, 2020 – 223 days
Smackdown Tag Team Champions	World Wrestling Entertainment	Oct 12, 2020 – 88 days
WWE Tag Team Champions	World Wrestling Entertainment	March 14, 2025 -

Honors	Sponsor	Year
Triple Crown Champion - NXT Tag Team title - Raw/World Tag Team title - Smackdown/WWE Tag Team title	World Wrestling Entertainment	June 1, 2019 March 2, 2020 Oct 12, 2020
Tag Team of the Year	World Wrestling Entertainment	2020

ANGELO DAWKINS

Gary Gordon who wrestles under the name Angelo Dawkins was a competitive athlete in his hometown Fairfield, Ohio. He later competed in football, track and amateur wrestling at Harper College in Illinois. He joined the WWE's NXT brand in June 2012. He competed for the NXT championship in 2015 and mostly wrestled in singles matches for the next two years. In February 2017, he participated in a mixed tag team match with Montez Ford and Liv Morgan. In July, Dawkins and Ford debuted as a tag team and won their first match against The Metro Brothers.

While holding the tag team titles in Evolve wrestling, Dawkins also competed in singles matches. In February 2019, he defeated Eddie Kingston in a singles match. The following month, the Street Profits lost their titles to Kingston and Joe Gacy. Dawkins also challenged JD Drake for the World Wrestling Network title but was unsuccessful. Nicknamed "The Curse of Greatness," Dawkins continues to wrestle in singles and tag team matches. His finishing move is the sit-down powerbomb.

MONTEZ FORD

Crawford was born in Chicago. As a kid, he became interested in professional wrestling during the WWE's Attitude Era. In high school, he was a standout track star before joining the United States Marine Corps. He had no prior wrestling experience before signing a contract with the WWE. As a Marine, Crawford scored a perfect 300 on the physical fitness test. His natural athleticism and aerial maneuvers were enough to convince bookers to take a chance with him.

"The military background has 100% helped me and my athletic background has 100% helped me into this WWE transition. I think by having those two backgrounds with me has helped me to be successful in this field."[16] Ford had his first televised match in 2016 and was instantly paired with Dawkins. The two captured gold within a short time and were the fastest tag team in WWE history to reach the triple crown status. After a long drought, the Street Profits once again are the WWE tag team champions. Ford is married to WWE superstar Bianca Belair.

---

[16] Montez Ford Interview with The Five Count - http://thefivecount.com/audio-posts/an-evening-with-wwes-montez-ford/#google_vignette

The Prime Time Players

The Prime Time Players, a tag team consisting of Darren Young and Titus O'Neil, had a brief but successful run in World Wrestling Entertainment. Before they became tag team partners, O'Neil and Young started their careers on NXT's fifth television season called *Redemption* in 2011. O'Neil and Young were rivals initially. Their in-ring feud was halted after Young's pro trainer Chavo Guerrero Jr. was released from his contract and he was suspended. Young returned on November 16, 2011, and attacked O'Neil. In January, their feud ended with O'Neil defeating Young and verbally insulting the fans. The duo debuted as a tag team in January 2012 on the WWE's NXT developmental brand. When O'Neil's former partner Percy Watson refused to join him, O'Neil solidified his heel status by attacking Watson. Alex Riley came to Watson's aid and O'Neil formed an alliance with his former foe Darren Young. After defeating Watson and Riley, they started feuding with Jimmy and Jey Uso.

Young and O'Neil debuted on SmackDown in April and defeated The Usos. In June, they officially started calling themselves The Prime Time Players. In July, Young and O'Neil were successful in their attempts to win the tag team titles from Kofi Kingston and R-Truth. They had another shot at the titles at *SummerSlam* but again were unsuccessful. At the September 15, 2013, *Night of Champions* event, they lost another bid for the tag titles from The Shield (Roman Reigns and Seth Rollins). After Young was pinned in a match against Curtis Axel and Ryback, ONeil turned heel and attacked Young. He officially disbanded the group and formed a short-lived partnership with Heath Slater while Young recovered from ACL surgery.

On the February 16, 2015, episode of Raw, O'Neil helped Young who was under attack from The Ascension. The duo reunited and started making comedy skits aimed at other tag teams. They successfully goaded the others into an eventual five-team challenge for the tag team titles. Unfortunately for the duo, O'Neil was pinned and The New Day claimed the titles. The Prime Time Players again earned a title match at *Money in the Bank*. At the June 14, 2015, pay-per-view event, O'Neil and Young defeated The New Day to become the WWE tag team champions. However, they lost a rematch against The New Day at *SummerSlam*. After failing to regain the titles, they would focus on singles competition. O'Neil was on a quest for the United States championship while Young challenged for the Intercontinental title. Both were unsuccessful in their attempts at single's gold. O'Neil and Young started another feud against each other in 2016. They both feuded and competed in singles matches until Young was released in October 2017.

Major Championships and Accomplishments		
Title	Promotion	Dates
World Tag Team Champions	World Wrestling Federation	June 14, 2015 – 69 days

DARREN YOUNG

Frederick Douglas Rosser III was born in Union County, New Jersey. He played football briefly at Farleigh Dickinson University but soon focused on professional wrestling. He made his wrestling debut in 2002 for the Independent Wrestling Federation and later Chaotic Wrestling. He won the IWF heavyweight title and later the East Coast Mid-Atlantic title in the East Coast Wrestling Association in Newark, Delaware. He made brief appearances for WWE in 2005 and 2006 before signing a contract with Florida Championship Wrestling. He debuted on NXT's first season in February 2010. After his career in WWE, he competed in the King of Trios tournament for Chikara and later signed with New Japan Pro Wrestling in 2020. The next year, he signed with the National Wrestling Alliance and was a contender for the NWA world television title but failed to defeat Da Pope (Elijah Burke).

TITUS O'NEIL

Thaddeus Michael Bullard was born in Boynton Beach, Florida. He was an All-American football player at Suwannee High School in Live Oak, Florida. He played college football for the University of Florida under head coach Steve Spurrier. He graduated in 2000 and played in the Arena Football League from 2003-2007. He signed a developmental contract in 2009 with WWE's Florida Championship Wrestling. He teamed with Damien Sandow to win the FCW Florida tag team titles. He joined NXT's second season and was the first person eliminated. However, he was selected to appear on the fifth season of NXT also where he feuded and eventually partnered with Darren Young. After The Prime Time Players tag team dissolved, he started a new gimmick called the Titus Brand and later Titus Worldwide. He teamed with Apollo Crews but was unsuccessful in winning the tag team championship. In 2018, Dana Brooke and Crews left Titus Worldwide and the gimmick faded.

On the May 20, 2019, episode of *Raw*, O'Neil became the inaugural 24/7 champion. His brief title reign lasted less than one minute as he was pinned by Robert Roode. O'Neil was hoping to join The Hurt Business but was attacked instead. He lost his final WWE match to Bobby Lashley in less than two minutes. After his in-ring career, he became a WWE Global Ambassador and was heavily involved in charitable work in the Tampa Bay area. On April 6, 2021, he was awarded the Warrior Award in honor of his charitable work and inducted into the WWE Hall of Fame Class of 2020.

Honors	Sponsor	Year
Shad Gaspard/Jon Huber Memorial Award	Wrestling Observer Newsletter	2021
WWE Hall of Fame	World Wrestling Entertainment	2020

The New Day

They are one of the most successful tag teams in WWE history. Kofi Kingston, Xavier Woods and Big E, known collectively as The New Day currently hold records in the tag team division. They compete under the Freebird Rule – a gimmick created by the Fabulous Freebirds during the NWA era where any two of the three members were allowed to defend the titles. Essentially, all three members are recognized as champions. Thus, it might be hard to believe that once Kofi Kingston and Big E were good singles wrestlers but for some reason were not successful as a tag team. After a series of losses, on July 21, 2014, Xavier Woods came to the ring and confronted the duo. He challenged them to stop being nice guys. "You cannot move ahead by shaking hands, kissing babies, singing and dancing like a puppet. You cannot move ahead by always doing what you're told. It is our time to find purpose, because we do not ask any longer. Now, we take" (Kelly, 2024). Woods once worked in TNA as Consequences

Creed and won the tag team title with partner Jay Lethal. He offered to manage the team and they found instant success.

The New Day's first gimmick was a babyface black gospel vignette. The early promo featured Woods as a James Brown-like choir director proclaiming "a new day is coming." The trio was on a winning streak and even had a shot at the tag team titles at *WrestleMania 31*. However, their gimmick was rejected by fans. On the March 31, 2015, episode of *Raw*, the fans loudly chanted "new day sucks!" They soon turned heel. At April's *Extreme Rules* pay-per-view, The New Day won their first of many tag team championships. In June, they lost the titles to The Prime Time Players. The New Day regained the titles at *SummerSlam* in August. This reign was the longest in WWE history until their record was broken by The Usos in 2022. The trio won the titles a record 8 times. They are the third team to become triple crown tag team champions in the WWE. As singles wrestlers, both Kingston and Big E held the WWE championship. Woods is a King of the Ring tournament winner. After being out of action due to legitimate injury, Big E was expelled from the group in December 2024.

Major Championships and Accomplishments		
Title	Promotion	Dates
Raw/World Tag Team Champions (5 times)	World Wrestling Entertainment	April 26, 2015 – 49 days
		Aug 23, 2015 – 483 days
		Oct 12, 2020 – 69 days
		March 15, 2021 – 26 days
		April 19, 2025 – 12 + days
Smackdown Tag Team Champions (7 times)	World Wrestling Entertainment	July 23, 2017 – 27 days
		Sept 12, 2017 – 25 days
		Aug 21, 2018 – 55 days
		July 14, 2019 – 62 days
		Nov 8, 2019 - 110 days
		April 17, 2020 - 92 days
		Oct 9, 2020 – 2 Days
NXT Tag Team Champions	World Wrestling Entertainment	Dec 10, 2022 – 56 days

Honors	Sponsor	Year
Triple Crown Champion - Raw/World Tag Team - Smackdown/WWE Tag Team - NXT Tag Team	World Wrestling Entertainment	April 26, 2015 July 23, 2017 Dec 10, 2022
Best Gimmick	Wrestling Observer Newsletter	2015
WWE Wrestlers of the Year	Rolling Stone	2015
Tag Team of the Year	Pro Wrestling Illustrated	2015, 2016
Best Moment/Angle of the Year	CBS Sports	2019

KOFI KINGSTON

Kofi Kingston is a triple crown singles, tag team and grand slam champion in WWE. He has held the WWE championship, four-time intercontinental champion, three-time United States champion and is a seven-time Raw and Smackdown world tag team champion. He made a guest appearance on the television shows *Kickin It* and *Let's Make a Deal*. In 2017, he and fellow New Day members published the book, The Book of Booty: Shake It. Love It. Never Be It.

BIG E

Big E is a former WWE champion, two-time WWE intercontinental champion, two-time Raw tag team champion, six-time SmackDown tag team champion and a Money in the Bank winner in 2021. He has made television appearances on several programs since 2015. He also appeared in the film *Countdown* and *Escape the Undertaker*.

XAVIER WOODS

Austin Watson was born in Columbus, Georgia. While attending Furman University in Greenville, South Carolina, he started wrestling part time with the Ultimate Christian Wrestling promotion. He later joined the Greenville-based World Wrestling Council where he developed the Austin Creed character. The gimmick was based on the flamboyant fictional boxer Apollo Creed from the *Rocky* movies. He joined NWA Anarchy and was voted wrestler of the year in 2006 by the fans. Creed held the tag team championship with partner Hayden Young. In 2007, while still in college, he decided to try out for Deep South Wrestling. At the tryout, he met Kofi Kingston. Deep South cut ties with World Wrestling Entertainment just before issuing Woods a contract. He won the DSW heavyweight title on July 12, 2007, and held it until the company closed on October 11. Three days later he appeared on TNA wrestling's *Bound for Glory* pay-per-view as Rasheed Lucius "Consequences" Creed. He teamed with Ron "The Truth" Killings as the replacement for NFL star Adam "Pacman" Jones. The duo was known as Truth and Consequences until Killings left the company. In 2008, he competed for the X Division title but was unsuccessful.

On the October 30, 2008, episode of *Impact!*, Creed joined forces with Jay Lethal, AJ Styles, Samoa Joe and other younger wrestlers forming a faction called The Frontline to compete against the Main Event Mafia. Lethal chose Creed as his partner in December and they defeated Beer Money to win the world tag team titles.

Xavier Woods - Major Championships and Accomplishments		
Title	Promotion	Dates
TNA World Tag Team Champion	Total Non-Stop Action Wrestling	w/ Jay Lethal (Dec 16, 2008 – 26 days
Raw/World Tag Team Champion	World Wrestling Entertainment	7 times
WWE Tag Team Champion	World Wrestling Entertainment	5 times
NXT Tag Team Champion	World Wrestling Entertainment	Dec 10, 2022 – 56 days

Honors	Sponsor	Year
King of the Ring	World Wrestling Entertainment	2021
Most Popular Wrestler	NWA Anarchy	2006

Private Party

The tag team known as Private Party consists of New York City natives Isiah Kassidy and DaQuentin Redden aka Marq Quen. Kassidy was born in New York City in 1997. He made his wrestling debut in August 2015. DaQuentin Redden made his wrestling debut in 2001. Marc Quen was a tag team champion in NEFW and EPWE with Alex Reyes. He tagged with Isiah Kassidy in 2015 to win the House of Glory tag team title. They went on to win other tag team titles on the independent circuit including Fight the World (FTW), Game Changer Wrestling (GCW), Pro Wrestling Magic (PWM) and the Warriors of Wrestling (WOW) tag team championships before joining AEW.

Private Party signed with AEW on April 22, 2019. They were unsuccessful in their debut match – a triple threat match – against Best Friends and SoCal Uncensored. Later that year, Private Party defeated The Young Bucks but lost to the Lucha Brothers in the semi-final round of the tournament to determine the inaugural AEW World tag team champions. They continued to compete for the title but were unsuccessful. In January 2021, they competed briefly in Impact

Wrestling. Private Party defeated the team of Chris Sabin and James Storm to earn a shot at the titles. Unfortunately, they were unable to dethrone The Good Brothers for the Impact world tag team title.

In 2023, Quen was sidelined for the year due to injury. He returned in January 2024 and reunited with Kassidy. On October 12, they challenged The Young Bucks for the championship but were defeated. However, two weeks later at *Fright Night Dynamite*, they defeated The Young Bucks to become world tag team champions. Private Party successfully defended the titles for 84 days until losing to Bobby Lashley and Shelton Benjamin who were known collectively as The Hurt Syndicate.

Major Championships and Accomplishments		
Title	Promotion	Dates
AEW World Tag Team Champions	All Elite Wrestling	Oct 30, 2024 – 84 days

The Hurt Syndicate

The Hurt Syndicate is a pro wrestling team competing in AEW consisting of Bobby Lashley, Shelton Benjamin and manager/trios partner MVP. The group was originally called The Hurt Business in WWE and also included Cedric Alexander. They were a dominant team during what became known as the WWE ThunderDome era where fans could attend virtual events during the COVID-19 shutdown. At their peak, the Hurt Business members held the tag team titles and the WWE Championship.

The Hurt Business was formed in May 2020 when MVP announced himself as the manager who would take his client Bobby Lashley back to the WWE championship. On June 14, 2020, Lashley challenged Drew McIntyre for the WWE championship but lost due to interference from his storyline wife Lana. MVP attempted to recruit Apollo Crews into the stable. When Crews refused, Lashley attacked him with the hurt lock – his version of the full nelson. MVP defeated Crews in a non-title match and declared himself United States champion with newly designed belt. Crews had to withdraw from a scheduled title match, MVP declared himself the official United States champion. Upon his return to action, Crews defeated MVP and claimed both belts. Shelton Benjamin was recruited after MVP and Lashley helped him win the 24/7 title from R-Truth. With the addition of Benjamin, the group became known as The Hurt Business.

The Hurt Business started a feud with Crews, Ricochet and Cedric Alexander. At *SummerSlam*, MVP lost again to Crews. However, at *Payback*, Lashley won the United States title from Crews. Shelton Benjamin subsequently won the 24/7 title two more times during this period. In a 6-man tag team match on September 7, Alexander turned heel and attacked his partners and became the newest member of The Hurt Business. In November, Alexander and Benjamin teamed up to defeat The New Day in a non-title match. They lost the subsequent rematch before capturing the Raw Tag Team titles at *TLC: Tables, Ladders & Chairs* on December 20. Lashley's quest to win the WWE championship was realized on March 1, 2021, when he defeated The Miz in a lumberjack match on Raw. Briefly, The Hurt Business held the major singles and tag team championships in WWE. However, just two weeks later Alexander and Benjamin would lose the tag team titles causing Lashley to attack and kick them out of the group. However, MVP said The Hurt Business was still active but only consisted of him and Lashley. He successfully defended the title against Drew McIntyre, Kofi Kingston, Goldberg and Randy Orton before losing to Big E.

The faction had a short-lived reunion in late 2021 after Alexander and Benjamin helped Lashley fight off an attack from The New Day. In January 2022 Lashley disbanded the faction claiming that he worked alone. The two attacked Lashley which officially dissolved the union. MVP and Lashley left the WWE in 2023 over disagreements with how they were being used in the company. MVP debuted in AEW in September 2024 while Benjamin and Lashley joined him in October. The trio reunited and renamed the group, The Hurt Syndicate. On January 22, 2025, Benjamin and Lashley dethroned Private Party to capture the AEW world tag team titles. MVP primarily serves as the manager but he participates in 6-man or trios matches along with Benjamin and Lashley. On May 14, 2025, MJF (Maxwell Jacob

Friedman) became the fourth member of the Hurt Syndicate after several weeks of being denied the required unanimous vote from all three members. MJF is a former AEW International title holder and the longest reigning AEW world heavyweight champion.

Major Championships and Accomplishments		
Title	Promotion	Dates
RAW Tag Team Champions	World Wrestling Entertainment	Dec. 20, 2020 (Benjamin & Alexander) – 84 days
AEW World Tag Team Champions	All Elite Wrestling	Jan. 22, 2025 (Lashley & Benjamin) – 50 + days

BOBBY LASHLEY

Bobby Lashley is a champion mixed martial artist (MMA) and professional wrestler. He has a 15-2 record in MMA with 12 wins by knockout or submission. He is a former Xtreme Fight Night heavyweight champion and Shark Fights heavyweight champion. In professional wrestling, he is a former 4-time TNA world heavyweight champion, 2-time WWE champion, 2-time ECW champion and a tag team world champion in All Elite Wrestling. Lashley is a triple crown TNA champion and a grand slam WWE champion.

CEDRIC ALEXANDER

Cedric Alexander Johnson was born in Charlotte, North Carolina. After training to become a professional wrestler at George South's Pro Wrestling School, he joined Ring of Honor wrestling in 2010. Alexander joined forces with Caprice Coleman and formed C&C Wrestle Factory. They competed for the RoH world tag team championship but never captured the titles. As a singles competitor, Alexander lost two major belt challenges for the RoH television title against Jay Lethal and the world title against Michael Elgin. He left the promotion in May 2016.

After Ring of Honor, he appeared as a competitor in the WWE's Cruiserweight championship tournament. He faced Enzo Amore on January 8, 2018, and won the match by count out, thus Amore retained the title. They were scheduled for a rematch at the *Royal Rumble* but the match was cancelled and Amore was released. At *WrestleMania 34*, Alexander defeated Mustafa Ali capturing the cruiserweight title. He lost the title to Buddy Murphy after 181 days as champion. During the 2019 Superstar Shakeup, Alexander was drafted to *Raw*. He won the 24/7 title from R-Truth and immediately lost it to EC3. In April 2020, he became a tag partner with Ricochet. After Lashley, Benjamin and MVP injured Apollo Crews, Alexander and Ricochet started feuding with The Hurt Business. After losing to The Hurt Business, they approached Alexander and offered him a chance to join the group. He refused. Alexander later pinned Benjamin to win the 24/7 title, only to lose it back later that night. On September 7, 2022, The Hurt Business fought Alexander, Ricochet and Crews in a 6-man tag team match. During the match, Alexander turned on his partners and joined The Hurt Business.

The original Hurt Business with Cedric Alexander

On December 20, 2020, Alexander and Benjamin defeated The New Day to win the Raw tag team titles. Upon losing the titles back to The New Day in March, Lashley lambasted the duo and kicked them out of the group. Afterwards, the tag team went on a losing streak. Alexander became critical and insulted Benjamin thus ending their alliance. However, in September 2021, Alexander and Benjamin came to Lashley's aid against The New Day. The move teased a reunion but it did not happen. Alexander won the 24/7 title for a third time by pinning Reggie but soon lost the belt to Dana Brooke. On June 5, 2022, at *Hell in a Cell,* Alexander helped Lashley and MVP win a handicap match against Omos. On August 8, Alexander defeated Benjamin in a singles match which appeared to end their partnership. Alexander and Benjamin teamed up again in January and continued to work as a tag team until Benjamin was released from the company on September

21, 2023. Alexander returned to singles action appearing on *SmackDown*. He became partners with Ashante "Thee" Adonis in February 2024. Alexander and Adonis appeared on NXT in July. They quietly disbanded and Alexander began mentoring Je'Von Evans. He competed on the NXT brand until his release on February 7, 2025. He currently competes on the independent circuit.

Cedric Alexander - Major Championships and Accomplishments		
Title	Promotion	Dates
24/7 Champion	World Wrestling Entertainment	June 24, 2019 – <1 day Aug 13, 2020 - <1 day Nov 22, 2021 - <1 day
NXT Cruiserweight Champion	World Wrestling Entertainment	April 8, 2018 – 119 days
Raw/World Tag Team Champion	World Wrestling Entertainment	w/Shelton Benjamin (Dec 20, 2020) – 84 days
PXW Heavyweight Champion	Premiere Wrestling Xperience	May 25, 2014 – 357 days
PXW Innovative Television Champion	Premiere Wrestling Xperience	Mar 29, 2013 – 15 days

SHELTON BENJAMIN

Shelton James Benjamin is among the rare breed of highly decorated amateur wrestlers who was able to successfully transition into professional wrestling. Benjamin was born in Orangeburg, South Carolina. He compiled a 122-10 overall record in high school wrestling and was a two-time state heavyweight wrestling champion (1993 and 1994). After high school, he attended Lassen Community College. He won the National Junior College Athletic Association (NJCAA) championships in both wrestling and track & field. He briefly attended NC State University on a football scholarship in 1995 but returned to finish his sophomore year at Lassen. After junior college, he transferred to the University of Minnesota on a wrestling scholarship. He was an all-American twice in the NCAA heavyweight division. After graduating, he became an assistant wrestling coach at Minnesota and helped train Brock Lesnar. Instead of trying out for the 2000 Summer Olympics, Benjamin opted to turn pro. In January 2000, he signed a developmental contract with the WWE and was assigned to Ohio Valley Wrestling.

At OVW, Benjamin was paired with Lesnar and they won the OVW Southern Tag Team championship three times. Benjamin also tagged with Redd Dogg Begnaud (Rodney Mack) and again won the tag team championship. He joined the SmackDown roster in December 2002 and teamed with Charlie Haas. Kurt Angle managed the duo and they became a part of Team Angle. After a month, they won the WWE tag team titles from Eddie and Chavo Guerrero, Jr. After losing the titles to Eddie and new partner Tajiri, Angle fired them from Team Angle. Benjamin and Haas regained the titles and started referring to themselves as "The World's Greatest Tag Team." They lost the titles again to Los Guerreros and Benjamin was drafted to the *Raw* brand. At *Raw*, he began a feud with members of Evolution. Benjamin defeated Triple H three times and scored a victory over Ric Flair before losing to Intercontinental champion Randy Orton. He later defeated Chris Jericho for the title at 2004's *Taboo Tuesday* pay-per-view. He lost the title to Carlito ending at 244 days which was the longest reign for the Intercontinental championship until the streak was broken by Gunther. In February 2006, he regained the title from Ric Flair. He lost the title and regained it for a third time by defeating Rob Van Dam. He lost the title to Johnny Nitro at *Vengeance*.

When Charlie Haas returned, they reignited The World's Greatest Tag Team. The duo competed for a few months before Benjamin was drafted to ECW. His hair was dyed blonde and he started calling himself "The Gold Standard." In 2008, he was drafted to *SmackDown* where he defeated Matt Hardy for the United States heavyweight title. On March 20, 2009, he lost the title to MVP. He was released on April 20, 2010, and returned to the independent circuit. He competed in different promotions and won the World Wrestling Council's universal heavyweight title and the Millennium Wrestling Federation's heavyweight title. He reunited with Haas in Ring of Honor in September 2010. On April 1, 2011, they won the Ring of Honor tag team titles. In December, they lost the titles to the Briscoe Brothers. They regained the titles from the Briscoe Brothers in May but lost the titles in June to Kenny King and Rhett Titus. Benjamin joined New Japan in 2012. During his tenure at New Japan, he teamed with MVP as "Black Dynamite." He competed for the intercontinental title but was unsuccessful.

Benjamin returned to the WWE in 2017. He initially teamed with Chad Gable and they were fan favorite babyfaces. They defeated The Usos for the tag team titles but the decision was reversed. Gable was drafted to *Raw* and the team dissolved. After switching brands again, he attacked Apollo Crews and joined the Hurt Business. During his run with the faction, he won the 24/7 title three times and was Raw tag team champion with Cedric Alexander. In 2024, he joined AEW. He and Lashley defeated Private Party to win the AEW tag team titles.

Shelton Benjamin - Major Championships and Accomplishments

Title	Promotion	Dates
RoH World Tag Team Champions (2 times)	Ring of Honor	w/Charlie Haas (April 1, 2011) – 266 days w/Charlie Haas (May 12, 2012 (w/Charlies Haas) 43 days
WWC Universal Heavyweight Champion	World Wrestling Council	July 31, 2010 – 119 days
WWE Intercontinental Champion	World Wrestling Entertainment	Oct 19, 2004 – 244 days Feb 20, 2006 – 68 days May 15, 2006 – 40 days
WWE United States Heavyweight Champion	World Wrestling Entertainment	July 20, 2008 – 240 days
WWE 24/7 Champion	World Wrestling Entertainment	July 20, 2020 – 14 days Aug 13, 2020 - >1 day Aug 13, 2020 – 6 days
WWE (Raw) World Tag Team Champion	World Wrestling Entertainment	w/Charlie Haas (Feb 4, 2003) – 100

		days
		w/Charlie Haas (July 1, 2003) – 76 days
		w/Cedric Alexander (Dec 20, 2020) – 84 days
AEW World Tag Team Champion	All Elite Wrestling	w/Bobby Lashley (Jan 22, 2025) – 70 + days

Honors	Sponsor	Year
100-meter dash champion	National Junior College Athletic Association (NJCAA)	1996
National Wrestling Champion	National Junior College Athletic Association (NJCAA)	1996
NCAA All-American	National Collegiate Athletic Association	1997 & 1998
Tag Team of the Year (w/Charlie Haas)	Pro Wrestling Illustrated	2003

MONTEL VONTAVIOUS PORTER (MVP)

Montel Vontavious Porter or MVP as he's commonly known, is not only the manager of the Hurt Syndicate but also an accomplished in-ring wrestler. MVP is two-time WWE United States champion, WWE tag team champion (with Matt Hardy) and the inaugural IWGP Intercontinental champion.

Hassan Hamid Assad was born Alvin Antonio Burke, Jr. in the predominantly African American Liberty City area of Miami, Florida. He joined a gang at age 12 and at 16 was sentenced to 18 years in prison for armed robbery and kidnapping. In prison, he met a correctional officer who was also a wrestler on the independent circuit. He began his career in 2002 after being trained by Soulman Alex G and Norman Smiley. Assad started wrestling under the name Antonio Banks originally before developing the MVP persona. MVP first appeared on SmackDown in August 2006 in segments flaunting his arrogance while surrounded by women and bodyguards. He initially feuded with Kane and later U.S. heavyweight champion Chris Benoit. After failing to capture the title from Benoit at *WrestleMania* and *Backlash*, MVP won the U.S. heavyweight title at *Judgement Day* 2007. A month later, he successfully defended the title with a signature win over Ric Flair. While U.S. champion, MVP teamed with Matt Hardy to win the tag team titles. They lost the titles to John Morrison and The Miz. The following April, MVP lost the U.S. title to Matt Hardy. MVP regained the title for a second time on March 20, 2009, by defeating Shelton Benjamin. He lost the title to Kofi Kingston.

In 2011, he signed with New Japan Pro Wrestling. In May, he became the inaugural IWGP Intercontinental champion by defeating Toru Yano. He lost the title to Masato Tanaka on October 10 after a 148 day-reign as champion. After two years with the company, he decided to leave New Japan and returned to the United States. He joined Total Nonstop Action (TNA) Wrestling on January 30, 2014. After wrestling control of TNA from president Dixie Carter, he named himself the number one contender for the world heavyweight title. He was supposed to win the title, however, MVP could not compete in the match due to a torn meniscus. In January, he formed the Beat Down Clan (BDC) to assist Bobby Lashley. Lashley turned on the BDC. In February, MVP unsuccessfully challenged Lashley for the title. He left the promotion in July due to creative differences. From 2013-2019, MVP wrestled on the independent circuit. He competed in Tommy Dreamer's House of Hardcore, Booker T's Reality of Wrestling,

Lucha Underground and a few other independent promotions. On October 10, 2016, he won the universal heavyweight championship from All Pro Wrestling. In February 2018, he won the Big-League Wrestling promotion's world heavyweight title. After a brief stint in Ring of Honor, he returned to the WWE in January 2020.

MVP signed a new agreement to return to the WWE as a wrestler, manager, commentator and producer. He made his appearance at the Royal Rumble where he was soon eliminated by Brock Lesnar. At *Money in the Bank*, MVP was scheduled to face R-Truth but was replaced by Bobby Lashley. At that time, MVP started managing Lashley. On July 20, Shelton Benjamin joined the group and they became known as The Hurt Business. The stable continued until April 2022 when MVP turned on Lashley and started managing Omos. In August, his contract expired. He returned again to the independent circuit.

In September 2024, MVP made his surprise debut for All Elite Wrestling (AEW) at *Grand Slam*. MVP confronted Swerve Strickland's manager Prince Nana and offer to take over as Strickland's manager. Shelton Benjamin appeared the next week and they reformed their former stable but this time calling themselves the Hurt Syndicate. On October 30, Bobby Lashley debuted and they attacked Strickland and Nana. MVP made his in-ring debut for AEW at December's *Maximum Carnage* where the Hurt Syndicate defeated Private Party. Away from the wrestling industry, Assad holds a black belt in Brazilian jiu-jitsu. He has recorded hip-hop songs since 2011. His third single, "Return of the Ronin" was his entrance song while competing in TNA.

MVP - Major Championships and Accomplishments		
Title	Promotion	Dates
IWGP Intercontinental Champion	New Japan Pro Wrestling	May 15, 2011 – 148 days
WWE United States Champion	World Wrestling Entertainment	May 20, 2007 – 342 days March 17, 2009 – 72 days
WWE World Tag Team Champion	World Wrestling Entertainment	Aug 28, 2007 (w/Matt Hardy) – 76 days

Honors	Sponsor	Year
Most Improved	Wrestling Observer Newsletter	2007
Most Underrated	Wrestling Observer Newsletter	2008
Comeback of the Year	Pro Wrestling Illustrated	2020

Bianca Belair and Jade Cargill

When Bianca Belair and Jade Cargill joined forces, they became one of the strongest, toughest, smartest and sexiest tag teams in the history of women's professional wrestling. The two-time WWE women's tag team champions were both elite athletes from other sports before becoming professional wrestlers. Belair and Cargill won the WWE women's tag team titles on May 4, 2024, at *Backlash* held in France. They held the belts for 42 days before losing them without either champion being pinned. They lost the titles in a triple threat tag team match when Zoey Stark was pinned. Belair and Cargill regained the championship at the *Bash in Berlin* event on August 31, 2024. After Cargill was mysteriously attacked and injured in the parking lot, Belair chose Naomi as her partner to defend the titles in Cargill's absence. Belair and Naomi lost the titles to Liv Morgan and Raquel Rodriguez on the February 24, 2025 episode of *Raw* after outside interference from Dominik Mysterio.

Major Championships and Accomplishments		
Title	Promotion	Dates
WWE Women's Tag Team Champions	World Wrestling Entertainment	May 4, 2024 – 42 days Aug 31, 2024 – 177 days

BIANCA BELAIR

Bianca Belair currently holds the record as the longest reigning Raw Women's Champion at 420 days. She is one of two women to win the main event match at WrestleMania. She is a two-time WWE women's champion, SmackDown women's champion, two-time tag team champion and *Royal Rumble* winner. She has appeared on the television shows *Love & WWE: Bianca & Montez*, *Celebrity Family Feud* and *Bel-Air*.

Bianca, Jade and Naomi once shared the Women's Tag Team Championship.

JADE CARGILL

Jade Cargill, a chiseled 5-foot, 10-inch, 160-pound statuesque figure, has been an athlete her entire life. She started playing basketball at age six in Gifford, Florida. Cargill played for the Amateur Athletic Union's Orlando Comets in 2009. Later, she played basketball at Jacksonville University and was named to the Atlantic Sun preseason first team during her senior year. After graduating, she modeled and played basketball in France. In 2018, a mutual friend introduced her to Mark Henry. She initially attended Face 2 Face wrestling school in Georgia and later trained at the WWA4 Academy and Nightmare Factory with Q.T. Marshall and Dustin Rhodes.

She made her wrestling debut with All Elite Wrestling on November 11, 2020, by interrupting Cody Rhodes. She feuded with Cody and his wife Brandi which led to a tag team match with Shaquille O'Neal as Cargill's special guest tag team partner against Rhodes and Red Velvet. Cargill and O'Neal won the high-profile match. Cargill won her first singles match on March 17, 2021, which started a winning streak. She continued to win matches leading up to her victory over Ruby Soho to capture the inaugural TBS Championship on January 5, 2022. Her reign lasted until May 28, 2023, when she lost an open challenge match to Kris Statlander. The loss ended her winning streak at 60 matches and 508 days, which made her the longest reigning champion in AEW history. After taking time off, Cargill did "the honors" by losing a rematch to Statlander on *Rampage* ending her initial AEW career.

In September, she started training at the WWE's Performance Center in Orlando. Her debut match was at January 2024's *Royal Rumble*. At *WrestleMania*, she competed in a six-woman tag team match with Naomi and Belair against Damage CTRL. She participated in the 2024 Queen of the Ring tournament but was eliminated by Nia Jax. After regaining the tag team championship with Belair, Cargill was mysteriously attacked backstage just before November's *Survivor Series*. Belair chose Naomi as her new tag team partner in Cargill's absence. When Cargill returned to action on March 1, 2025, she attacked Naomi. The surprise twist was shocking until Naomi publicly revealed that she was the mysterious attacker. Cargill used her signature chickenwing facebuster, a move she dubbed "Jaded" to defeat Naomi at *WrestleMania 41*. Cargill was inspired to become a wrestler by former powerlifter/wrestler Chyna along with Jackie Moore and Jazz. Her hairstyle was inspired by the X-Men character Storm. Cargill has appeared on the television shows *Rhodes to the Top* and *Celebrity Family Feud*. She also holds a master's degree in child psychology.

Jade Cargill - Major Championships and Accomplishments		
Title	Promotion	Dates
WWE Women's Tag Team Champion	World Wrestling Entertainment	w/Bianca Belair (May 4, 2024) – 42 days w/Bianca Belair and Naomi (Aug 31, 2024) – 177 days
AEW TBS Champion	All Elite Wrestling	Jan 5, 2022 – 508 days

Honors	Sponsor	Year
Rookie of the Year	Pro Wrestling Illustrated	2021
Rookie of the Year	Wrestling Observer Newsletter	2021
Breakout Star – Female	All Elite Wrestling	2022
Tag Team of the Year	Pro Wrestling Illustrated	2024

Blunt Force Trauma

In 2022, flamboyant manager Aron Stevens assembled a team designed to wreak havoc on the National Wrestling Alliance. He transformed singles wrestlers Rodney Mack and Marshe Rockett into Damage and Carnage known collectively as Blunt Force Trauma (BFT). On the November 30 episode of *NWA Powerrr,* Rockett and Mack came to the ring wearing black face masks a la WCW's Doom and squashed opponents David Powers and Eddie Vero. Carnage spent the next few weeks participating in the NWA Champions Series. On February 11, 2023, at the *Nuff Said* pay-per-view, Blunt Force Trauma challenged La Rebelion but lost the match due to disqualification. In the Crockett Cup tournament, BFT defeated La Rebelion in the quarterfinals but lost to Mike Knox and Trevor Murdoch in the final round. Two months later at the NWA 75th Anniversary Show, BFT successfully defeated La Rebelion for the NWA world tag team championship on the first night. On day two, they retained the title against Knox and Murdoch. They successfully defended the titles at *Samhain* and *Hard Times 4* pay-per-views. They lost the titles to Knox and Murdoch on June 1, 2024, at *NWA Back to the Territories* event.

Major Championships and Accomplishments		
Title	Promotion	Dates
NWA World Tag Team Champions	National Wrestling Alliance	Aug 26, 2023 – 280 days

CARNAGE

Marshe Rockett, who wrestles as Carnage, made his professional wrestling debuted in 2005 for Windy City Pro Wrestling. He wrestled on the independent circuit until signing with TNA/Impact Wrestling on March 24, 2016. While working for the promotion, he competed for the X Division title and the Impact Grand Championship but was unsuccessful in every attempt. After slightly more than a year, he left Impact on November 1, 2017. Rockett returned to the independent circuit where he found success in several promotions. In March 2021, he debuted for NWA Powerrr. Rockett pursued singles titles but has been unsuccessful. He teamed with Slice Boogie in a tournament for the world tag team titles but was eliminated in the first round. On February 8, 2022, he teamed with Jordan Clearwater and Tyrus but lost to Rodney Mack and The End. He continued to compete in singles competition but was unsuccessful in attempts to win both the NWA national championship and the world television championship. Rockett found success when he joined with Rodney Mack and manager Aron Stevens to form Blunt Force Trauma.

RODNEY MACK

Rodney Begnaud is an accomplished professional wrestler and mixed martial artist. Begnaud started wrestling on the independent circuit after training with the Junkyard Dog. He debuted in 1988 as Redd Dogg. After learning the ropes in the Southwestern independent wrestling territories, he signed with Extreme Championship Wrestling in 2000 as a member of Da Baldies. After ECW closed its doors, Begnaud signed with the WWE and went to the Ohio Valley region. While in Ohio Valley, he and Shelton Benjamin formed The Dogg Pound. His signature victory in OVW was winning the Southern Tag Team championship in July 2002. He moved up to the main roster the following year and made his first appearance on *Smackdown* on January 16, 2003. Redd Dogg replaced Bull Buchanan as John Cena's enforcer. After one appearance, he jumped to *Raw* and was renamed Rodney Mack. On *Raw*, Mack restarted Teddy Long's Thuggin' and Buggin' faction (Caldwell, 2009). Thuggin' and Buggin' Enterprises started as a group of all Black wrestlers who worked the race angle because they were held down by the system. Mack competed in a series of so-called "White Boy Challenges" which were essentially squash matches against white opponents. Mack was undefeated until he found himself on the receiving end of a squash match when he lost to Goldberg in 30 seconds (Ziegler,2003). Mack formed a partnership with Christopher Nowinski, a white wrestler who joined the group because he was also held down by "the man." The two were a successful tag team until Nowinski suffered a career-ending injury and was forced to retire. Mark Henry later placed Nowinski and he and Mack had success until a knee injury in November 2003 sidelined Mack. When he returned to action, instead of the main roster, he worked dark matches and for Ohio Valley. On November 4, 2004, he along with his wife Jazz, were released from their WWE contracts.

Mack returned to the independent circuit wrestling for NWA Cyberspace. In 2005, he and Jazz opened Downsouth Championship Wrestling but the company folded in 2007. In 2006, he and Jazz returned to WWE working for the ECW brand. However, both along with several other wrestlers were released on January 18, 2007. Mack returned to the independent circuit once more. He won the All-American Wrestling Tag Team title with Heidenreich on May 18, 2008 but they were forced to vacate the titles due to interference. He took three years off after the birth of his twins. In 2011, Mack won the NWA Mississippi Heavyweight Championship. He also won the AIWF Southwest title on March 21, 2016. For the last 10 years, he has primarily competed in for NWA Anarchy. After a championship drought, Mack turned to a new gimmick. He partnered with Carnage and on August 26, 2023, they won the NWA world tag team titles.

Major Championships and Accomplishments		
Title	Promotion	Dates
NWA Texas Heavyweight Champion	NWA Southwest	Nov 27, 1998 – 68 days July 29, 1999 – 34 days May 26, 2000 – 126 days
OVW Southern Tag Team Champion	Ohio Valley Wrestling	w/Shelton Benjamin (July 17, 2002) – 175 days

Honors	Sponsor	Year
Southern Wrestling Hall of Fame	Iconic Heroes of Wrestling	2011

Harlem Heat

As the song "Rap Sheet" booms throughout the arena, two imposing figures march down the ramp. Booker T looks at partner Stevie Ray, then turns to the camera and says "somebody's gonna get hurt." To which Stevie Ray replies, "now can you dig that, suckas!" Perhaps the most dominant tag team in professional wrestling during the 1990s was Harlem Heat. Stevie Ray (Lash Huffman) and his young brother Booker T. (Booker T. Huffman) started their wrestling careers in Houston under the tutelage of Polish American veteran wrestler Ivan Putski (Jozef Bednarski). In the late 1980s, Putski had a wrestling school and his own independent wrestling promotion called Western

Wrestling Alliance (WWA). The brothers debuted as singles wrestlers. In the WWA, Lash was known as Super Collider and Booker T used the moniker G.I. Bro. When the WWA folded, the Huffman brothers joined the Global Wrestling Federation (GWF) in 1992.

In the Dallas-based GWF, they met "Hot Stuff" Eddie Gilbert who devised the idea of putting the brothers together as a tag team instead of singles wrestlers. The Huffman brothers rose through the ranks quickly and captured the GWF Tag Team titles in July 1992. Their first title run only lasted a week. However, they soon regained the titles by defeating the Blackbirds (Iceman King Parsons and Action Jackson) in September. They would soon lose the belts due to Booker T suffering an injury that required surgery. In 1993, the Ebony Experience returned to action and won the titles in February for a record third time. They dropped the belts in May to the Sicilian Stallions (Guido Falcone and Vito Mussolini) when they left the promotion for World Championship Wrestling.

On June 22, 1993, the Ebony Experience made their debut in WCW as Harlem Heat. Lash was named Kane and Booker T was known as Kole. The original gimmick was to portray the brothers as prisoners in shackles managed by Colonel Rob Parker. But the racially insensitive storyline was dropped. Harlem Heat became villains by teaming with Sid Vicious against 2 Cold Scorpio, Ron Simmons and Marcus Alexander Bagwell. In July 1994, after a series of high profile matches on television and pay-per-view, the brothers ended the managerial services of Col. Parker and changed their names to Booker T and Stevie Ray. At the *Clash of the Champions* in November 1994, Harlem Heat acquired Sensuous Sherri as their new manager and she helped them defeat The Nasty Boys. They later renamed her Sister Sherri. On December 8, they won their first of 10 titles by defeating Stars and Stripes (The Patriot and Marcus Alexander Bagwell). The match was televised on January 14, 1995 – a month after the title change took place.

In an interview, Stevie Ray said: "I knew we were going to be the champions. I knew it. It was just something that was eventually going to happen and we knew it. We knew we were the best tag team around there and we knew slowly but surely, we're gonna be what we were supposed to become and that's what we worked on. And it was a challenge to us. So, when it happened it really wasn't a surprise because in our minds, we were champions already (Uhuru, 2023).

After losing the titles to the Nasty Boys, they regained the championship for their second title reign. Harlem Heat lost the titles to Col. Parker's Stud Stable (Dick Slater and Bunkhouse Buck). They regained the titles for the third time at Fall Brawl 1995 with interference from The Nasty Boys. They lost the titles the next day Monday Nitro to The American Males (Marcus Alexander Bagwell and Scotty Riggs). They regained the titles in October for their fourth title run. After losing the belts to Sting and Lex Luger in January 1996, they won the title for the fifth time by winning a triangle match between Luger and Sting and Rick and Scott Steiner in June. Booker T and Stevie Ray lost to the Steiner Brothers on July 24 but defeated them in a rematch three days later for their sixth tag team title run. On September 23, they lost the belts to Rocco Rock and Johnny Grunge, known as Public Enemy. On October 5, they defeated the Public Enemy in a rematch for their seventh title. Harlem Heat dropped the belts at Halloween Havoc to the New World Order's (nWo) Outsiders (Scott Hall and Kevin Nash).

After losing the titles, Harlem Heat became babyfaces and fired Col. Parker. In July, they also fired Sister Sherri after costing them a match against Public Enemy. At *Road Wild* (Aug 9, 1997) Jacqueline became their new manager and helped Harlem Heat defeat Buff Bagwell and Scott Norton. After competing in singles matches for a while, they reformed the Harlem Heat and challenged Bam Bam Bigelow and Chris Kanyon for the tag team titles. At *Road Wild*, Harlem Heat won the title for the eighth time. They lost the titles to Barry and Kendall Windham on August 23. However, they regained the titles in the rematch at Fall Brawl for the ninth time. On October 18, Harlem Heat lost to The Filthy Animals (Konnan and Rey Mysterio). Just six days later, Harlem Heat won the world tag team titles for an unprecedented tenth time by winning a triple threat match against the Filthy Animals and The First Family.

In November 1999, Creative Control arrived in WCW and made several moves which impacted the brothers. Creative Control attacked Buff Bagwell during a match against Stevie Ray, cost him at shot at the world heavyweight title. Later the same night on Nitro, Creative Control attacked Booker T causing Jeff Jarrett to advance in the tournament. Stevie Ray was suspended by Creative Control. Booker T challenged Jarrett and Creative Control to a Harlem Street fight and was saved by a female bodybuilder named Midnight. Midnight later joined Harlem Heat. Stevie Ray returned from suspension and rescued Midnight from an attack by Curt Hennig. During a match against The Revolution, Midnight was injured and Booker T left Stevie Ray alone when he tended to Midnight. Stevie Ray grew to resent Midnight's presence in the group. Stevie Ray would eventually turn on the two and attack both Booker T and Midnight. The two brothers fought at *Souled Out* in January 2000 where Booker T was attacked by Big T (Ahmed Johnson) who made his debut. Stevie briefly formed Harlem Heat 2000 with Big T as his partner. The team had little success and disbanded in June when WCW released Big T from his contract.

Booker T and Stevie Ray reunited again in July to defeat Jeff Jarrett and Rick Steiner in a final match before WCW was sold. They had another reunion in Booker T's Reality of Wrestling promotion on February 21, 2015. They defeated The New Heavenly Bodies to capture the Reality of Wrestling tag team titles. They vacated the championship after a month without a title defense. In 2019, Harlem Heat was inducted into the WWE Hall of Fame.

Major Championships and Accomplishments		
Title	Promotion	Dates
WCW World Tag Team Champions	World Championship Wrestling	Dec 8, 1994 – 164 days
		May 3, 1995 – 28 days
		Sept 17, 1995 – 1 day
		Sept 27, 1995 – 117 days
		June 24, 1996 – 30 days
		July 27, 1996 – 58 days
		Oct 1, 1996 – 26 days
		Aug 14, 1999 – 9 days
		Sept 12, 1999 – 36 days
		Oct 24, 1999 – 1 day
GWF Tag Team Champion	Global Wrestling Federation	July 31, 1992 – 7 days
		*Sept. 1992 – 52 days? (exact date the title won is unknown but they lost the titles on Oct 23)

		Feb 26, 1993 – 70 days
ROW Tag Team Champion	Reality of Wrestling	Feb 21, 2015 – 21 days

Honors	Sponsor	Year
Tag Team of the Year	Pro Wrestling Illustrated	1995, 1996
Tag Team Award	Cauliflower Alley Club	2018
WWE Hall of Fame	World Wrestling Entertainment	2019

BOOKER T.

Booker T. Huffman, Jr. is a semi-retired wrestler and announcer for the WWE's NXT brand. He also co-owns the Houston-based Reality of Wrestling promotion. Booker T has held two championship titles in TNA and is a grand slam champion in both WCW and WWE. Overall, he has held over thirty titles throughout his career.

STEVIE RAY

Laslon "Lash" Steven Huffman is a semi-retired wrestler and podcaster. He is known for his time in WCW where he was a 10-time world tag team champion and world television champion. He is also a three-time tag team champion and held the North American heavyweight title in Global Wrestling Federation. Stevie Ray is best known as a member of Harlem Heat but he also carved his own niche as a solo competitor. During Booker T's fifth title reign as WCW world television champion, he was injured and ruled unable to compete. In his absence, Stevie Ray used Power of Attorney to defend the title. He held the title for 28 days before losing to Chris Jericho. Still seeking singles gold, he was offered a chance to join Hollywood Hogan's nWo Hollywood or the Black & White as they were known because of their colors. Booker T. refused to join either faction of the nWo but remained cordial with his brother. Stevie Ray began using the slapjack weapon to knock his opponent unconscious. By 1999, infighting started over who would was the group's leader. Stevie Ray emerged victorious in a fatal four-way battle over Horace Hogan, Vincent and Brian Adams to claim leadership of the Black & White.

Meanwhile, Booker T was fending for himself alone many times against the other wrestling factions. Stevie Ray started helping Booker T again and they reunited. Harlem Heat won the tag team titles three more times after their reunion. The harmony would soon be disrupted again when a new manager named Midnight arrived in late 1999. Stevie did not want Midnight to manage the group and he feuded with Booker T. After losing a match against Midnight, Stevie attacked Booker T and Midnight. He left the group and formed Harlem Heat 2000 with Big T (formerly Ahmed Johnson), Kash and J. Biggs. They defeated Booker T at *SuperBrawl X* on February 20, 2000 and won the rights to the name. The group soon disbanded in May and Stevie went back to aiding Booker T. He "retired" from in-ring action and became a commentator for WCW *Thunder*. After Vince McMahon bought WCW in 2001, Stevie Ray didn't join Booker T and other top performers on their sojourn to the WWE. Harlem Heat is a sacred property to Stevie Ray. The tag team was formed to promote an image of strong, fearless and positive black men.

In an interview on Ryback's *Conversations with the Big Guy* podcast, Stevie Ray explained the legacy of the group: "This is the thing: I wanted people to remember Harlem Heat as an ass-kicking tag team of color, you see what I'm saying? I didn't want us to be something else. I didn't want us to turn into a Doink the Clown, so I'm not saying that they would have done this with Harlem Heat, but I didn't want to lose the edge that we once had as Harlem Heat." Stevie Ray wrestled briefly on the independent circuit for the WWA, Reality of Wrestling and in 2015 he won the WildKat wrestling's heavyweight championship. In 2016, he started his radio show called *Straight Shooting with Stevie Ray*, a podcast and he frequently appears as a guest on different podcasts and at wrestling shows across the country.

Stevie Ray - Major Championships and Accomplishments		
Title	Promotion	Dates
GWF North American Heavyweight Champion	Global Wrestling Federation	Feb 5, 1993 – 145 days
WCW World Television Champion	World Championship Wrestling	July 13, 1998 – 28 days
ROW Tag Team Champions	Reality of Wrestling	Feb 21, 2015 – 21 days
WPW Heavyweight Champion	WildKat Pro Wrestling	May 16, 2015 – 182 days

Conclusion

Over the years, professional wrestling has continued to increase in popularity. The WWE's signature pay-per-view event *WrestleMania* is now two days and its flagship television program *Raw* is now streamed to a global audience on Netflix. According to *Forbes*, AEW is the third largest combat sports promotion behind the Ultimate Fighting Championship (UFC) and WWE. In 2024, the UFC was valued at $11.3 billion followed by WWE with a distant $6.8 billion and AEW at $2 billion (Teitelbaum, 2025). As the market size has increased, so have the opportunities for the wrestlers including African Americans.

It is nearly impossible to capture all of the Black champions and the world titles they have won in one publication. Many are still active so their statistics are more likely to have changed by the time this book reaches the market. Since the original publication in 2009, the number of Black and African American world champion wrestlers – especially females have doubled. As the largest wrestling promotion, WWE has several championships that it considers world titles since the acquisition of WCW and ECW in the early 2000s. They also have two world titles for women – the WWE Women's Championship and the Women's World Championship. WWE has also introduced a battle royal and intercontinental championship for women wrestlers. The rise of AEW and Ring of Honor will also provide more opportunities for both men and women to capture world titles.

References

Annino, C. (2024, February 25). *African American pro wrestling pioneers finally get justice.* ProWrestlingPost.com. https://prowrestlingpost.com/african-american-pro-wrestling-pioneers/

Arnold, M. (2021, January 13). *The untold story of Bobo Brazil: The Jackie Robinson of professional wrestling.* Daily DDT. https://dailyddt.com/2021/01/13/the-untold-story-of-bobo-brazil-the-jackie-robinson-of-professional-wrestling/

Atlas, T., & Teal, S. (2010). *Atlas: Too much...too soon.* Crowbar Press.

Barrasso, J. (2024, March 14). *Carmelo Hayes-Trick Williams match officially set for Stand & Deliver.* Sports Illustrated. https://www.si.com/fannation/wrestling/wwe/carmelo-hayes-trick-williams-match-officially-set-for-stand-deliver

Bernstein, J. (2003, March 30). *WrestleMania XIX breaks attendance record at SAFECO field.* WWE Corporate. https://web.archive.org/web/20140313010924/http://corporate.wwe.com/news/2003/2003_03_30.jsp

Blassie, F., & Greenberg, K. E. (2004). *Legends of Wrestling: "Classy" Freddie Blassie: Listen, you pencil neck geeks.* Pocket.

Boston Wrestling. (2019, January 27). *Tony Atlas shoots on Saba Simba WWF run; 1997 return w/ Rocky Maivia: Memories & legends #2.15.* YouTube. https://www.youtube.com/watch?v=GAj6nTF2NhA

Caldwell, J. (2009, January 29). *Torch trivia 1/28: Answer to who John Cena teamed with six years ago at a WWE house show.* PWTorch.com. https://pwtorch.com/artman2/publish/Torch_Trivia_27/article_29617.shtml

Carey, I. (2025, March 16). *Mercedes Mone defeats Indi Hartwell in first indie match since 2012*. F4W/WON. https://www.f4wonline.com/news/aew/mercedes-mone-defeats-indi-hartwell-in-first-indie-match-since-2012/

Chappell, C. (2025, February 17). *Even after 20 years, Captain America's introduction of Isaiah Bradley feels as relevant as ever*. ScreenRant. https://screenrant.com/captain-america-comic-brave-new-world-truth-isaiah-bradley/

Clark, A. V. (2022, May 24). *Why did Sasha Banks and Naomi Walk out on WWE?*. Vulture. https://www.vulture.com/2022/05/sasha-banks-naomi-wwe-walkout-suspension.html

Cofield, S. (2009, May 16). *Pro wrestler Lashley destroys Cook in 24 seconds*. Yahoo Sports.https://web.archive.org/web/20160315160520/https://ca.sports.yahoo.com/mma/blog/cagewriter/post/Pro-wrestler-Lashley-destroys-Cook-in-24-seconds?urn=mma%2C163814

Cosper, J. (2019). *The Original Black Panther: The Life & Legacy of Jim Mitchell*. Eat Sleep Wrestle, LLC.

Djeljosevic, D. (2023, November 2). *The Gangstas: 10 things fans should know about ECW's most controversial tag team*. TheSportster. https://www.thesportster.com/the-gangstas-ecw-controversial-tag-team-facts-trivia/

Eckinger, H. (2006, June 12). Hot moves: heat dancers' hopes for stardom. Miami Herald. Retrieved from http://www.miami.com/mld/miamiherald/14792810.htm.

Erdman, C., Jenkins, D., Gawley, P., Prada, L., Cichacki, S., Valens, A., Fike, A., & Caramela, S. (2024, August 9). *The forgotten story of the first black female wrestlers*. VICE. https://www.vice.com/en/article/the-forgotten-story-of-the-first-black-female-wrestlers/

Finnegan, A.J., & Finnegan, J. (2024, October 4). Hulk Hogan, Kevin Nash and the Fingerpoke of Doom! Pro Wrestling Stories. https://prowrestlingstories.com/pro-wrestling-stories-hulk-hogan-kevin-nash-fingerpoke-of-doom/

Genzlinger, N. (2019, November 25). Ethel Johnson, early black wrestling star, is dead at 83. The New York Times. https://www.nytimes.com/2019/11/25/sports/ethel-johnson-dead.html

Giri, R. (2014, September 25). *Vader talks saving Sid Vicious' life, leaving WCW, Ron Simmons making history, Eric Bischoff, Hogan.* Wrestling Inc. https://www.wrestlinginc.com/news/2014/09/vader-talks-saving-sid-vicious-life-581395/

Greene, D. (2019, June 18). *Nyla Rose quietly makes history as AEW's first transgender wrestler.* SI. https://www.si.com/wrestling/2019/06/18/aew-nyla-rose-transgender-wrestler-history

Greer, J. (2021, March 29). *The Pioneers: Bobo Brazil, the first African-American Megastar.* Last Word on Pro Wrestling. https://lastwordonsports.com/prowrestling/2019/02/06/the-first-african-american-megastar-bobo-brazil/#google_vignette

Harkulich, C.M. (2018). Sasha Banks, the Boss of NXT. In A.D. Horton (Ed.), Identity in Professional Wrestling: Essays on Nationalism, Race and Gender (pp. 148-161). Essay, McFarland & Company Publishers.

Helwani, A. (2022, April 4). *Sasha Banks breaks into tears after her first WrestleMania win with Naomi.* TNT Sports. https://www.youtube.com/watch?v=EJW-8ojgbYY

Highspots Wrestling Network. (2022, January 25). *Ernie Ladd interview (full interview).* YouTube. https://www.youtube.com/watch?v=_6Xg0YBFUOU

Hogg, K. (2020). From Chitlins to Championships: Limited Opportunities for African American Professional Wrestlers. In *Sports in African American life: Essays on history and culture.* essay, McFarland & Company, Inc., Publishers.

Hornbaker, T. (2007). *National Wrestling Alliance: The untold story of the monopoly that strangled professional wrestling.* ECW Press.

Jack, N., & Norman, J. (2020). *New Jack: Memoir of a Pro Wrestling extremist*. McFarland & Company, Inc., Publishers.

Johnson, M. (2022, May 17). *Lots more on the Sasha Banks-Naomi walkout last night at Raw*. PWInsider. https://www.pwinsider.com/article/159007/lots-more-on-the-sasha-banksnaomi-walkout-last-night-at-raw.html?p=1

Johnson, S., & Oliver, G. (n.d.). *"The Big Cat" was seldom tamed*. Slam Wrestling. https://archive.ph/20130115065905/http://slam.canoe.ca/Slam/Wrestling/2007/03/11/3732079.html

Johnson, S., Oliver, G., Mooneyham, M., & Dillon, J. J. (2012). *The Pro Wrestling Hall of Fame: Heroes and icons*. ECW Press Independent Publishers Group distributor.

Kelly, C. (2024, July 28). *The New Day and being black in WWE*. VICE. https://www.vice.com/en/article/the-new-day-and-being-black-in-wwe/

Kerrick, G. (1980). The Jargon of Professional Wrestling. *American Speech*, 55(2), 142-145.

Klein, G. (2012). *The King of New Orleans: How the Junkyard Dog became wrestling's first black superhero*. ECW.

Lady Wrestler: The amazing, untold story of African American women in the ring. (2016). USA. Retrieved from https://www.ladywrestlermovie.com/.

Lady Wrestlers. (1952, February 21). *Jet*, 56–58. Retrieved from https://books.google.com/books?id=K0MDAAAAMBAJ&pg=PA56#v=onepage&q&f=false.

Lambert, J. (2022, March 4). *Big E: Kofi Kingston and my WWE title runs weren't too drastically different*. Fightful News. https://www.fightful.com/wrestling/big-e-kofi-kingston-and-my-wwe-title-runs-weren-t-too-drastically-different

Laprade, P., & Murphy, D. (2017). *Sisterhood of the Squared Circle: The history and rise of women's wrestling*. ECW Press Ltd.

Lelinwalla, M. (2016, July 22). Q&A: superstar Sasha Banks talks battle ground event, cousin Snoop Dogg and living her dream. BET. https://www.bet.com/article/wcgoig/qa-wwe-superstar-sasha-banks-talks-battle-ground-event

Litsky, F. (2007, March 14). *Ernie Ladd, hall of famer in football and Pro Wrestling, dies at 68.* The New York Times. https://www.nytimes.com/2007/03/14/sports/football/14ladd.html

Mahjouri, S., Brookhouse, B., Campbell, B., Blackburn, P., & Crosby, J. (2025). WWE and TNA Wrestling announce multi-year partnership as wrestlers will appear on both NXY and TNA Impact. CBSSports.com. https://www.cbssports.com/wwe/news/wwe-and-tna-wrestling-announce-multi-year-partnership-as-wrestlers-will-appear-on-both-nxt-and-tna-impact/

Malcolm, M. (2022, February 4). *The first black women's champion: Ethel Johnson.* WrestleTalk. https://wrestletalk.com/features/the-first-black-womens-champion-ethel-johnson/

Marlan Gary Funeral Home Chapel of Peace. (2018, September 22). Ethel Blanche Hairston Obituary. https://www.thechapelofpeace.com/obituaries/ethel-blanche-hairston

Mathews, B. (2023, February 25). *Ron Simmons: Untold tale behind becoming WCW champion.* Pro Wrestling Stories. https://prowrestlingstories.com/pro-wrestling-stories/ron-simmons/

Mendhe, A. (2021, March 6). Identities of Apollo Crews' guards revealed. Sportskeeda. https://www.sportskeeda.com/wwe/news-identities-apollo-crews-guards-revealed

Mrosko, G. (2021, February 1). *Alicia Fox returned, entered the Royal Rumble, won the 24/7 title, then lost it all.* Cageside Seats. https://www.cagesideseats.com/wwe/2021/1/31/22259557/alicia-fox-returned-royal-rumble-won-24-7-title-then-lost-it-all

Mrosko, G. (2025, June 10). *R-Truth cuts his own hair on Raw to become Ron Killings.* Cageside Seats.

https://www.cagesideseats.com/wwe/2025/6/9/24446409/r-truth-cuts-his-own-hair-wwe-raw-ron-killings

Mukherjee, S. (2025, May 28). Rich Swann reveals what really happened during his arrest for public intoxication. Ringside News. https://www.ringsidenews.com/2025/05/28/rich-swann-reveals-what-really-happened-during-his-arrest-for-public-intoxication/

New Jack, & Norman, J. (2020). *New Jack: Memoir of a Pro Wrestling extremist*. McFarland & Company, Inc., Publishers.

National Wrestling Alliance. (2021, December 17). *A tribute to Jazz | NWA hard times 2*. YouTube. https://www.youtube.com/watch?v=YOKNwL8hvgU

Ojst, J. (2023, January 10). *Bobo Brazil, Bearcat Wright, and Art Thomas - Champion pioneers*. Pro Wrestling Stories. https://prowrestlingstories.com/pro-wrestling-stories/bobo-brazil-bearcat-wright-art-thomas/

Ojst, A. J., & Ojst, J. (2025, April 22). *Oscar and the surprising story of men on a mission*. Pro Wrestling Stories. https://prowrestlingstories.com/pro-wrestling-stories/oscar-men-on-a-mission/

Powell, J. (2003, March 31). *WWE shines at WrestleMania XIX*. Slam Wrestling. https://web.archive.org/web/20150630142306/https://slam.canoe.com/Slam/Wrestling/2003/03/31/55003.html

Powell, J. (2021, May 10). *Booker T: Wrestling's consummate performer*. Slam Wrestling. https://slamwrestling.net/index.php/2000/06/18/booker-t-wrestlings-consummate-performer/

PWInsider - WWE News, Wrestling News, *WWE. Oscar reveals why he was kicked out of Men on a Mission, why P.N. News failed, details on the M.O.M. reunion, and more in his first ever shoot interview* | PWInsider.com. (2009, September 16). https://pwinsider.com/article/41503/oscar-reveals-why-he-was-kicked-out-of-men-on-a-mission-why-pn-news-failed-details-on-the-mom-reunion-and-more-in-his-first-ever-shoot-interview.html?p=1

Riper, T. V. (2013, June 19). *The NFL's truly most valuable players*. Forbes. https://www.forbes.com/2006/12/22/mvp-nfl-bargain-biz-cx_tvr_1222nflmvp.html?sh=3edb76f56660

Rickard, M. (2018). *Tag team spotlight: The soul patrol*. Merchandise & Memories. https://www.merchandiseandmemories.com/tag-team-spotlight-the-soul-patrol

Rogers, R. (2023, December 11). *Mark Henry on winning the Arnold Classic: Vince McMahon said win or get fired! Wrestling with Rip Rogers podcast*. https://www.youtube.com/watch?v=ryPNqfj_JDo

Sam, D. (2018, October 26). *Step into the ring with WWE NXT star Bianca Belair - if you dare*. Andscape. https://andscape.com/features/step-into-the-ring-wwe-nxt-star-bianca-belair/

Sapp, S. R. (2021, August 17). *Jonathan Gresham on Black Wrestlers getting respect, Forbidden Door, ROH / 2021 Shoot Interview*. www.fightful.com. https://www.youtube.com/watch?v=VfcKD1IF9LA

Saxton, B. (2016, September 1). Ember Moon talks about overcoming rejection, her legendary trainers and making it to NXT. WWE. https://www.wwe.com/shows/wwenxt/article/ember-moon-long-journey-to-a-dream

Shabazz, D. (2023, December 2). Interview with Ric Flair. personal.

Shabazz, D. (2024, November 3). Interview with Ron Simmons. personal.

Sledge, P. (2020, June 6). *Bobo Brazil: 6 things to know about one of Wrestling's first black superstars*. CinemaBlend. https://www.cinemablend.com/television/2547498/bobo-brazil-things-to-know-about-one-of-wrestlings-first-black-superstars

Staff. (2024, September 30). *Mercedes Moné blames Vince McMahon for WWE exit.* Wrestling On Fannation. https://www.si.com/fannation/wrestling/wwe/mercedes-mone-blames-vince-mcmahon-for-wwe-exit#:~:text=I%20left%20for%20many%20different,me%20and%20I%20left%20WWE.

Staff. (2022, May 30). *Official WWE statement on Sasha Banks & Naomi.* WWE. https://www.wwe.com/article/official-wwe-statement-sasha-banks-naomi

Staszewski, J. (2022, May 24). *WWE's Sasha Banks-Naomi Pettiness won't fix the real problem.* New York Post. https://nypost.com/2022/05/24/wwes-sasha-banks-naomi-pettiness-only-feeds-real-problem/

Teitelbaum, J. (2025, January 21). *The most valuable combat sports promotions 2024.* Forbes. https://www.forbes.com/sites/justinteitelbaum/2024/04/18/the-most-valuable-combat-sports-promotions-2024/

Tello, C. (2015, August 6). Layla announces retirement from WWE: WWE.com exclusive interview. WWE. https://www.wwe.com/inside/layla-retires-from-wwe

Terry, B. (2021, February 24). Impact Wrestling sanctions TNA world heavyweight championship. Last Word on Pro Wrestling. https://lastwordonsports.com/prowrestling/2021/02/23/impact-wrestling-tna-world-heavyweight-championship/

Titus, P. (2024, October 11). Becoming Trick Williams: How former South Carolina football walk-on achieved WWE stardom. The State. https://www.thestate.com/sports/college/university-of-south-carolina/usc-football/article293356259.html

Tynes, T. (2025, March 11). *From The Rock to Bianca Belair: 15 greatest black wrestlers ever.* BET. https://www.bet.com/article/d2znws/greatest-black-wrestlers-ever

Ucchino, R. (2024, November 15). Is WWE fake? The truth behind wrestling's scripted drama and real dangers.

Wrestling On Fannation. https://www.si.com/fannation/wreslting/is-wwe-fake

Uhuru, T. (2023, October 22). What Happened to Stevie Ray of Harlem Heat? https://www.youtube.com/watch?v=vQUlRcFwPAU

Van Vliet, C. (2024, January 25). Why Moose choose TNA over WWE or AEW. YouTube. https://www.youtube.com/watch?v=6UJpnweB4cg

WOL Staff. (2025, March 7). *Breaking barriers: Ethel Johnson's legacy and the untold story in "Queen of the Ring."* WOL. https://woldcnews.com/3405616/ethel-johnson-queen-of-the-ring/

WWE. (2022, April 3). *Banks and Naomi emotional after winning tag team titles.* YouTube. https://www.youtube.com/watch?v=bZocsATPKQ8

YouTube. (2020, October 26). *The Gangstas on Jim Cornette, Smokey Mountain & More.* RF Video Vault. https://www.youtube.com/watch?v=mBOrRggHWbg

YouTube. (2024, January 10). *Former WWE superstar Victoria Crawford fka Alicia Fox Interview.* The Tantalizing Tony Wrestling Show. https://www.youtube.com/watch?v=yYzRpdLw2Tc

YouTube. (2024, July 2). *Mercedes Moné reveals why she left WWE + addresses being an unsafe wrestler.* YouTube. https://www.youtube.com/watch?v=7isFj9MlSG8

Ziegler, J. (2003, June 23). *411's Live WWE Raw coverage 06.23.03 – Goldberg's MSG debut, Orton & Foley backstage.* 411mania.com. https://411mania.com/wrestling/411s-live-wwe-raw-coverage-06-23-03-goldbergs-msg-debut-orton-foley-backstage/

Acknowledgements

This edition would not be possible without the first eBook published by my brother Julian L.D. Shabazz in 2009 and the foundation he laid by chronicling black wrestlers in 1999. I want to thank Jamie Hemming from *Slam Wrestling* magazine who was a dedicated wrestling historian and journalist who left us too soon. I also want to thank Mark Henry who was very supportive of my desire to revive Julian's work and helped me contact other wrestling historians and insiders. Special thanks to author/wrestling historian John Cosper for invaluable insight into the history of African American wrestlers especially in the Ohio Valley region. Also, I want to again thank *Slam* Magazine and various wrestling collectors for providing historical facts and photos of the wrestlers. Thanks to the following podcasters Vince Russo, John Poz at Two Man Power Trip, Monte & The Pharoah, Wrestling While Black, Black Rasslin' and Attitude Era. And a special thanks to wrestlers Stevie Ray, Ron Simmons and "Nature Boy" Ric Flair who allowed me to interview them for the book.

Photo Credits: All wrestler photos are provided courtesy of Blueyedchap2000 except for the following: Ethel Johnson – Hillbilly Warehouse, Private Party – Sam's World; Tyrus, Swerve Strickland, Athena, The Acclaimed and Mercedes Mone – Crush Photography; Xavier – Slam Magazine; Prime Time Players – R.J. Wrestling; Black Machismo – Wrestle Warehouse; Sasha Banks and Naomi and Lethal Consequences – Power Pro Wrestling; Rich Swann, Moose – Autographs, Cards and More; The Hurt Syndicate – Wrestling Posters Worldwide; Jay Lethal – Cheap Time Collectibles.

Index

AEW. *See* All Elite Wrestling
Alicia Fox. *See* Victoria Crawford
All Elite Wrestling, *10, 103, 122, 125, 144, 146, 162, 163, 170, 179, 195, 198,
    227, 239, 241, 242, 243, 267, 270, 277, 279, 283, 284, 285*
Angelo Dawkins, *251, 254*
Anthony Bowens, *242, 244*
Antonio Inoki., *32*
Apollo Crews, *144, 157, 200, 258, 268, 271, 275*
Art Thomas, *39, 43, 45*
Athena, *177, 178, 179*
Awesome Kong, *102, 162*

Babs Wingo, *24, 25, 26*
Bearcat Wright, *29, 31, 32, 38*
Bianca Belair, *10, 115, 121, 130, 149, 150, 281, 282, 301*
Big E, *135, 136, 138, 139, 144, 154, 155, 156, 157, 260, 261, 264, 269, 298,*
    See The New Day
Big Ryck. *See* Ezekiel Jackson
Bill Watts, *44, 57, 217*
Billy Wolfe, *23, 24*
Bobby Lashley, *141, 145, 146, 157, 187, 252, 259, 267, 268, 270, 277, 278,
    279*
Bobo Brazil, *35, 36, 37, 38, 45, 46, 295, 297, 300, 301*
Booker T, *69, 75, 76, 78, 107, 115, 173, 226, 278, 286, 287, 288, 289, 291, 292*
Brodus Clay.. *See* Tyrus
Bruno Sammartino, *11*
Bubba Smith, *48*
Buddy Rogers, *37, 45*
Butch Reed, *56, 214, 215, 217, 218, 220*

Cedric Alexander, *136, 268, 269, 271, 272, 273, 275, 277*
Charlotte Flair, *120, 126, 150*

D'Lo Brown, *69, 114, 245*
Darren Young, *156, 256, 258*
Dwayne Douglas Johnson, *67*

ECW, *58, 87, 88, 89, 106, 109, 115, 116, 134, 141, 142, 143, 146, 147, 164, 165, 166, 211, 236, 246, 247, 248, 249, 250, 270, 275, 294, 296, 297, 298*, *See* Extreme Championship Wrestling
Ed Don George, *30*
Edouard Carpentier, *31, 51*
Edward "Bearcat" Wright, *28*
Ernest "Ernie" Ladd, *47*
Ernie Ladd, *11, 49, 50, 295, 297, 298*
Ethel Johnson, *24*
Extreme Championship Wrestling, *58, 87, 88, 246, 250*
Ezekiel Jackson, *165*

Fabulous Freebirds, *57, 215, 219, 260*
Fabulous Moolah, *89, 110*
Freddie Blassie, *31, 45, 49*

Gene Kiniski, *32, 37*
Gene LaBell, *31*
Goldust, *76, 84, 94, 113*
Grand Slam Champion, *85, 127, 140, 171*

Harlem Heat, *64, 76, 78, 81, 286, 287, 288, 289, 292, 302*
Harley Race, *206, 210*
Hulk Hogan, *70, 73, 169, 210*

Ivan Koloff, *56*

Jack Brisco, *206*
Jack Johnson, *28, 206*
Jacqueline Moore, *63*
Jade Cargill, *10, 115, 130, 131, 151, 152, 179, 281, 283, 284*

Jay Lethal, *99, 167, 168, 173, 226, 227, 261, 264, 265, 271*
Jazz, *87, 88, 89, 102, 284, 300*
Jerry Lawler, *113, 229, 233*
Joe Frazier, *36*
Joe Louis, *36, 45*
Jonathan Gresham, *169, 170, 172, 174*
June Byers, *25, 27*

Kansas City Chiefs, *48, 217*
Keith Lee, *196, 198, 238, 241*
Kia Stevens. *See* Awesome Kong
Killer Kowalski, *31*
Kofi Kingston, *93, 97, 133, 137, 144, 156, 256, 260, 263, 264, 269, 278, 298*,
    See The New Day

Layla, *108, 109, 110, 302*
Lou Thesz, *31, 45, 46, 86, 118*

Mabel, *206, 229, 230, 231, 232, 233, 234, 235, 237*
Mark Henry, *69, 112, 115, 150, 182, 211, 283, 304*
Marva Scott, *24, 25, 27*
Max Caster, *242, 243, 244*
Mercedes Mone, *119, 122, 224, See* Sasha Banks
Michelle McCool, *102, 109*
Mildred Burke, *24, 25*
Mo, *229, 230, 231, 232, 233, 235*
Montez Ford, *151, 251, 254, 255*
Moose" Ojinnaka, *186*
Mustafa, *136, 245, 246, 247, 249, 271*
MVP, *134, 144, 268, 269, 271, 272, 275, 277, 278, 279, 280*

Naomi, *69, 106, 120, 122, 124, 128, 129, 130, 151, 152, 192, 222, 223, 224,
    281, 282, 283, 284, 296, 297, 301, 302, 303*
National Wrestling Alliance, *10, 11, 25, 35, 37, 42, 53, 60, 89, 90, 91, 96, 103,
    173, 193, 194, 216, 220, 236, 258, 297, 300*
National Wrestling Association, *10*

New Jack, *245, 247, 248, 249, 250, 297, 300*
NWA. *See* National Wrestling Alliance
Nyla Rose, *161, 297*

Oscar, *228, 229, 233, 234, 300*

Pat Patterson, *206*
Peter Maivia, *67, 68, 69, 206*
Private Party, *266, 267, 269, 275, 279*

Regis Philbin, *49*
Ric Flair, *37, 169, 215, 217, 218*
Rich Swann, *106, 181, 183*
Ring of Honor, *98, 99, 100, 162, 167, 168, 169, 170, 171, 172, 175, 176, 178, 179, 180, 185, 187, 190, 196, 227, 240, 271, 275, 276, 279, 294*
Rocky Johnson, *36, 67, 68, 204, 206, 211, 236*
Rocky Maivia. *See* Dwayne Johnson
Ron Killings, *92, 264*
Ron Simmons, *55, 56, 57, 59, 69, 76, 114, 214, 215, 216, 219, 287, 296, 299, 301*
R-Truth. *See* Ron Killings

Samoa Joe, *10, 94, 98, 136, 168, 179, 197, 240, 264*
Sasha Banks, *106, 119, 122, 129, 130, 131, 149, 150, 222, 223, 224, 296, 297, 298, 301, 302*
Shelton Benjamin, *134, 136, 144, 146, 267, 268, 269, 273, 276, 278, 279*
Stevie Ray, *76, 81, 82, 83, 84, 86, 286, 287, 288, 289, 291, 292, 293, 302*
Swerve Strickland, *10, 144, 195, 196, 240, 241, 279*

Teddy Long, *115, 215, 218, 219*
Terry Funk, *206*
Tha Gangstas, *114, 245, 246, 247*
The Rock. *See* Dwayne Johnson
The Usos, *135, 137, 156, 252, 256, 261, 275*
The Wild Samoans, *50, 69*
Tiger Conway, *49*

Titus O'Neil, *135, 156, 256*
Tony Atlas, *68, 204, 206, 209*
Tony Khan, *242*
Trick Williams, *199, 200, 201, 295, 302*
Trinity. *See* Naomi
Triple Crown Champion, *73, 85, 126, 153, 160, 176, 185, 190, 254, 263*
Tyrus, *191, 193*

Van Vader, *55, 57*
Verne Gagne, *11*
Victoria Crawford, *105, 106, 107, 303*
Vince McMahon, *50, 113, 122, 129, 136, 143, 200, 205, 211, 223, 233, 292, 301*
Vix Crow. *See* Victoria Crawford

World Championship Wrestling, *32, 34, 53, 56, 60, 63, 76, 78, 82, 83, 85, 215, 216, 220, 247, 287, 290, 293*
World Wrestling Entertainment, *27, 34, 38, 42, 46, 61, 66, 71, 73, 76, 85, 86, 90, 93, 96, 97, 107, 111, 115, 116, 118, 124, 126, 127, 131, 138, 139, 140, 147, 148, 152, 153, 158, 160, 166, 180, 184, 198, 202, 209, 212, 213, 225, 241, 253, 254, 259, 262, 263, 264, 265, 270, 273, 276, 280, 282, 284, 291*
World Wrestling Federation. *See* World Wrestling Entertainment
WWE. *See* World Wrestling Entertainment

Xavier Woods, *135, 136, 138, 139, 156, 192, 227, 260, 265, See* The New Day

A NOTE FROM THE AUTHOR

A book of such magnitude will undoubtedly include some unintentional errors, omissions, etc. The authors would appreciate, for the purpose of keeping future editions as accurate and complete as possible, if readers will send all corrections and/or additions to: david_shabazz@yahoo.com

For more books by David L. Shabazz

Visit: DavidLShabazz.com
or find him on social media @DavidLShabazz

Scan the QR code to visit DavidLShabazz.com for a preview of upcoming books, articles and more.

www.ingramcontent.com/pod-product-compliance
Lightning Source LLC
Chambersburg PA
CBHW071149070526
44584CB00019B/2725